Rethinking Media Pluralism

Rethinking
Media Pluralism

Kari Karppinen

FORDHAM UNIVERSITY PRESS · NEW YORK · 2013

Library of Congress Cataloging-in-Publication Data

Karppinen, Kari.
  Rethinking media pluralism / Kari Karppinen.
      p. cm. — (Donald McGannon Communication
Research Center's Everett C. Parker book series)
  Includes bibliographical references and index.
  ISBN 978-0-8232-4512-3 (cloth : alk. paper) —
  ISBN 978-0-8232-4513-0 (pbk.)
  1. Mass media—Political aspects—Europe.
  2. Mass media policy—Political aspects—Europe.
  3. Multiculturalism—Europe. I. Title.
  P95.82.E85K37 2012
  302.23—dc23
                                    2012021677

Printed in the United States of America
15 14 13   5 4 3 2 1
First edition

CONTENTS

ACKNOWLEDGMENTS

This book brings to a close several years of research, including many detours, and I want to thank all my colleagues and friends who have offered their encouragement or advice over these years. In particular, I am grateful to Hannu Nieminen for his advice and encouragement throughout the project. Many thanks also to the editor of the Everett C. Parker Book Series, Philip M. Napoli, for his support and comments along the way.

The Department of Media and Communication Studies in the University of Helsinki and my colleagues there have offered a productive but relaxed setting for working on this project. My thanks also go to the Centre for the Study of Democracy at the University of Westminster and the Donald McGannon Communication Research Center at Fordham University for visiting fellowships that greatly influenced this book.

Des Freedman, Peter Dahlgren, Hallvard Moe, Laura Juntunen, and the anonymous reviewers at Fordham University Press have all offered valuable comments on the manuscript in its different stages. Thanks also to David Kivinen for his proofreading help.

Rethinking Media Pluralism

INTRODUCTION

Media pluralism and diversity are values that few would oppose in principle. Access to a broad range of different political views and cultural expressions constitutes a fundamental value in media policy as well as in theories of the relationship between media and democracy. Opinions on the meaning and nature of media pluralism as a theoretical, political, or empirical concept, however, are many, and they embody some of the central conflicts in contemporary thinking about the role of media in society. The aim of this book is to analyze the ambiguities involved in and controversies surrounding the concept of media pluralism in two ways: by deconstructing the normative roots of the concept from the perspective of democratic theory, and by analyzing its different uses, definitions and underlying rationalities in current, mainly European media policy debates. Building on the critique developed here of the uses of pluralism and diversity in media studies and policy discourses, I will then argue for a more critical conception where media pluralism is understood not only in terms of variety or choice, but more broadly as a normative value that refers to the distribution of communicative power in the public sphere.

Although concerns for media pluralism in its different guises are by no means new, it seems that they have continued to gain increasing prominence in recent academic and political debates. This emphasis can partly be linked to the broader renaissance of pluralism in political thought. The theories and concepts underlying normative views of media and democracy have clearly taken a pluralist or antiessentialist turn in recent decades. Consequently, it is difficult to establish any universally recognized standards for evaluating media performance and quality. As normative judgments based on quality or truth have become increasingly problematic, definitions of public interest in the context of culture and media have shifted even more towards emphasizing pluralism and diversity. As John Keane (1999, 3) has noted, normative questions about the media, whether they concern the structure and organization or the quality of contents, are hard to answer with anything but platitudes about the need for diversity, balance, and variety.

Notions of pluralism and diversity also seem to invoke a positive resonance in media policy, so much so that they permeate a major part of the arguments in current media policy debates. Des Freedman (2005) notes in his study of UK and US media policy that contemporary policy documents are littered with positive references to pluralism and diversity, signaling their rise as a key justification for emerging regimes of media regulation. Keen to avoid the patronizing claim to "know what is best for the people," defenders of public interest in media policy increasingly plead for values such as pluralism, diversity, openness, and creativity (De Bens 2007, 11). Hence, it can be argued that pluralism is not only an indisputable value but also one of the few politically correct criteria for assessing media performance and regulation.

Based on the fundamental principles of liberal democracy and a democratic public sphere, a plurality of viewpoints and perspectives in the media can be considered a self-evident value. Yet, this consensus in principle has not stopped disagreements about the definition of media pluralism, let alone its proper implementation or institutionalization. In part, this ambiguity can be traced to the nature of pluralism as a social value. According to Gregor McLennan (1995, 7), the constitutive vagueness of pluralism as a general social and philosophical value gives it enough ideological flexibility so that it can signify reactionary things in one phase of the debate and progressive things in the next. Similarly in media policy, the positive resonance of pluralism and diversity has been used in arguments for various and often incompatible objectives: for free competition and consumer choice as well as for further public intervention and regulation.

The ambiguity of media pluralism as a descriptive and evaluative concept is only amplified by recent technological developments and the proliferation of new media forms. In a sense, it seems almost ironic that the concepts of pluralism and diversity have become so popular in media policy discourse at a time when the public has access to more media outlets and information than ever before.

As Keane (1999, 8–9) puts it, "the wide and conflicting spectrum of available criteria for deciding what counts as quality pushes towards pluralist conclusions—towards a policy of 'letting hundreds of flowers bloom.' This has the paradoxical effect of encouraging audience segmentation, still further growth in the quantity of media possibilities and outputs, and yet more disputes about whether the effects are more or less pluralistic, more or less in the public interest." This also raises the legitimate question of whether media pluralism really amounts to anything more than an empty catchphrase. According to Denis McQuail (2007b, 42), arguments for pluralism or diversity "sound at times like arguments on behalf of virtue to which it is hard to object." Yet the inclusiveness and multiple meanings of the concept also expose some of its limits, so "we should perhaps suspect that something that pleases everyone may not be as potent a value to aim for and as useful a guide to policy as it seems at first sight" (ibid.).

According to another commentator, "notions of pluralism, diversity and the marketplace for ideas are at best vague and malleable, at worst adjusted to the purpose of whoever invokes them" (Tambini 2001, 26). Looking at contemporary media policy debates and the range of objectives advocated by the positive value associated with the concepts of pluralism and diversity, it is easy to agree.

Nevertheless, media pluralism remains a key concept in both critical media studies and contemporary media policy. The basic premise of this book is that it is relevant not only to analyze its different uses and to articulate its problems in the context of contemporary media policy, but to also rethink the purpose and value of media pluralism as a critical concept.

MEDIA PLURALISM AS AN AMBIGUOUS OBJECTIVE

Notions of media pluralism and media diversity are often used interchangeably in discussions of media performance and policy, and there is some confusion about the distinction, or a possible hierarchy, between these two concepts.[1] Although the primary purpose of this book is not to propose new systematic definitions, I assume here an initial conceptual hierarchy whereby media diversity is understood in a more neutral, descriptive sense, as heterogeneity on the level of contents, outlets, ownership or any other aspect of the media deemed relevant; whereas media pluralism, as a broader socio-cultural and evaluative principle is understood as referring to the acknowledgment and preference of such diversity, which also requires some schematization of its relationship to democracy or other societal values. Consequently, I use the concepts of diversity or plurality primarily when referring to the empirical

---

[1] The concept of media diversity is more commonly used in the United States, whereas media pluralism is the favored term in recent European media policy debates. The existing definitions of the concepts are discussed in detail in Chapter 4.

fact of plurality, while pluralism, as an *ism*, refers more explicitly to a value orientation that considers multiplicity and diversity in ideas and institutions a virtue.

The reason why media pluralism and not diversity appears in the title of this book is a reflection of my interest in the underlying values and ideologies of media policy. This distinction is not commonly established in the media policy literature, and in any case both these concepts are umbrella terms whose flexibility and ambiguity are the very focus of this book. This does not then remove the ambiguity that arises from the fact that both pluralism and diversity are often used normatively as well as descriptively, both as normative justifications for policies and as empirically measurable and assessable constructs. For the sake of clarity though, I will mainly use the term media pluralism instead of diversity, except when following the terminology used in the source material.

In its broadest sense, media pluralism refers to some of our most taken-for-granted assumptions about media and democracy: the broad belief that the media ought to reflect different interests, values and cultures in society, and provide public access to the widest possible range of voices. On closer analysis, it becomes clear that the concept has multiple dimensions and that it can be analyzed on several levels, ranging from media structure and ownership to content and use. The context in which pluralism is considered can also vary from local markets to the global information infrastructure. These different levels and aspects of pluralism are further discussed in Chapter 4.

Attempts at a systematic definition of media pluralism are further complicated by the seemingly contradictory or even paradoxical relationship of its different aspects to one another (see van Cuilenburg 1998). An increased number of media channels or outlets, for instance, can mean more choice for consumers, but this does not necessarily translate into better provision for minorities or a fairer distribution of communicative power in any broader sense. Increasing competition in the media market can lead to more diverse media content or to further homogenization, depending on the perspective one takes. Attempts to promote one form of pluralism through national ownership or content requirements may well undermine other forms of pluralism. As I discussed in Chapter 5, new media technologies and the proliferation of online information also seem to multiply, rather than solve, questions about the nature and relevance of concerns for media pluralism.

Indeed, at a time when the Internet offers a world of choice and diversity far greater than the old media ever did, the whole emphasis on pluralism and diversity as media policy values may seem questionable. However, if one takes a broader view than just that of consumer choice, it is clear that despite all its promises, the Internet will not be able to resolve the asymmetries of communicative power between different social actors or between cultural producers and cultural consumers.

While much of the debate on media pluralism deals with market structure or media ownership, the underlying, fundamental concern is usually with media content, or more precisely, with what people actually see and hear in the media. In this sense, the changing information environment raises the question as to whether pluralism should refer to the information that is potentially available or to the information that citizens actually access and use. Even though a wider range of sources may give increased choice, many studies report that there is no corresponding effect on citizens' access to relevant information. On the contrary, it has been argued that due to the ability of consumers to filter information, an increased diversity of supply may in fact reduce exposure to different views (see Hindman 2009; Sunstein 2007; Webster 2007). While some commentators argue that the abundance of media available today implies an undeniable dispersal of power, others fear that audience fragmentation paradoxically may lead away from the ideal of a pluralistic public sphere where different perspectives and views meet and engage in dialogue.

In any case, it is easy to notice that different aspects of pluralism may be at variance with one another, which raises the question as to what kind of pluralism it is that we are really looking for. Drawing on the recent research literature and policy debates, I will attempt to make sense of this ambiguity by breaking down the different levels at which pluralism is discussed and by deconstructing the normative assumptions underlying its various uses. In other words, in line with the main focus of this book, the different levels of analysis are not discussed here because of their empirical utility, but because they entail radically different assumptions about the nature of pluralism as a normative value.

Understood broadly, the notion of media pluralism also interfaces with a number of policy issues, from traditional concerns with media ownership and market structure, the remit and status of public service broadcasting, and the role of alternative and community media to issues of copyright, control of information and access to new media technologies. Yet as a broader policy principle or an underlying value, it is not reducible to any of these particular issues.

The premise of this book is that structural changes in the media environment raise questions not only about regulatory tools, but also about what ultimately is valuable in media pluralism. This is not to deny the need for further empirical studies about the scope and implications of actual changes in media structures or the effectiveness of different regulatory tools. In this book, however, media pluralism is by design treated as a normative principle whose value derives more from political philosophy and democratic theory than from empirical evidence.

THE VALUE OF PLURALISM FOR DEMOCRACY

There are many different brands of pluralism in social sciences, including cultural pluralism, political pluralism and philosophical pluralism. According to McLennan (1995), pluralism is therefore best treated not as a proper *ism* or a distinctive school of thought, but as a concept in the social sciences that raises a series of problems that can apply to a range of different fields. The concern here is primarily with pluralism as a political and normative principle for evaluating the relationship between media and democracy. Therefore I draw mostly on political philosophy and theories of the public sphere, and only selectively on debates about multiculturalism or other fields where the concept may be equally debated.

As a political principle, pluralism was long associated with a specific school of thought in American political science. This "empirical democratic theory," developed by authors such as Robert Dahl (1956), presented pluralism as a polyarchical political system where a wide array of interest groups compete with one another over the outcome of political decisions and where no one group is able to dominate the political process.

Widely criticized for their narrow conception of the political and naïve assumptions about the workings of political power, these claims of empirical pluralism have long been dismissed by radicals as a thinly veiled ideological defense of liberal democracy that underestimated the imbalances of power in Western society, and that were designed to prevent any radical transformation of the status quo (Wenman 2008). However, over the past thirty years the concept of pluralism is said to have undergone a remarkable renaissance, so that it is now invoked widely—and in a positive manner—by liberals and radicals alike (McLennan 1995; Wenman 2008).

Indeed to a certain extent, the value of pluralism for democratic politics and the public sphere is self-evident. Politics presupposes different values and interests, and it is easy to agree that the media should somehow reflect these differences. Yet the exact meaning and nature of pluralism as a normative principle remains highly contentious and elusive, not only in terms of evaluating the performance of the media but also more generally in social and political theory.

One source of difficulty is that pluralism does not itself identify any specific qualities, values or virtues that need to be advanced or protected, except that of differentiation itself. According to philosopher Louise Marcil-Lacoste (1992), pluralism entails a certain ambiguity "between the overfull and the empty." On the one hand, it suggests abundance, flowering and expansion of values and choices, but on the other hand, it also evokes emptiness. To recognize or promote plurality in some context is to say nothing about the nature of its elements and issues, their relations and value. From this it follows that pluralism can combine both critique and evasion. It involves critique of all monisms and their foundational claims. Yet there is also evasion, Marcil-Lacoste argues, in terms of its refusal to develop substantive normative positions concerning social, political and economic finalities.

As McLennan (1995) notes, it may seem that all things plural, diverse and open-ended are automatically to be regarded as good. But in deconstructing the value of pluralism, we are faced with questions of the following order: Is there not a point at which healthy diversity turns into unhealthy dissonance? Does pluralism mean that anything goes? And what exactly are the criteria for stopping the potentially endless multiplication of valid ideas? In other words, what are the limits of pluralism, and what distinguishes it from relativism? In the context of an increasingly complex and at least in some sense diversified media landscape, the crucial question remains as to how pluralism should be conceptualized as a political value without falling into the trap of flatness, relativism, indifference, and an unquestioning acceptance of market-driven difference and consumer culture (McLennan 1995, 83–84).

As Denis McQuail (2007b, 43) puts it, "it is possible to have more diversity, without any more of what we really value." This kind of ethos of evasiveness and vacuousness is not foreign to contemporary debates in media studies and media policy either. If there is no rational basis or common standard for evaluating the media, it is feared that relativism will take over and the politics of difference will lead to the "politics of indifference." Given that pluralism is a notion that almost everyone can embrace and that does not impose any limits, its flip side is that it indicates no specific content and hardly resolves the problems associated with media structure and democratic regulation of the media.

Given the inherent ambiguity of pluralism as a social or political value, it is hardly surprising that controversies over its precise meaning are also at the heart of contemporary debates in democratic theory. In this book I demonstrate the different conceptions of pluralism by distinguishing three main approaches to democracy and the public sphere: liberal, deliberative, and radical-pluralist models. This distinction is more useful as a heuristic tool than a rigid categorization. The purpose is not to argue that the three approaches are mutually exclusive, clearly delineable theoretical traditions.

The concept of liberalism, for instance, is itself notoriously difficult to define and there is also considerable overlap between the three approaches. Yet, despite their indeterminacy, I use these approaches as general entry points into the discussion on the value of pluralism for democracy.

Theoretically, the notion of media pluralism is most commonly grounded in the metaphor of the "free marketplace of ideas" or different theories of the public sphere. These can roughly be equated with dominant liberal-pluralist and deliberative frameworks of democratic theory, respectively.

Liberal theorists of democracy have long seen pluralism and the clash of divergent opinions and interests in various realms of social life as mediating progress (Bobbio 1990, 21–24). This point was perhaps most famously made by J. S. Mill (1948), who defended freedom of speech by arguing that all opinions, whether true or false, must have their place in public so that their merits can be openly evaluated. The basic principles of political liberalism, such as the dispersion of power and the critique of monistic ideas of truth and common good, still provide the foundation for media pluralism as a political and philosophical value. The legacy of liberal pluralism for media regulation, however, has been far from unproblematic, and much has been written about the abuse and misunderstanding of concepts such as freedom of speech and the marketplace of ideas in media policy (see, for example, Peters 2004; Splichal 2002).

In particular, I argue that in neo-liberal media policy discourses, pluralism is often reduced to a doctrine of free markets and individual choice in a way that is in sharp contrast to the more philosophical defense of pluralism in political liberalism. According to the oft-repeated critique, individual freedom of choice and the marketplace model fail to account for relations of power and other structural constraints and obstacles that limit public communication. The problem is that metaphors such as the marketplace of ideas imply that the marketplace itself provides a natural and neutral logic for the operation of the media, ignoring the ways in which the market itself can act as a form of censorship that privileges some voices and excludes others. Given the long tradition of critique from the critical political economy of communication, the notion of free choice in the marketplace of ideas has thus proved an inadequate framework for conceptualizing the complex nature of media pluralism as a broader public interest value.

Instead of the market model, much of the discussion on media pluralism in the social sciences and critical media studies has been grounded in theories of deliberative democracy and the public sphere. While much of the debate on the media and the public sphere still draws upon Jürgen Habermas's (1989) early use of the concept, the public sphere has become broadly understood in media studies as a general context of interaction where citizens get informed and where public discussion takes place. In this general sense of the concept, the voicing of diverse views and access to a wide range of information and experiences are rarely questioned as preconditions for effective participation in public life.

However, the public sphere approach and its theoretical background have also attracted intense criticism in both political theory and in media studies. Reflecting the renewed emphasis on pluralism and difference in social and political theory, deliberative models of democracy and the public sphere have been particularly criticized for overemphasizing social unity and rational consensus. For many, the public sphere is an inherently old-fashioned, over-rationalistic concept that bears no relevance in the contemporary media landscape. Although Habermas's ideas have been rather selectively adopted into media studies and media policy, and his later revisions of the public sphere theory have often been neglected (Habermas 1992; 1996a; 2006; see also Brady 2004; Dahlberg 2005b; Garnham 2007), there remains a sentiment that fresher perspectives are needed to conceptualize the democratic role of contemporary media.

As an alternative approach that can serve as a normative basis for debates on media pluralism, this book discusses the recent radical-pluralist or ago- nistic models of democracy that so far have received much less consideration in media studies. As alternatives to the liberal and deliberative models of democracy, radical-pluralist or agonistic theories of democracy have recently attracted much discussion in political philosophy, yet they have only oc- casionally surfaced in debates on the role of the media (see Carpentier 2011; Carpentier and Cammaerts 2006; Dahlberg and Phelan 2011; Karppinen 2007; Karppinen, Moe, and Svensson 2008).

The radical-pluralist approach, associated with political theorists such as Chantal Mouffe, Ernesto Laclau, William Connolly and Bonnie Honig, has typically criticized both liberal and deliberative models of democracy for their conceptions of pluralism and unequal relations of power. Emphasizing the ineradicable nature of power relations and the democratic value of dis- sent and conflict, the radical pluralist approach can be viewed as an attempt to repoliticize the discourse of pluralism. In contrast to the allegedly rationalistic and monistic thrust of the Habermasian public sphere approach, radical pluralism can easily be considered to resonate better with the chaotic and complex nature of the contemporary media landscape.

A central argument in this book is that radical democratic pluralism must also be distinguished from views that celebrate all kinds of multiplicity and difference as signs of emancipation. Instead, the aspect of radical pluralist perspectives that is most interesting to media studies is the fundamental role of power relations. Drawing on theories of radical democratic pluralism, it can then be argued that a critical notion of media pluralism must be able to account for the difference between the sheer number of voices, the number of different voices, and above all their relationship with existing power structures in society. As a consequence, media pluralism can be understood to be more about power relations and less about defining or defending differences as such.

The radical pluralist approach, which I examine here primarily through Chantal Mouffe's (1993; 2000; 2005) work, is thus interesting in two ways. First, it offers a fundamental critique of both liberal and deliberative approaches to the public sphere and democracy. Secondly, and perhaps more importantly, it also provides criticism of postmodern approaches that celebrate all multiplicity and diversity without paying attention to the continued centrality of the questions of power and exclusion in the public sphere—a critique that arguably has passed unnoticed in much of the reception of Mouffe's work in media and cultural studies. While the radical pluralist approach is not without contradictions of its own, its emphasis on asymmetries of power and its revaluing of dissent and contestation provide an interesting basis for discussing the value of media pluralism in contemporary media policy.

THE POWER OF DEFINITIONS AND THE POLITICS OF CRITERIA

If the concept of pluralism is theoretically controversial, no less so are its political uses. While different uses of pluralism and diversity in various media policy discourses are easy to find practically all around the world, the present book will focus particularly on recent media policy debates in Europe. The notion of pluralism itself is by no means new in media policy, but it seems to have featured even more prominently in recent European policy discussions. A commitment to media pluralism is now at the heart of communications policy at both national and supranational levels. Apart from the renaissance of pluralism in social theory, other reasons for its political appeal have to do with more mundane factors, including its antipaternalist resonance and perceived neutrality and measurability.

In the European context, the normative basis for much of the debate on media pluralism can be found in declarations such as the European Convention for the Protection of Human Rights and Fundamental Freedoms (1950), which in rulings by the European Court of Human Rights has often been interpreted to associate freedom of expression with diversity of information in a way that obliges governments to protect, and if need be, to take positive measures to safeguard and promote media pluralism (see Council of Europe 2009). More recently, the phrase "freedom and pluralism of the media shall be respected" has also been enshrined in the Charter of Fundamental Rights of the European Union. Moreover, a number of other policy documents since the 1990s—including the European Commission's (2007a) recent "three-step" initiative to advance debate on media pluralism by developing a common monitoring approach—have entrenched the position of media pluralism as one of the basic values of European media policy.

Despite the status of media pluralism as one of the fundamental values of European media policy, its uses in policy documents, political statements, and academic literature demonstrate just how broad and ambiguous the notions of pluralism and diversity are. As Des Freedman (2005, 16) illustrates, even developments such as the media law that entrenched Silvio Berlusconi's control of Italian television or the consolidation of Rupert Murdoch's media empire have been defended on grounds that they "provide greater plurality" or "foster diversity of voices."

One way to address the ambiguity of media pluralism as a policy objective is thus to look at the contradictions between the approaches taken by different actors and stakeholders in these debates. While pluralism has traditionally been mobilized in European media policy to defend institutions such as public service broadcasting and to support alternative media, press subsidies and other interventionist means, the analysis of recent debates seems to illustrate how references to pluralism and diversity also feature in deregulatory and market-oriented policy documents. This can be seen to reflect a broader paradigm shift in European media policy towards a neoliberal regime, which assesses the value of public communication in terms of the social relations of market exchange and individual consumer choice (Kaitatzi-Whitlock 2005; Michalis 2007; van Cuilenburg and McQuail 2003; Venturelli 1998).

Because of the fetishizing of choice and competition under the labels of pluralism and diversity, Freedman (2008, 79) has gone so far as to argue that these principles have been reduced to convenient justifications to secure public consent for the marketization of the media. Contestation of these notions is thus closely associated with more general shifts in contemporary media policy. Whereas public service broadcasting, for instance, has traditionally relied on a notion of media pluralism that is not only about individual freedom of choice but about the needs of society at large, current neoliberal policy reforms increasingly seem to rely on a more quantitative notion of pluralism and diversity.

Aside from these distinctively European concerns, issues of media pluralism and diversity have also received considerable debate in the United

States, where questions around media diversity surfaced as a matter of public interest in connection with the revision of media ownership rules especially in the early 2000s. This process, which culminated in the different ways to define and measure media diversity, also provoked surprisingly strong public debate (see, for example, Baker 2007; Freedman 2008; Howley 2005; Napoli 2007). As many analysts have noted, the level of public involvement and controversy prompted by proposals for less stringent ownership regulation and the prospects of increased consolidation was at the time largely unprecedented.

As yet there has been no public involvement on this scale in Europe, although issues related to media ownership or the role of public service broadcasting, for instance, are no less topical in Europe. In any case, developments in both Europe and the United States have made it clear that although media pluralism may command broad respect by virtue of its undisputed value for democracy and a vital public sphere, there is no consensus on its meaning either as an abstract principle or as a tangible policy objective. As is the case with so many normative concepts used in politics, including values such as freedom or democracy, problems arise immediately when concepts are used to argue for specific policies. In the case of media pluralism, recent attempts to operationalize the concept into empirically measurable and "objective" indicators of media policy have arguably intensified the stakes of this contestation.

As is the case with many other contentious issues in media policy, the issues discussed in this book illustrate a broader division between economic and democratic rationalities. Media pluralism can be conceptualized as a quantifiable commodity value or as a broader social and political value (Baker 2007; McQuail 2007b, 44). Reflecting a broader trend towards economic arguments in media policy, media pluralism has been increasingly conceptualized in contemporary media policy in terms of market competition and consumer choice.

In European media policy, the shift towards a more quantifiable conception of media pluralism has been evident in attempts to develop concrete criteria for the measurement of pluralism. Despite political disagreements about the meaning of the concept, pluralism is not treated in policy discussions merely as a matter of opinion—like quality, which is in the eye of the beholder. Instead of viewing it as a justification for policy initiatives or another abstract dimension of media freedom, there is a clear tendency to treat pluralism as an objective and tangible construct that can be empirically measured.

Reflecting this tendency, the European Commission recently appointed a major study aimed at creating a monitoring tool for the measurement of media pluralism in EU member states (ICRI et al. 2009). While the merits of such an endeavor can be debated, it certainly makes it even more relevant to problematize the concept itself. As not all aspects of pluralism are equally amenable to empirical measurement, the tendency to seek empirical indicators raises obvious questions as to what rationalities and assumptions these efforts rest on, what implications they have, and what aspects they ignore. Any definition of media pluralism will entail choices about what is important and what criteria are deemed valid for making that assessment. More critically, these endeavors also raise the question as to whether the concept of media pluralism is better suited to the endless assessment needs brought about by New Public Management than to serious reflection about the state and performance of current media systems.

As noted, one of the reasons for the popularity of pluralism in current media policy probably lies in its apparent measurability and the illusion of neutrality it conveys (see McQuail 2007b). As both politicians and political theorists are increasingly keen to avoid "ideological thinking" and the dangers of elitism and paternalism, pluralism and diversity have emerged as some of the few politically correct criteria for assessing the performance of the media. The emphasis on empirical measurement and expert knowledge, however, is hardly neutral in regard to different conceptions of pluralism and the public interest. From a critical perspective, it is easy to interpret the emphasis on empirical and objective data as echoing the current neoliberal policy discourse and its vision of a society driven by individualistic cost-benefit thinking.

According to many critics, the fetishizing of scientific data also functions to marginalize the public from the policy process by reserving it exclusively for the experts, lawyers, and lobbyists who are in prime position to supply the sort of information that policy makers demand (Freedman 2008; Napoli and Seaton 2007). As has become clear in the American debates on diversity indexes as well as in recent European media policy debates about indicators of pluralism, public value and market impact tests and other metrics, the reliance on empirical data also opens up another crucial arena for definitional power. The stakes involved in what I call "the politics of criteria" are discussed in more detail in Chapter 7.

TOWARD A CRITICAL NOTION OF MEDIA PLURALISM

The contradictions involved in the use of pluralism as a catch-all value in media policy do not necessarily mean that media pluralism as such has become an anachronistic concept in critical media studies. Part of the purpose of this book is to critically analyze different normative, political, and empirical uses and definitions of media pluralism and to trace their underlying values and political rationalities. Yet the aim is not only to deconstruct its different definitions, but also to rethink normatively its meaningful scope and to propose some outlines for a more radical conception of media pluralism.

The critical argument made in the book regarding contemporary media policy debates is that the principle of media pluralism is too often either reduced to an empty catchphrase or conflated with individual issues such as media ownership, consumer choice, or free competition. To reclaim the notion as a meaningful normative principle, I will draw on democratic theory as well as contemporary media policy research and argue that media pluralism should be understood more broadly in terms of the distribution of communicative power. Instead of consumer choice or a blind celebration of all multiplicity, the principle of media pluralism would thus be associated with the aim of balancing existing structural asymmetries in communicative power and supporting political equality.

The central argument is that we need a broader conception of media pluralism that is concerned not only with specific empirical indicators, and that is not reducible to specific issues such as media ownership or competition, but with broader social and political values. Edwin Baker (2007, 16) has argued in the context of media concentration and democracy that an egalitarian political order inevitably relates to the distribution of expressive power. For Baker (2007, 7), this implies that as a central political institution, the media need to be structurally egalitarian in order to allow a "wide and fair dispersal of power and ubiquitous opportunities to present preferences, views, visions." Basing my argument in democratic theory, I will further argue for a conception of media pluralism that refers broadly to a more democratic distribution of power and influence in the public sphere.

Instead of seeing pluralism and diversity as something that could simply be measured through the number of outlets or channels available, the expanded notion brings back the normative and political aspect into the concept of media pluralism. After critically engaging with its uses, I argue that there is a need to reclaim the concept of media pluralism from its technocratic and reductionist uses for the critical purpose of identifying and evaluating new forms of power, exclusion, dominance, and concentration of communicative power that are emerging in the contemporary media environment.

Theoretically, such a definition leans on the recognition of power asymmetries as inherent to the media and the public sphere. Some social actors will always be in a better position than others to make their voice heard. The risk of what can be called *naïve pluralism* is that these questions of power are veiled or ignored under the illusion of communicative abundance or limitless choice. Unequal relations of power remain a persistent and prominent feature of the field of media policy and media institutions, and there is no reason to think that technological or any other developments will lead to spontaneous harmony. This underscores the continued relevance of both theoretical and empirical attempts to uncover and analyze structural hierarchies of power that influence and shape the contemporary media environment.

Markers of plurality in the media should thus rest not on the multiplication of genres, media forms, or markets alone, but on the actual success of media systems in providing opportunities and competences for different groups and individuals to participate in public life. Identifying the new forms of power, exclusion, dominance, and concentration of communicative power that are emerging in the contemporary media environment is of course to a great extent an empirical question that needs to be investigated by media and communication researchers. Yet pluralism is also an open-ended value whose precise consequences are open to political and public debate. Furthermore, it will lead to questions of how alternative conceptions of democracy suggest different ideals concerning the "fair distribution of communicative power."

BETWEEN POLITICAL IDEAS AND POLICY ANALYSIS

My approach is mainly theoretical and conceptual rather than empirical in nature. I discuss the concept of media pluralism primarily as a political and philosophical value rather than as an empirical fact or an object of measurement. In the latter part of the book, however, I also engage in empirical analysis of policy documents to examine and illustrate different political uses of media pluralism in current (mainly European) media policy discourses. The primary rationale and focus of the book, however, is not to provide a comprehensive review of existing policy measures or to produce policy recommendations, but to clarify the intellectual bases and provide new theoretical resources for the debate on media pluralism as a normative and a political value.

The aim is to break down and analyze the political rationalities and theoretical assumptions that underpin contemporary debates on media pluralism in both academic research and policy making. The approach adopted is therefore positioned at the interface between normative political philosophy and empirical analysis of policy argumentation.

It follows that the approach is also explicitly normative and political, which means calling into question the traditional fact-value dichotomy that has dominated much of academic policy analysis. Definitions and knowledge, about politically contested concepts in particular, are never neutral, and it is not the purpose of this book to provide any objective or nonideological definitions of the key concepts in focus. The approach is also deconstructive in the sense that it is written more for the purpose of critical reflection than for the needs of policy implementation or regulation. The overall aim is therefore more to stimulate academic and political debate rather than settle disputes and disagreements.

With this in mind, the book is based on the broad premise that as well as exploring policy choices, interests, and institutions, media policy analysis must also pay attention to the role of ideas and ideologies that underlie the formation of policy principles and paradigms. Departing from the mainstream understanding of policy analysis, the focus of the book is particularly on the contestation of concepts and definitional power involved in this process. This raises questions over how the uses of different concepts legitimate and justify certain political aims and practices, and how they politically frame problems that guide decision makers' considerations and the possible alternatives open to them. The focus on ideas also implies a broader proposition that discussions in media studies and also in media policy can benefit from engagement with broader developments in contemporary political philosophy and democratic theory. It has often been argued in both general public policy studies and in the media policy context in particular that there is a need to bridge the gap between political theory and public policy analysis (Anderson 1987; Fischer 2003; Freedman 2008; Mosco 1996). In the context of media policy, Georgina Born (2006, 111) has noted that normative arguments in media studies and media policy alike tend to suffer from an absence of grounding in political philosophy and recent currents in democratic theory; instead, they have "baulked at the challenge of founding ideas for reform on normative rationales." Similarly, Denis McQuail (1997) has argued that the academic variant of media policy analysis has typically been long on realism, anxious to appear economically and technologically literate, and rather short on idealism and fundamental criticism.

This shunning of normative theories and ideologies is compatible with the established academic division of labor, in which normative and ideological questions are considered the domain of political philosophy, while policy studies deal more with the empirical and causal models that seek to explain policy making in terms of (material) interests and rational behavior. Arguably, this division of labor is only further reinforced by developments in contemporary media policy. According to many scholars, contemporary media policies are increasingly driven by pragmatic, mostly technological or economic, concerns instead of grand ideologies or normative theories. For McQuail (2007a, 11), the subordination of cultural and political issues to technological and economic considerations also involves a shift away from public discourse towards one where professional expertise or economic logic trump aspirations and beliefs. As he puts it, "the dog of media policy is increasingly being wagged by the tail of technology with its inbuilt industrial and economic ramifications" (ibid., 11). Contemporary debates on media pluralism and its empirical indicators also bear witness to these trends.

The problem with this is that the avoidance of values tends to make traditional policy research inherently conservative. Policy research that is concerned with evaluating policy choices or developing performance indicators often assumes that the subject matter of research is self-evident and independent of any theoretical frameworks. Instead it leans on models of economics and tends to see politics in terms of competing interests that more or less balance each other out. Most accounts of public policy making have thus focused on how policy outcomes are determined by prevailing institutional arrangements that structure the interests and behavior of economic and political agents. As Frank Fischer (2003, 4–5) has argued, policy analysis, in a somewhat caricatured form, tries to translate political and social issues into technically defined ends to be pursued by administrative means. For radical critics like Fischer, the tendency to neglect the role of ideas and values in policy has reduced much of policy analysis to depoliticized scientism that offers no genuine alternatives to established ways of thinking.

Rather than using traditional methods of policy analysis, this book draws more on the postpositivist policy analysis literature and its focus on the political implications of contestable policy presuppositions (Anderson 1987; Dryzek 1990; Fay 1975; Fischer 1998; Fischer 2003). Postpositivism, or postempiricism, here refers to a broader meta-theoretical critique of the dominant neopositivist methodologies in the social sciences. In the context of public policy analysis, it is associated particularly with an emphasis on the argumentative and discursive character of policy making and the use of interpretative and qualitative methods.

Instead of viewing theoretical ideas and concepts as some kind of static background assumptions, it is more useful for the purposes of this book to regard ideas and concepts, too, as a site of constant definitional struggle and political contestation. Based on these premises, my approach departs from the behaviorist or institutional modes of explanation of traditional policy analysis in favor of a more critical and interpretative approach, which holds that ideas and their expression in both politics and academic debates should as a kind or aspect of political action in its own right (see Finlayson 2004, 530–31).

It follows that policy goals or the criteria applied to assessing them are never self-evident, but always dependent on the theoretical and conceptual tools used to define them. Although policy makers may feel that they are involved in a rather dull process of problem solving, media policy, as viewed in this book, is a deeply political phenomenon (see Freedman 2008, 1).

The concepts and theoretical paradigms examined in this book are also real in the sense that they have a decisive influence in explanation. They frame political debate and determine the range of issues that are deemed important and the solutions that are possible. Although media policy practice, and to some extent its research, have moved away from explicit ideological and normative concerns, there are still guiding principles and values, whether they are explicit or not. It is only that changes in the fundamental principles that guide policy are often more subtle and harder to discern when policy discussions are couched in pragmatic concerns over technology or economics.

Ideas are not treated in this book simply as instrumental tools used by self-interested agents. Instead, ideas and concepts are beliefs that affect the range of policy options considered by actors as well as actors' perceptions of their interests. As Colin Hay (2004) notes, concepts and ideas provide interpretative schemas that limit the scope of policy making by defining the targets and goals of policy and delineating the range of instruments and settings that are considered legitimate.

The concept of media pluralism is thus conceived in this book as an object of political contestation in itself; it is a meeting point for different demands rooted in different social values, interests, and visions of democracy. The book is premised on the idea that the contestation of any normative and political concepts can be analyzed on at least three levels: in normative and theoretical debates, in their political, strategic or rhetoric uses, and on the level of implicit political rationalities and evaluation criteria on which political considerations rely. These different levels of analysis tend to imply different modes of discourse, often associated with different research approaches.

Yet without privileging any of these as grounds for objective knowledge production, all three levels can be seen as arenas of definitional contestation in which certain ideas and political rationalities are institutionalized and normalized. This furthermore implies the aim of illustrating how contested political ideas move from one domain to another, from theory to politics and further to the informational practices of governance, and how they are transformed in the process.

To illustrate this, I will heuristically employ the concepts of political rationalities and governmental technologies. According to Nikolas Rose and Peter Miller (1992), any forms of governance can be analyzed in terms of their political rationalities, "the changing discursive fields within which the exercise of power is conceptualized, the moral justifications for particular ways of exercising power by diverse authorities, notions of appropriate forms, objects and limits of politics and conceptions of the proper distribution of such tasks." Governmental technologies, on the other hand, refer to the "complex of mundane programs, calculation, techniques, apparatuses, documents and procedures through which authorities seek to embody and give effect to governmental ambitions" (ibid., 175).

The concepts of political rationalities and governmental technologies are often associated with a broader neo-Foucauldian framework of governmentality and its focus on understanding and analyzing the rationales and techniques of political power and public policy (see Dean 1999; Foucault 1991; Rose 1999; Rose and Miller 1992). Central to this perspective is the recognition that the activities of government and regulation are always bound up with developments in knowledge and the powers of expertise. In short, it is premised on the assumption that ideas and action are mutually constitutive. As Hay (2002, 258) argues, "it is the ideas actors hold about the context in which they find themselves, rather than the context itself, which ultimately informs the way in which they behave." This implies that definitions and interpretations of concepts such as media pluralism can have political effects independently of actual empirical changes in media structures or the interests of the parties involved.

The recognition of governing as a complex activity that cannot be viewed simply in terms of implementing a particular political or normative theory makes political rationalities conceptually distinct from political philosophies or ideological doctrines. It also means that political rationalities cannot be divorced from the mechanisms or technologies through which thinking about government is put into effect. The incorporation of philosophies or theories into governmental practice always requires connection with administrative techniques and forms of calculation that modify, if not transform, the original theories and their objectives.

Such techniques, it is argued, contribute to the governing of a certain area of social life as "intellectual machinery" that renders the world thinkable and amenable to regulation (Rose and Miller 1992; Rose 1999). In other words, governing a sphere requires that it can first be depicted in such a way that it can enter the sphere of conscious political calculation. Events need to be transformed into political language, and furthermore into information, reports, and statistics. And although necessary, these can never be neutral in the sense that they are always bound to specific political rationalities.

Empirical indicators of media pluralism analyzed in this book are prime examples of the kind of intellectual machinery that serves to move the abstract concept of media pluralism into the realm of political calculation and action.

According to Rose and Miller (1992, 178), political discourse is, by definition, "a domain for the formulation and justification of idealized framings for representing reality, analysing it and rectifying it." From this perspective, analyzing policy is not so much about unraveling the meaning of concepts or words such as freedom, pluralism, or democracy, but rather about finding out what they do, the way they function in connection with other elements, what they make possible, the sentiments they mobilize, and the regimes of truth they constitute (Rose 1999, 29–30).

In emphasizing the role of ideas, the purpose of this book is not to conflate social reality and our ideas about social reality, or to reduce politics to mere discourses or language games. Politics is not just about ideas but also about socio-economic conflicts between different interests, and the varying power of different interests to influence policies. As McQuail (2007a, 14) puts it, reasons underlying media policy involve "an intricate mixture of pragmatic self-interest and more fundamental values." The role of fundamental values is not always explicit or even intentional, but concepts or principles can acquire a certain status and meaning both because of intentional attempts to define them and because of contingent factors related to the policy process. It needs to be emphasized that the main aim here is not to explain causes of policy choices, but rather to understand different political rationalities by making them visible and providing an intellectual basis for further arguments and alternative political imaginaries. For the purposes of this book, then, ideas matter regardless of whether they are presented as coherent ideologies or as ad hoc justifications for policy choices.

In addition to emphasizing the role of ideas in public policy, the approach chosen here also draws broadly on the traditions of critical theory and a critical realist philosophy of science. According to Iris Marion Young (2000, 10), we can talk of critical theory as a general theoretical approach, meaning socially and historically situated normative analysis and argument. Critical theory, in this sense, does not derive its principles from philosophical premises about morality, human nature, or the good life, but instead reflects on existing social relations and processes to identify what we experience as valuable in them. Theoretical ideals are not descriptions or blueprints that correspond to reality. Instead, they allow thinkers and actors to reflect on reality from a distance, reveal deficiencies in contemporary political arrangements, illuminate new structures and relations, and envision alternative future possibilities (ibid.).

The use of theory in this context does not then imply constructing grand theoretical systems, but as Nick Couldry (2008, 161) puts it: "theory is useful only if through its relative generality it enables us to engage better with the particular, that is, for better tools with which to practise our suspicion towards totalising claims, whether by academics, politicians, or media executives."

New knowledge is never based on new observations alone, but it is built upon previous theories and concepts, which in turn can be conceived as causes for the formation of new theories and concepts. In line with a broader critical realist philosophy of science, this book will thus focus on the preexisting theories that inform the development of particular concepts. The purpose of this is to open the theoretical background of unwanted social or political practices to new lines of criticism (see Patomäki 2002, 152–55; Sayer 2000). Rethinking the terms of political theory and policy discourse is therefore about opening up a new space for both political thought and action. As such, the approach denies the relativism of postmodern perspectives, whose only aim is to deconstruct different discourses or language games for their own sake. As Andrew Sayer (2000, 47) argues, "critical realism accepts 'epistemic relativism,' that is the view that the world can only be known in terms of available descriptions or discourses, but it rejects 'judgemental relativism'— the view that one cannot judge between different discourses and decide that some accounts are better than others."

THE STRUCTURE AND SCOPE OF THIS BOOK

Part I of this book focuses on the values and assumptions behind the notion of media pluralism, particularly from the perspective of political philosophy and democratic theory. I argue that different theories of democracy and the public sphere suggest different conceptions of pluralism and have different assessments of its value. Part II of this book traces the political rationalities behind different uses and definitions of the concept of media pluralism and analyzes how they have been generated and mobilized in European media policy. In particular, the policy uses of media pluralism are analyzed through two cases or exhibits. The first empirical exhibit discusses recent attempts to define media pluralism as a common objective for European media policy. In the second case, I analyze different uses of pluralism and diversity in the context of recent debates on the role and legitimacy of public service media.

Revealing the vagueness of the concept, both cases illustrate how media pluralism is routinely employed to argue for opposite goals; for both expanding and limiting the role of public service media, and for both increasing and decreasing the regulation of the commercial media industry. In addition to the obvious conflict between economic and more cultural or democratic rationalities, both cases also reveal a tendency to avoid explicitly ideological arguments and to treat media policy as a matter of pragmatic administration. One part of this tendency, I argue, is that in the context of

European media policy, media pluralism is increasingly understood as an empirically measurable variable instead of a normative value grounded in democratic and political values. Against this background, Part II critically analyzes the various empirical indicators of media pluralism and discusses their normative implications and underlying rationalities.

The actual research material used consists of three broad categories of texts: theoretical literature, which provides the normative basis for debates on media pluralism; the policy documents, position papers and studies that provide definitions and arguments about media pluralism as a policy objective; and the empirical studies and reports that have sought to operationalize and measure media pluralism as a tangible indicator of media structure or performance. The overall time frame of the study extends roughly from the early 1990s to the present. The institutional context of the analysis lies at the European level, which mostly means policy discussions within the European Union (EU). In addition, I also refer to the documents of the Council of Europe and various other interest groups and organizations that lack the binding force of more formal modes of media governance, but that nevertheless have influenced the terms of European policy debates by means of expert reports and nonbinding recommendations. In analyzing the actual political arguments and justifications used in media politics, the research material consists of texts that have constructed and contested the objectives and rationalities of European media policies, such as reports, directives, declarations, advisory opinions, speeches, discussion papers, as well as studies that have documented these.

Most of the material is collected around the two empirical case studies. The first concerns the conceptual contestation around attempts to outline a common European approach to the issues of media concentration and pluralism. Although there is no coherent supranational regulatory framework and much of the regulatory competence remains with individual member states, the debate within the EU since the early 1990s offers a particularly interesting example of the different values, interests and definitional struggles that issues around media pluralism raise. The main documents analyzed here consist of successive documents on the topic by both the European Commission (EC) and the European Parliament, and in particular the EC's recent three-step initiative for advancing debate on media pluralism (see EC 2007a).

The second case study deals with the debates on public service media, which has been another major arena for struggles between contradictory tendencies in European media policy. The key document here is the EC's Broadcasting Communication (EC 2009), which sets out the rules for state aid to public service broadcasting. Both these initiatives also involved a consultation process that included written contributions from various stakeholders, including the media industry, professional associations, and civil society organizations.

Finally, a third set of research material used in the book involves reports and studies that have explicitly attempted to operationalize media pluralism as an empirically measurable construct. This includes both academic and policy-oriented studies, including the recent study commissioned by the EC to develop concrete empirical indicators for measuring media pluralism in EU member states (ICRI et al. 2009).

One obvious issue that rises from this choice of research material concerns focus on the European level. The choice to deal with supranational European debates can reasonably be challenged on the grounds that questions concerning media pluralism and most other culturally and socially sensitive media policy issues still remain under the explicit competence of individual EU member states. Even though I have chosen to examine debates on the European level, I do not want to suggest that there are no national differences in policy approaches or that the supranational level has superseded national policies in importance. National governments and regulators often defend the interests of their national media companies, their own distinctive cultural and social models, or other aspects considered vital to national interests.

An alternative strategy for analyzing the different definitions and uses of media pluralism could have involved a comparison of different national contexts, including differences between the United States and Europe or between different European countries. However, there is also clearly an emerging common European media policy discourse, which covers an increasing number of issues and which not only reflects the positions of EU member states but also increasingly shapes the terms of media policy discussions. It can thus be assumed that, despite their limitations, supranational policy debates have had a significant impact on national policies and acted as a catalyst for the convergence of different policy approaches across Europe and perhaps beyond (see Harcourt 2005).

Because of the EU's nature as a supranational polity, analyses of EU-level policy often tend to focus on questions of jurisdiction, competence, and the interplay between different levels and sites of decision making. My purpose here, however, is to use the European-level debates as an example to illustrate some contradictions in the definitions and uses of media pluralism and to offer new critical perspectives on its meaningful uses. As a policy arena that is strongly characterized by conflicting interests and different policy traditions, rather than coherence or consensus, the European debates serve this purpose well. This book thus differs from most existing accounts in that it does not focus on the policy process or on institutional competencies, but rather on the argumentation used and its underlying principles, values and rationales (for more detailed institutional analyses of European media policy, see, for example, Collins 1998; Harcourt 2005; Kaitatzi-Whitlock 2005; Levy 1999; Michalis 2007; Sarikakis 2004).

Instead of aiming at a comprehensive treatment of European media policy or even the regulations regarding media pluralism, the analysis is guided by the critical aim to illustrate different rationalities, deconstruct their normative assumptions, and to open up new theoretical perspectives to understanding and deploying media pluralism as a normative value in future academic and political debates. In this sense, this book is also an attempt at scholarly self-reflection, since academic research is of course itself one of the institutions of intellectual machinery that produce the conceptual frames for political discourse. As Fischer (2003, 35) argues: "the recognition that scientific expertise is itself shaped by power and politics is the first step toward a discursive understanding of the policy process."

Recognizing that policy issues and available alternatives are socially and discursively constructed has clear critical and normative implications as well. In line with theories of radical and plural democracy, which I discuss in Part I, this book emphasizes that concepts such as pluralism, democracy, and freedom have no ultimate rational foundation (see Mouffe 1993, 145). Instead, the concepts and rationalities of political thought are always indeterminate and open to a multitude of interpretations. The role of critical research itself is to offer these interpretations and to create new articulations that will serve as a basis for real political alternatives.

PART I

Theorizing Pluralism and the Public Sphere

The following three chapters address the assumptions underlying the debate on media pluralism from the perspective of contemporary political philosophy and democratic theory. Beyond the general consensus that the public sphere requires a broad range of voices, the exact meaning and implications of pluralism as a normative principle remain controversial and arguably undertheorized in both media studies and political theory. While much of the debate on media pluralism as a policy goal or as an object of empirical measurement takes it for granted that pluralism is important for democracy, there is less agreement on why and how: What is the purpose of media pluralism? What are its problems and limits? And what norms or theoretical models should we use to conceptualize and justify it?

In line with the approach outlined in the introduction, the idea here is that it is relevant to engage with democratic theory, not only in order to highlight the gap between the ideals and the reality but also to question the normative assumptions and arguments made in contemporary academic and political debates.

The following chapters draw on discussions within the fields of both political philosophy and media studies. In particular, I will deconstruct the standard assumptions and readings of different theories of democracy adopted in media studies. My goal is thus to challenge the theoretical models and metaphors such as the marketplace of ideas and the public sphere that are commonly invoked in media policy and to question their established interpretations.

Taking some distance from the attractiveness of pluralism as a common sense principle, the following chapters highlight some of the differences among political theories, all of which, on the surface, appear to advocate a pluralistic public sphere as a central value. Chapter 1 distinguishes three different models of democracy and the public sphere, and analyzes their implications for conceptualizing media pluralism. Chapter 2 problematizes the implications of the revival of pluralism in contemporary social and political theory and raises some questions about the ambiguities and problems associated with its application in media studies. Finally, Chapter 3 synthesizes some of the arguments and discusses their implications for critical media studies and for a rethinking of the notion of media pluralism.

CHAPTER 1

Three Models of Democratic Pluralism

Although much of the confusion surrounding the notion of pluralism in media studies stems from its different uses in different contexts, there is also an inherent element of ambiguity within the concept of pluralism itself. As is the case with most *isms* that carry significant political implications, pluralism is an essentially contested concept that is subject to endless arguments about its interpretation and implications.

It is questionable then whether it is possible to mount any general defense of pluralism, because pluralism itself is so plural; it exists in several versions that can be incompatible with one another. Rather than as a specific ideology or a school of thought, McLennan (1995) argues that pluralism is best conceived as a general intellectual orientation whose specific manifestations would be expected to change depending on the context.

Even in the field of political theory, however, the concept of pluralism has several meanings. It may stand for the empirical claim that different people hold different values, or for the normative view that such plurality is desirable. As a consequence, classic liberal philosophers, empirical political scientists, and contemporary theorists of radical difference and identity politics have all employed pluralism as a political value, yet they all emphasize different aspects and have diverging views on how best to realize the notion.

In this chapter, I will illustrate different ways of conceptualizing pluralism as a democratic value by distinguishing three traditions or categories of democratic theory, all of which have to varying degrees also influenced academic and political debates on media and democracy. My aim is not to categorize different models of democracy as such, but rather to deconstruct some of the most commonly used normative frameworks used in media studies and to rethink their implications especially from the point of view of how they conceptualize pluralism as a value in public communication.[1]

My discussion is structured by examining three different approaches that build on critiques of the other approaches. All have been used to justify different conceptions of the role of media in a democracy, and they espouse a different version of pluralism.

> Liberal pluralism. Contemporary media politics and the debate on media pluralism in particular are still largely grounded in the basic values of political liberalism, such as individual freedom, personal development, dispersion of power and self-government. However, the legacy of many liberal political theorists for media politics is controversial and contested. One of the best examples is the metaphor of "the free marketplace of ideas," which today is one of the dominant models for conceptualizing the value of pluralism and diversity in the media. Although associated with many classical liberal theorists, it has been argued that the metaphor probably reflects more the contemporary ideological belief that market behavior paradigmatically represents freedom. Below, I will demonstrate the controversial legacy of liberal political theory by focusing on the idea of the marketplace of ideas and its problematic association with the ideas of J. S. Mill and other liberal political theorists.
>
> Deliberative democracy. While the liberal discourse of the marketplace of ideas is still powerful in policy rhetoric, much of the discussion in academic debates on media and democracy leans on the framework of deliberative democracy and the concept of the public sphere, which some claim is now the quintessential "God-term" in scholarly debates over media and democracy (Gitlin 1998, 168). One of the central ideas of deliberative democracy is the attempt to reconcile disagreements and the fact of pluralism through the idea of a rational-critical public sphere and discursive formation of public opinion. However, there is tension between the framework of deliberative democracy and its pluralist critics, who argue that the emphasis on rational deliberation

---

[1]For more thorough attempts to categorize theories of democracy and the public sphere, see Christians et al. (2009), Cunningham (2002), Curran (2011), Ferree et al. (2002), and Held (2006).

and consensus ignores unequal relations of power, the depth of social pluralism, and fundamental value differences. For these reasons, the deliberative approach, often associated with Jürgen Habermas's work (1989, 1996, 2006) is increasingly read in media studies as a defense of an outdated and overtly pessimistic ideal which has little practical relevance in contemporary societies.

Radical pluralism. Finally, as an alternative to the former two, more established models, I discuss the recent radical-pluralist theories of democracy and their critiques of both deliberative democracy and traditional liberal pluralism. Radical-pluralist or agonistic theories of democracy here refer to theories in which the public sphere is conceived as a site for political struggle and conflict, and not only as a site for the formation of common will or consensus (Connolly 1991; Connolly 1995; Connolly 2005; Honig 1993; Mouffe 1993; Mouffe 2000; Mouffe 2005). While many of these theorists have recently gained prominence in political philosophy, in the field of media studies their perspectives have been used more as oppositional discourses to criticize the biases and flaws in the existing normative frameworks. This has raised doubts over whether they have anything worthwhile to contribute to more concrete or institutional questions. The implications and potential significance of the radical-pluralist approach for media studies and media policy are discussed here mainly by reference to the political philosophy of Chantal Mouffe. Mouffe's radical democratic pluralism provides a fundamental critique of the deliberative approach to the public sphere and democracy, and this critique has significant consequences for current debates on media and democracy. Perhaps more importantly, however, I argue that her approach provides an equally strong critique of naïve pluralism that celebrates all multiplicity and diversity, without paying attention to the continued centrality of the questions of power and exclusion in the public sphere.

Each of the three approaches outlined above offers a distinct conceptual framework for understanding media pluralism: for liberal pluralists it is the marketplace of ideas and individual choice; for deliberative democrats pluralism is a means to improve the epistemic quality of public deliberation and discursive reconciliation of disagreement; and finally, radical pluralists criticize both for unnecessary idealizations and instead focus on the continuous contestation of power relations and hegemonic structures.

LIBERAL PLURALISM AND THE FREE MARKETPLACE OF IDEAS

In political science, the term pluralism is often still associated with a mid-twentieth century strand of liberal political science that drew attention to the existence of multiple centers of power and conceived democracy as the self-regulation of society through competition among groups over power and social privileges (Dahl 1956; see also Marcil-Lacoste 1992, 129; McLennan 1995, 35). As a central normative principle of liberal democracy, however, pluralism has a much longer history. Premised on the impossibility of unambiguously establishing truth, right or good, especially in social and political affairs, pluralism has been widely celebrated as the cornerstone of the liberal conception of democracy. Although liberalism can certainly mean many things, it can be argued that the general affirmation of individual freedom and pluralism over any collective substantive idea of the common good is central to all those different meanings.

Most conceptions of pluralism share the basic assumption that values or conceptions of the good cannot be reduced to any single hierarchy. The epistemological foundation of pluralism therefore consists in opposition to monism and the view that diversity is a social good that prevents the dominance of one particular idea (Smith 2006, 21–22). Value pluralism, as discussed by philosophers such as Isaiah Berlin (1969, 167–69), maintains that there are no single right answers to questions of value. Similarly, John Rawls (1996, xviii) famously argued that political liberalism begins with the recognition that disagreement and conflict between "incompatible yet reasonable" moral doctrines is an enduring feature of contemporary societies and an ineradicable element of their political institutions. More recently, the inescapable plurality of reasonable arguments and its consequences for moral philosophy have also been extensively discussed by Amartya Sen (2010).

From a liberal perspective, in contrast to more community-centered or unitary views of society, pluralism, variety, and conflict between differing views are commonly seen as fruitful and as being a necessary condition for human progress. Antagonism is seen as mediating progress, and the clash of divergent opinions and interests, in the realm of argument and in economic competition, as well as struggles in the political domain, can be seen as inherently positive (Bobbio 1990, 21–24).

One of the most famous and influential arguments for the social desirability of disagreement and diversity and their contribution to intellectual and social progress was made by philosopher John Stuart Mill, whose *On Liberty* discusses freedom of thought and discussion as essentially an argument about the importance of disagreement in a democratic political culture. In short,

Mill argues that first, any opinion that is being suppressed may possibly be true; secondly, in practice most beliefs are neither wholly true nor wholly false, so only by allowing for the expression of contrary opinions can the whole truth be uncovered; and third, even if the opinion is false, it is only through full and frequent discussion that it can be rationally rejected and prevented from becoming a dogma (Mill 1948, 15–40). Therefore, the only effective way to deal with erroneous or dangerous ideas is to refute them, not to suppress them.

In keeping with the general opposition to monism, pluralism also implies that political power should be dispersed and not be allowed to accumulate in the hands of the few. These principles, which are broadly accepted as the basis of liberal democracy, also form the essence of media pluralism as a normative value. Their interpretation, however, is constantly contested in theories of media and democracy.

The strength of liberal pluralism derives from the intuitive normative appeal of its basic principles, and in this sense the ideas of philosophers such as Mill, Berlin, and Rawls still provide an eloquent rationale for thinking about media pluralism as a political value. The dispersion of power and the critique of any monistic ideas of truth remain key justifications in political philosophy with which to defend freedom of speech and its close association with the principle of media pluralism. The purpose here is not to argue that the salience of these principles as such has diminished. In fact, many of the theories that are discussed below can be placed within the liberal tradition, even when there is polemic against some of its interpretations.[2] The interpretation of the abstract principle of pluralism, and its implications and differing emphases within the liberal tradition, however, continue to be intensely contested in both political philosophy and politics. More often than not, this is also the case when the principle is applied to theorize the role of the media as modern social and political institutions.

Perhaps most influentially, the implications of the liberal tradition for thinking about media and democracy have been guided by the classic *Four Theories of the Press*, which presents the "Libertarian theory of the press"

---

[2]Chantal Mouffe (2000, 18) acknowledges her debt to the liberal tradition by recognizing that the acceptance of pluralism, understood as "the end of a substantive idea of the good life," is the single-most important defining feature of modern liberal democracy that sets it apart from ancient models of democracy. In this sense, pluralism is understood not merely as a fact, as something that must be dealt with, but rather as an axiological principle that is "constitutive at the conceptual level of the very nature of modern democracy and considered as something that we should celebrate and enhance" (ibid., 19).

as a development of the philosophical principles found in the writings of philosophers such as John Milton, Thomas Jefferson and J. S. Mill (Siebert, Peterson, and Schramm 1963). The metaphor of the free marketplace of ideas, which in *Four Theories* is explicitly assigned to Mill, leads to the assumption that the mass media operate under the guiding principle of free enterprise and that all media compete in an open market, where their success depends on the public which it seeks to serve (ibid., 52).

Four Theories thus clearly establishes the articulation between diversity of ideas and the idea of "free competition in the market place of information, opinion, and entertainment." Although the authors acknowledge that the ideal of free markets can never completely reflect reality, there remains a clear commitment to the idea that "the less government becomes involved the better" (ibid., 53). Even though it discusses many of the shortcomings of free markets and introduces the "social responsibility theory" as its alternative, this articulation carries some fundamental normative implications. The conception of "the marketplace of ideas," in particular, has arguably strengthened an implicit rational choice ontology and the economic vocabulary of consumer choice and competition in discussions on media pluralism.

Subsequently, the liberalism of Mill and other early advocates of free speech has often been interpreted in a way where pluralism, variety, and choice are seen as the opposite of state oppression or paternalism, as constructing a narrative of media history as a continuum from public regulation and censorship towards ever increasing freedom for both producers and consumers of the media (see Curran 2002, 4–8). According to Nicholas Garnham (2000, 168), the liberal-pluralist approach has consequently taken a narrow view on the relationship between media and politics, describing it as one between media that were supposedly free because they were market-based and the institutions of representative party democracy.

Critical theorists, in turn, have criticized conventional liberal pluralism for its strategic avoidance of political economy and the unequal opportunities open to different social actors (see McClure 1992, 118). The problem in applying liberal theories of the free press to contemporary conditions lies in their assumption that political power is the main external threat to individuals who are otherwise naturally capable of expressing their opinions (Keane 1991, 36–38). This "free information-flow" paradigm views the media themselves as free and as neutral conduits of information, and fails to represent the ways in which information and opinions are embedded in communicative practices and the structure of the media which set agendas, and constrain possible choices and thereby shape public debates. Consequently, liberal pluralist perspectives ignore the questions of unequal cultural and economic power that arise from cultural production itself. As Keane (1991, 89) argues, liberal models of the media have developed a "fetish of market competition," which ignores the forms in which communication markets themselves restrict pluralism and freedom of the media. In this sense, the liberal discourse of market competition and choice has largely failed to provide a compelling model on which to base any critical understanding of media pluralism.

This is not to say that all proponents of market doctrines would assume well-functioning media markets without acknowledging any market failures or needs for regulation, or even that choice and competition could not be regarded as valuable objectives as such. Issues related to asymmetries of power also arise in the market-consumer context, and it remains important to acknowledge that often media consumers simply still do not have much choice. Instead, the point is to question whether the marketplace is the only proper metaphor for conceptualizing the value of broader political objectives such as media pluralism.

Reflecting the dominance of this discourse, media policy discourses (especially in the United States but to a lesser extent in Europe as well) commonly conceptualize the need for plurality of opinion through the metaphor of the marketplace of ideas (for the genealogy of the concept, see Gordon 1997; Peters 2004). While the articulation of freedom and pluralism with the market has been influential, a number of critics have argued that the whole notion rests on implausible theoretical underpinnings (Baker 2007; Goodman 2004; Ingber 1984). By analogizing democratic discourse to market exchange, the model is all about competitive markets that can supply consumers with what they want. As such, it depends upon the prior existence of private, autonomous individual subjects who know their interests and who make rational choices in the marketplace. Furthermore, in assuming that each individual has equal access to the marketplace and that the marketplace itself is only a neutral mediator, the model is blind to the unequal relations of power (within media corporations and between those corporations and individual citizens) and the differences between groups and individuals in getting their voices heard. In short, it ignores that the media are not exempt from broader relations of power in society, as some social actors have more cultural, social, and economic resources than others to access the media. The model also ignores that the media themselves are structurally biased, as market-based media themselves privilege certain voices and prejudice against voices that are critical of consumer capitalism, for instance.

Consequently, the claim that the market maximizes plurality and choice (or that it is a proper model for conceptualizing plurality and choice) is routinely questioned in critical media studies. Instead, with the maximization of audience in mind, the media are seen to offer mass appeal content which leads to insufficient diversity and underrepresentation of particular audiences, privileges corporate speech, and silences non-commercial and non-market opinions and forms of life (Keane 1991, 77–89).

Many commentators have also argued that the metaphor and its corresponding tenets of minimal regulation and freedom of choice for consumers actually represent rather poorly the original ideas of free speech philosophers such as J. S. Mill (see Baum 2001; Gordon 1997; Splichal 2002). John Durham Peters (2004) has shown that a wide range of figures from Mill to Adam Smith have all been credited with inventing the marketplace of ideas metaphor, even though there is no evidence of any of them even using the phrase. As noted by Jill Gordon (1997), the market metaphor, more than representing Mill's views, probably reflects the current ideological belief that market behavior paradigmatically represents freedom. It is clear from the reading of *On Liberty* alone that Mill's central concern was with the quality and range of ideas presented in the public sphere. Mill even noted that the freedom of the press no longer needs to be protected from state tyranny, but more so from the "tyranny of the majority," a sort of social control that limits diversity of perspectives (Mill 1948, 13–14). Therefore, instead of recommending anything like a marketplace of ideas, Mill's wording suggests that beyond mere passive tolerance of all ideas, we must "encourage" and "countenance" the expression of minority opinions in particular (ibid., 42). Rather than advocating anything like a marketplace, which judges the merits of ideas and opinions based on their popularity, Mill argued that: "if either of the two opinions has a better claim than the other, not merely to be tolerated, but to be encouraged and countenanced, it is the one which happens at the particular time and place to be in a minority" (ibid., 42).

It is evident that Mill's case for free speech is essentially about the value of diversity, particularly minority opinions, and not about negative freedom of expression, let alone consumer choice as such. According to Bruce Baum (2001, 506–10), Mill was well aware of the connection between public opinion formation and the social relations of power. Mill's main concern was with equal access for different ideas to the public sphere, and because power is unequally distributed, the mere negative freedom of expression or the unregulated marketplace of ideas will not guarantee pluralistic public discussion.[3] Instead, in the marketplace of

---

[3] Mill begins his argument by noting that his concern is not primarily with defending liberty of press against corrupt or tyrannical government, but against any abuse of power (Mill 1948, 13).

ideas, the ideas that survive or prevail will be those espoused either by the most powerful or the most numerous in society. The metaphor therefore implies an outcome that runs counter to Mill's conception of freedom of expression and is conducive to the same "social tyranny" he wishes to prevent (see also Gordon 1997, 3).

Despite these problems, the discourse of market competition and choice is still central to media policy, and it frames much of the debate on media pluralism and diversity. As Keane (1991, 52) noted, the old language of "liberty of the press," shaped by the ethos of private market competition, has ensured that debates over media policies since the 1980s have largely been shaped in terms of individual choice, deregulation and market competition, while other public interest values sound increasingly hollow. Illustrating the problematic legacy of liberal political philosophy, the term "liberal" and liberalization have in contemporary media policy come to mean arguments for deregulation and for market-based media. Although there have been some attempts to build more critical theories of the media on the traditions of positive liberty or communication rights that might be closer to Mill's original intentions, basic liberal values such as freedom of communication have been largely reduced to rhetorical catchwords that are used to legitimate political decisions or to defend the interests of media corporations. According to Paul Jones (2000, 319), they are mainly used as "means of corporatist bargaining between owners of capitalized means of communication and the state."

For many critical theorists, the association with the defense of existing institutions of capitalist democracy still gives a bad name to liberal pluralism. In media policy literature, pluralist perspectives on politics and policy are still sometimes presented in contrast to critical perspectives, as views that see politics and policy making as a more or less balanced competition between multiple interest groups (see Freedman 2008, 25; Garnham 2000, 167).

While the various uses and abuses of liberal principles need not discredit the principles themselves, their use in media policy has given rise to fundamental confusions. The long tradition of critique against the free marketplace concept has made it clear that this is far from an adequate framework for conceptualizing media pluralism or any other than economic goals for media policy. In response to the ambiguity and misuses of the liberal discourse of freedom and choice in media policy, critical scholars have instead mostly employed the notion of the public sphere and the more recent deliberative or participatory models of democracy as a theoretical framework in which to seek grounding for the principles of media pluralism.

For the past few decades, the dominant strand of critical academic thinking about the relationship between media and democracy has been based on the concept of the public sphere and the so-called deliberative turn in democratic theory. Coinciding with broader concerns for revitalizing liberal democracy, the rise of the public sphere approach has been closely linked to critiques of both Marxist and conventional liberal traditions in political theory. Instead of theories of dominant ideology or the negative freedom of the press, the debate on media and democracy has consequently been increasingly couched in concepts such as the public sphere, civil society, and citizenship (Garnham 2000, 168–9). Proposed as reformed or radicalized ideals of liberal democratic theory, the ideas of deliberative democracy and the public sphere largely grow out of the rejection of economist models of democracy and their focus on the aggregation of private interests.

While the first use of the term *deliberative democracy* is credited to Joseph M. Bessette (1980), the increasing popularity of the deliberative or discursive conception of democracy, especially in media studies, is largely attributed to Jürgen Habermas's work.

One aspect of the difference between deliberative and the liberal model of democracy is clearly captured in Habermas's (1989) analysis of Mill in *The Structural Transformation of the Public Sphere*. According to Habermas, Mill recognized public opinion as a powerful force, but one that needs to be brought under control.[4] Public opinion thus came to be understood more as a compulsion towards conformity than as a critical force (Habermas 1989, 133). Overall, Mill and other liberal philosophers were ambivalent toward the public sphere and public opinion, thinking that its force must be limited, because of the tyranny of public opinion (ibid., 134). As a result, Habermas argues that public opinion became understood in most liberal democratic theories as a mere limit on power (ibid., 136). The project of deliberative democracy, in contrast, can be understood as an attempt to envision the role of the public sphere and public opinion in a more positive sense, not only in terms of negative liberty.

The common denominator for the various versions of deliberative democracy is the view that democracy is something more than just a process of fair bargaining and the aggregation of preexisting preferences. It is argued

---

[4]This is made clear by Mill (1948, 3) in the introduction to *On Liberty*, where he argues that the will of the people "practically means the will of the most numerous or the most active part of the people."

that true participation requires citizens to engage in informed discussion with other citizens. Therefore, in contrast to the liberal model of the marketplace of ideas, the public sphere approach provides a more expansive view of media and democracy that emphasizes the epistemic role of the media as an agency of public deliberation and debate. The public sphere approach thus replaces the metaphor of the market with that of a public forum or an arena, which consequently steers the focus away from the satisfaction of individual preferences towards discursive relationships and the formation of public opinion.

When employed in media studies, the concepts of public sphere and deliberative democracy are almost invariably traced back to the work of Habermas and his many followers and critics. Habermas (1998) himself has characterized the deliberative or discursive conception as the third model of democracy, beyond liberal and communitarian traditions. In contrast to these traditions, the deliberative approach denies the pluralism of fixed differences (individual or community) that lead either to the aggregation model of predefined individual interests or to irreducible community identities. Instead, it places the normative core of political community in public dialogue, where different perspectives can meet and potentially interact. The liberal emphasis on pluralism is thus complemented, and qualified, with an emphasis on rational-critical deliberation as a means of reconciling diverse informed opinions (see also Habermas 2006).

With their emphasis on public communication, the deliberative models of democracy have understandably provided a popular lens through which to theorize the relationship between media and democracy (see, for example, Curran 2002; Dahlgren 1995; Garnham 1992 and 2000; Jones 2000; Thompson 1995; Venturelli 1998). In approaches informed by deliberative democracy, the role of the public sphere is generally conceptualized in terms of open critical-rational discussion between free and equal citizens. As such, these approaches provide a normative ideal of the public sphere, which is free from government and corporate interests, inclusive, and aimed at understanding or agreement. As certain social institutions seemingly encourage this type of communication more than others, it also provides an explicitly normative framework, which has been employed in debates on media policy and the necessary institutional foundations of public debate. The hypothetical media system built around this ideal would provide an impartial arena for public debate over matters of common interest that is open to all, free from both state and market manipulation, and oriented to critical-rational formation of public opinion. In particular, much of the theoretical work on the justifications of public service broadcasting has been framed in the public sphere approach.[5]

Rather than signifying a close association with Habermas's normative-theoretical project, the term *public sphere* has become understood more generally as a conceptual resource or perspective on which much of the discussion on media pluralism is at least implicitly premised. The demand that access to the public sphere should be as open as possible to all citizens and all views has unquestionably provided a clear normative framework for debates on media pluralism and diversity in media policy (see Hitchens 2006, 50). James Bohman (2007) has recently argued that the model of deliberative democracy and the public sphere provides a clear basis for a positive, normative argument for dispersing media power more widely and so for raising the epistemic level of deliberative practices. In this sense, the public sphere approach and the framework of deliberative democracy undoubtedly give one answer to questions about the purpose of media pluralism.

However, the concept of the public sphere and its usefulness as a normative framework has also become increasingly contested. According to Habermas, democratic will-formation draws its legitimating force from procedures and institutions that "allow the better arguments to come into play in various forms of deliberation" (Habermas 1998, 242). This understanding of idealized rational-critical communication, however, is often claimed to have become inadequate in attempts to understand the complexities of contemporary mediated communication. The dynamic and complex nature of communication systems and the proliferation of different forms and modes of communication arguably weaken the appeal of the ideal of "rational communication" (see Keane 1999; 2009). Especially against the revival of pluralism in social theory and the postmodern questioning of universal theories and their visions of the common good, Habermas, and by extension many other deliberative democrats, are seen as defending an outdated and overtly pessimistic ideal of a unitary public sphere which has little relevance in contemporary mediated societies.

Furthermore, many critics have noted that the discussion on deliberative democracy tends to be highly abstract, and in concrete contexts its implications or feasibility have received much less research attention. Susan Stokes (1998)

---

[5]Habermas himself has not systematically applied the abstract ideals of deliberative democracy or the public sphere to the media or the design of any other social and political institutions (but see Habermas 2006). Regarding media politics, "the public sphere approach" thus refers here to the interpretation of his work in contemporary media studies. For its uses in theorizing the role of public service broadcasting, see, for example, Moe and Syvertsen (2008).

notes that despite their attractiveness in theory, deliberative ideals may in a number of practical contexts lead to pathological consequences. It is therefore not unproblematic to try to design or even assess social or political institutions such as the media based on some abstract rules of ideal discourse.

The questioning of the public sphere approach in recent social and political theory has also raised doubts over its relevance in media and communication studies. Uses of Habermas's conceptualization of the public sphere, in particular, have been criticized for failing to adequately theorize pluralism, openness and political equality, in at least three ways: critics say they are too rationalistic and thus exclusive in privileging certain communicative forms and cultural modes of discourse and overlooking fictional or rhetorical modes of communication, for instance; they draw the line between public and private in a way that excludes certain groups of citizens or political matters; and they overvalue agreement and universal norms, and thus deny difference, disagreement, and conflict as political and democratic resources.

One of the primary critiques of deliberative democracy is that it privileges a conception of rationality and reasonableness that turns into exclusionary norms (Young 2000, 45). Many critics see that the deliberative emphasis on communicative reason inevitably leads to supporting the status quo in terms of existing exclusions and inequalities. This is because in privileging rational argument and articulateness, the emphasis on communicative reason fails to acknowledge the normalizing tendencies involved in the designation of a particular form of communication as the rational, democratically legitimate norm (see, for example, Baumeister 2003; Benhabib 2002; Fraser 1992; Gardiner 2004; Villa 1992; Young 2000).

This criticism has had clear implications in media studies. According to Garnham (2000, 169–70), the public sphere approach has been used as a normative test against which to judge the performance of contemporary media in terms of either the rationality of their discourse or the range of views or speakers accorded access. However, there is a tension between these two criteria: a critique of the "dumbing down" or tabloidization of news, for instance, can be seen as an attack against the decaying rationality of the public sphere, yet the emphasis on public standards of argument may implicitly exclude those who are less capable of following those rules. The emphasis on pluralism and access to different voices, on the other hand, can lead to cultural populism, as in defending greater access for "ordinary people" to public debate traditionally dominated by the elites (ibid., 172).

It is evident that the concept of the public sphere includes a strong aspect of commonality and unity. The term public itself implies an orientation to issues of shared concern or to a collective space, which makes its relationship with the notion of pluralism particularly problematic. In most formulations of the public sphere, participants are in principle governed by the search for something like the general interest or common good. As a theoretical concept the public sphere is thus unavoidably associated with the task of constructing forms of social coordination that produce solidarity and commonality. This had led to the critique that it overemphasizes social unity and rational consensus while underestimating the depth of societal pluralism and the fundamental nature of value conflicts, both in the sense of cultural differences and structural conflicts of interest. The general thrust of deliberative democracy is thus seen to be too heavily dependent on the view that a benign social order must be grounded in the ideal of consensus. While social reality is increasingly conceived as a chaotic situation of diversity and complexity, the insistence on rational consensus is seen as "too idealized, too unrealistic, and too academic" (Rescher 1993, 165).

Overall, it is felt that the emphasis on consensus and universal criteria of rationality ignores the inequalities between social groups and their specific needs. Iris Marion Young (1997, 401) has argued that the defining characteristic of a public is plurality and that it is irreducible to a single denominator. Therefore, a conception of publicity that requires its members to put aside their differences in order to uncover the common good is considered to destroy its very meaning. Or as Bauman (1997, 202) puts it even more bluntly: "Habermas's 'perfect communication,' which measures its own perfection by consensus and the exclusion of dissent, is another dream of death which radically cures the ills of freedom's life."

Consequently, the relationship between pluralism and the commonality inherent in the notion of the public sphere has proved to be one of the central points of contention in recent democratic theory (see Bohman and Rehg 1997; Phillips 2000). It must be granted that much of the criticism is based on a rather simplified reading of deliberative democracy and especially its more recent versions, including Habermas's later work, which can be seen as advocating a much more plural conception of public spheres than its critics argue (see Brady 2004; Dahlberg 2005b; Dryzek and Niemeyer 2006; Garnham 2007; Habermas 1992; 1996; 2006). Yet regardless of how justified the critiques are, it can be argued that despite acknowledging the plurality of public spheres, Habermas continues to rely on rational consensus as a regulative ideal that guides deliberation and mediates various forms of pluralism. Even though genuine consensus is rarely achieved, Habermas insists that participants must continue to assume that rational consensus is possible in principle, for otherwise political disputes would forfeit their deliberative character and degenerate into purely strategic struggles for power.

Given these critiques, it has become the norm to speak about public spheres in the plural, and to acknowledge the impossibility of rational consensus in practice. Yet there remains a lingering sense that public sphere theory and deliberative democracy are still associated with certain Habermasian ideals of rational and power-free communication, which according to many critics can do little to help us understand the nature of existing mediated public spheres. Therefore, it is tempting to look for fresher perspectives in strands of democratic theory that have more firmly rejected the model of deliberative democracy and its underlying assumptions.

FROM RATIONAL CONSENSUS TO AGONISTIC PLURALISM

Building on the above critiques and problems of deliberative democracy, so-called radical-pluralist or agonistic models of democracy have recently emerged among the most prominent alternative strands of democratic theory.[6] Radical pluralist theories of democracy draw upon various strands of poststructuralism and postmodernism and typically take distance from the models of both liberal pluralism and deliberative democracy.

Like conventional liberal pluralists, radical pluralists are concerned with conflict and disagreement as unavoidable facts of politics. Their prescription of the realization of pluralism, however, differs from the model of competition between pregiven interests. In particular, contemporary radical pluralists have a different understanding of power and of how differences and identities are constructed (Connolly 1995; Cunningham 2002, 184). In this sense, notions of critical or radical pluralism share with deliberative democrats the rejection of views of democracy as based simply on the goal of aggregating individual or group preferences. Instead, they argue that despite its emphasis on diversity, conventional pluralism actually ignores structural inequalities between groups and individuals. Conventional interpretations of liberal pluralism are thus seen to give too much priority to past political settlements and power relations that are already established, which systematically tends to silence or ignore voices of difference and new forces of pluralization (Connolly 1995, xiv).

On the other hand, radical pluralists have also criticized theories of deliberative democracy by maintaining that civil society is not harmonious or unitary, but rather characterized by conflicts of interest and an irreducible pluralism of values. Consequently, theories based on the ideal of rational consensus or common good are seen by radical pluralists as not only utopian,

---

[6] *Radical pluralism* is used here as a general term for theoretical approaches known by such names as *agonistic pluralism, agonistic democracy,* or *radical and plural democracy* (see Wenman 2003).

but also necessarily exclusive. In this sense, radical pluralism can essentially be seen as an attempt to shift discourses of pluralism from a theory of the status quo to a progressive or transformative theory of democratic contestation.

There are two reasons for my choice to discuss the radical pluralist approach mainly through the work of Chantal Mouffe. First, her work provides one of the most prominent critiques of traditional liberal approaches and recent deliberative approaches to the public sphere and democracy, which clearly has consequences for current debates on media and democracy. Perhaps more importantly though, Mouffe offers an equally strong critique of the celebration of multiplicity and diversification as such, a critique that I argue has generally passed unnoticed in media and cultural studies.

For these reasons, I argue that Mouffe's approach is especially useful for illustrating many of the problems that arise in the debate on the value of pluralism in media politics, even if her approach itself may be open to many other criticisms in political philosophy (see, for example, Brady 2004; Crowder 2006; Fossen 2008; Knops 2007). The purpose of discussing the agonistic approach here is therefore not to argue for more pluralism as such. Instead, it serves to question the inclusiveness of current pluralistic discourses and emphasize the continued importance of analyzing the relations of power inherent in the public sphere. The agonistic model of democracy is discussed here as a possible theoretical basis on which the current ethos of pluralization can also be brought to bear on the level of media structures and politics in ways that avoid some of the problems of liberal and deliberative approaches. Before discussing its implications for media policy, however, let me first review some key characteristics of Mouffe's conception of agonistic pluralism.

If theories of deliberative democracy and the public sphere have essentially tried to reconcile the tension between pluralism and commonality by placing the emphasis on agreement among rational inquirers, the agonistic model of democracy advocated by Mouffe can be seen as its direct antithesis: "The belief in the possibility of a universal rational consensus has put democratic thinking on the wrong track. Instead of trying to design the institutions which, through supposedly 'impartial' procedures, would reconcile all conflicting interests and values, the task for democratic theorists and politicians should be to envisage the creation of a vibrant 'agonistic' public sphere of contestation where different hegemonic political projects can be confronted" (Mouffe 2005, 3). For Mouffe, democratic politics thus requires the constitution of collective identities around clearly differentiated positions and the real possibility of making a choice between them. She emphasizes the inevitability of conflict in political life and claims that open conflict of interests and vibrant clash of political positions are not only necessary for healthy democracy, but can also work as buffers against confrontations between nonnegotiable moral values and essentialist identities (Mouffe 1993, 6).

The underlying argument here is that the ideal of a rational-critical deliberative public sphere, just as the liberal model of the marketplace of ideas, fails to address power and existing forms of exclusion. Furthermore, deliberative democrats have not adequately theorized the themes of plurality and openness and therefore they inevitably exclude the articulation of difference and conflict from democratic deliberation. While emphasizing the positive aspects of political conflicts for democracy, Mouffe (2000, 103) acknowledges that there will always be a need for a certain degree of consensus in liberal democracy. However, this need not and cannot be a rational consensus based on the kind of common will envisaged by deliberative democrats. According to Mouffe (2000, 49), every consensus is provisional and exists as the temporal result of hegemony, a stabilization of power relations, and always entails some form of exclusion. Because the model of deliberative democracy envisages the availability of consensus without exclusion, it inevitably fails to theorize liberal-democratic pluralism in an adequate way.

In contrast to Habermas, for whom power-free communication is the regulative ideal, Mouffe thus affirms the permanence of power relations. The aim of radical democratic pluralism is therefore not the elimination of power relations, but their transformation so that they are made more compatible with democratic principles. For Mouffe, this requires above all the availability of different political alternatives and the continuing contestation of all hegemonic projects.

According to Mouffe, democracy should be conceived as agonistic confrontation or continued contestation of hegemonic power relations that does not even purport to pursue any final solution or common good. In other words, a fully achieved democracy is a conceptual impossibility, and for Mouffe (1993, 145), the substance of radical and pluralistic democracy is found in the open-ended contestation of all normative principles, not in their final definition or actual realization.

Radical democratic pluralism also calls for abandoning the essentialism dominant in the liberal interpretation of pluralism and acknowledging the contingency and ambiguity of social identities. Because identities are always contested and never fixed, a more dynamic understanding of differences and identities is needed. An agonistic public sphere is thus not only an arena for the formation of discursive public opinion, or the aggregation of predefined interests, but also a site for the formation and contestation of social identities.

A mistake that Mouffe (2005, 6) says is typical of both liberal and deliberative models of democracy is that they ignore the affective dimension of collective identifications and passions in politics. One of the key distinctions in Habermas's approach is the separation of private, the realm of irreconcilable value pluralism, and the realm of public, where rational consensus can be reached. According to Mouffe, what this separation really does is circumscribe a domain that would not be subject to the pluralism of values and where a consensus without exclusion could be established. In assuming that all differences could be relegated to the private sphere through the construction of a procedurally based rational consensus, deliberative democrats ignore the irresolvable nature of conflicts over political values. They "relegate pluralism to a non-public domain in order to insulate politics from its consequences" (Mouffe 2000, 33, 91–92).

Many others have also criticized liberal theorists' rationalist bias and purified models of political debate by arguing that deliberation is culturally embedded and never based on arguments only. Iris Marion Young (2000), for instance, has argued that deliberative models tend to be overly rationalistic and thus insufficiently egalitarian. By favoring educated and dispassionate rather than emotional forms of communication, they exclude the way in which most people communicate most of the time. Thus, it can be argued that some participants are advantaged over others in deliberative democracy, as some participants' naturalized modes of communication are closer to the legitimate normative mode than others.

In short, radical-pluralists thus argue that the universal-rationalist public sphere approach underestimates the challenge posed by social and cultural pluralism to the ideas of shared collective identity, all-encompassing political culture and political consensus, and to the possibility of common procedures or forms of deliberation that are purportedly value-neutral. While the revisions made by Habermas and his fellow deliberative democrats address the first point to some degree, the second point remains a major disagreement between deliberative democrats and their radical pluralist critics. Although even Habermas acknowledges the "fact of pluralism" and value-conflict as inevitable, he continues to defend the ideal of deliberative democracy as one based on the universal criteria of communicative rationality (see Baumeister 2003, 746).

From a radical-pluralist perspective, it can be asked whether it suffices that the arenas and levels of public debate have multiplied if there is still only one form of public reasoning, one universal standard of rationality. It can be argued that Habermas and many deliberative democrats have indeed come to grips with the fact of pluralism, but not with deeper meta-ethical pluralism, a view in which political life is characterized not by a search for common standards but by persistent conflict between incommensurable interests and values.

For these reasons, Habermas remains for many radical pluralists an archetypically modernist thinker whose aim is to achieve a high degree of rational purity and conceptual order typical of monistic discourses (Gardiner 2004, 30). From a radical pluralist perspective, the problem with such approaches thus lies perhaps as much in their universal and rationalist form as in their political substance.

On the other hand, many of the differences between the deliberative and agonistic models reviewed here also reflect the division of democratic theories into (1) those oriented to democratizing or rationalizing the procedures of decision-making and (2) those confined more explicitly to the processes of resistance and contestation as inherently valuable. As Bonnie Honig (1993, 2) writes, the radical pluralist approach finds its justification above all as a critique of political theorists that measure their success by the elimination of dissonance and conflict, and thus confine politics to the tasks of stabilizing moral and political subjects, building consensus, or consolidating communities and identities. Radical pluralism thereby explicitly aims to shift the emphasis of democratic politics to the processes of dislocation, contestation, and resistance.

It must be granted that such adversarial emphasis certainly also involves some apparent problems and limitations. For instance, it makes the radical pluralist approach susceptible to the criticism that it is obsessed with conflict and disagreement, thus ignoring issues related to governability and decision making. In discussing the media, the strong focus on the value of dissent and resistance admittedly also bears the risk of ignoring other values media pluralism can serve, such as fostering open-mindedness, cultural integration and mutual respect.

Having said that, the radical pluralist approach does provide a fresh contrast to the idealized conceptions of the marketplace of ideas or the public sphere, and as such it can contribute to a better understanding of media pluralism as a theoretical and normative concept, even if it remains only one partial perspective among many others.

While both adversarial and more consensus-oriented logics may have their merits, the role of the media has never been understood so much in terms of direct participation in state power or governance, but primarily in terms of critique of other centers of power. In his more recent work, even Habermas (1996, 359) has described the public sphere as a "warning system with sensors that, though unspecialized, are sensitive through society." The public sphere, and especially the mass media, can thus only be expected to "mobilize and pool relevant issues" and prepare the agendas for political institutions (Habermas 2006, 416). The media are peripheral political institutions and thereby relieved from the burden of solving problems or having to produce a rational solution to political questions. In this sense, it is easy to understand why an approach that emphasizes the aspects of contestation and dislocation (instead of the utopia of rationalizing society through some universal principles) seems particularly attractive in theorizing the chaotic and complex nature of the contemporary media landscape.

CHAPTER 2

Pluralization and Its Problems

In recent decades it seems that the normative theories and concepts used in theorizing the media in general have taken a marked pluralistic or antiessentialist turn. While notions such as quality, public interest, and common good have been more and more called into question in both theory and politics, pluralism has gained increasing prominence as a key principle for evaluating media performance. As an example of this kind of antiessentialism, John Keane (1992) has even argued that the political values of democracy and freedom of speech should be conceived as means and necessary preconditions for protecting philosophical and political pluralism, rather than as foundational principles themselves.

This reflects broader trends in social and political theory. Radical sociopolitical pluralism and the acceptance of multiplicity and pluralism in all social experiences, identities, and aesthetic and moral standards have arguably become the defining characteristics of the contemporary postmodern political condition (McLennan 1995). Although it carries some historical baggage, the negative connotations of pluralism have mostly faded, and it is understood as a positive recognition and affirmation of multiplicity and heterogeneity. Indeed pluralism today has a distinctly positive resonance that is hard to challenge.

In theorizing the public sphere, this positive resonance is most clearly evident in the rejection of a universal or singular idea of the public sphere in favor of a complex field of multiple, contesting public spheres, which even Habermas (1996; 2006) has now acknowledged. Reflecting on this new mainstream in political theory, Seyla Benhabib (1996, 87) argues that "the chief institutional correlate of deliberative democracy is a multiple, anonymous, and heterogeneous network of many publics and public conversations."

The pluralization of the public sphere, however, has not solved all problems. As noted above, one of the weaknesses of pluralism as an evaluative concept is that it is rather empty of specific meaning, except that of differentiation itself. It does not identify any qualities, values, and virtues that need to be advanced or protected (see Marcil-Lacoste 1992). This dilemma certainly also applies to the radical pluralist perspectives discussed above. In emphasizing the continuous contestation of all normative principles, the radical pluralist perspectives also concede that their own prescriptions are inevitably partial and provisional. Therefore, valuing pluralism as an end in itself will inevitably create problems of its own. Below I discuss some of these "pathologies of pluralism" before moving on to analyze their implications for thinking about the role of the media.

PATHOLOGIES OF PLURALISM

It is evident that pluralism does not constitute a linear value that provides an unambiguous basis for assessing the democratic quality of the public sphere. This is not only because there are endless disputes about the best way to realize or institutionalize genuine pluralism, but also because there is a need to define the limits of pluralism and reconcile it with other values that may be at variance with it.

While it has become commonplace to abandon the unitary model of the public sphere and speak instead of public spheres in the plural in political philosophy, it can be argued that at some point the emphasis on diversity and pluralism runs counter to the basic imaginary presuppositions of democracy itself. In particular, there is an inherent tension between pluralism and the idea of collective self-government. As Mouffe (2000, 64) has argued, there is a "democratic paradox" of how to envisage a form of commonality that is strong enough to institute a *demos* but nevertheless compatible with true religious, moral, cultural, and political pluralism. For Mouffe (2000, 5), as indeed for many other political philosophers, this highlights the paradoxical relationship between the liberal tradition, which emphasizes individual freedom and pluralism, and the democratic tradition, which emphasizes popular sovereignty and collective self-government.

This paradox also goes to the core of representative politics. Ulrich Beck and Elisabeth Beck-Gernsheim (2001, 28–89) argue that the number of negotiation systems cannot grow indefinitely, and it is not possible to admit more and more actors and views into political power, because that would only multiply the number of arenas of conflict without increasing the potential for consensus and coordination. Instead, the increasingly fragmented political structure also weakens the potential of political societies for the integration and aggregation of various public opinions into collective decisions (Beck and Beck-Gernsheim 2001, 28–29).

From this perspective, it can even be argued that the problem is not so much the lack of public spaces, but the inability to translate various expressions of public opinions into political decision making. As Nancy Fraser (2007) has acknowledged, from the point of view of the basic normative criteria in public sphere theory, communicative power generated in civil society must also somehow influence laws and administrative policies. If the participants in the public sphere no longer constitute a *demos*, how can public opinion be mobilized as a political force? If the function of the public sphere is to control and constrain political power, then the pluralization of public spheres raises questions about which publics are relevant to which powers. And who are the relevant members of a given public? No matter how many public spheres we imagine there are, they continue to be charged with relations of power and hierarchies in terms of their capacity to influence politics.

This ambiguity has become especially clear in contemporary media politics where, rather than expressing enthusiasm about new technological possibilities, many other commentators have voiced fears about the excessive fragmentation or atomization of the public sphere. While it is taken for granted that the media should provide access to a plurality of voices, the mass media are often also seen as a tool for integrating people into a political community and creating a shared arena for public debate. Consequently, it has been argued that growing social disintegration and cultural fragmentation can be counterproductive to the ideals of a democratic public sphere. It is feared that the proliferation of media outlets and audience segments may effectively undermine the capacity of mass media to shape common experiences, promote shared discourses and agendas and move public opinion. As Todd Gitlin (1998, 173) asks in his often quoted discussion of "public sphericules:"

> Does democracy require a public or publics? A public sphere or separate public sphericules? Does the proliferation of the latter, the comfort in which they can be cultivated, damage the prospects for the former? Does it not look as though the public sphere, in falling, had shattered into a scatter of globules, like mercury? The diffusion of interactive technology surely enriches the possibilities for a plurality of publics—for the development of distinct groups organized around affinity and interest.

What is not clear is that the proliferation and lubrication of publics contributes to the creation of a public—an active democratic encounter of citizens who reach across their social and ideological differences to establish a common agenda of concern and to debate rival approaches.

While many observers rightly celebrate the increasing individualization of political and social experience and envision new avenues of political engagement provided by networks and subpublics, the question remains whether the media should be as open as possible to any expressions, whether they should be somehow representative of existing social interests or subcultures, and whether there are perhaps some contents that everyone should see, regardless of their individual preferences or tastes?

Similarly, Sandra Braman (2007, 139–41) has criticized contemporary media policy discourse for the belief that the mere accomplishment of diversity, however that is measured, is sufficient to ensure an ideal type of democratic public sphere. Braman argues that diversity alone is not the final goal of media policy, but it is also necessary to consider the political efficacy of public discourse: what is said in public should have some effect on politics. The existence of a plurality of publics with their own media outlets does not necessarily resolve the question of political will-formation, and if pluralism is not considered primarily an end in itself but a precondition for a democratic public sphere, then it is necessary to consider more fully the idea of encounters and dialogue between different, antagonistic views and perspectives.

So while some celebrate the fragmentation of audiences and the rise of subaltern publics, others have continued to argue for the continuing necessity of a unifying political public sphere where discussion is aimed at agreement and concerted action within unified polity. Nicholas Garnham (1992) draws a distinction between the political public sphere that serves to make political decision making accountable to public opinion, and other public spheres that serve the purposes of identity and community construction. Both require mass media, but for Garnham (1992, 371) it is above all the political public sphere that must match the scale and scope of the polity, providing universal access and participation for all citizens. In contemporary media policy, this function is often assigned to public service broadcasting and other institutional arrangements that provide common spaces where different perspectives meet.

Overall, despite their apparent endorsement of pluralism and the plurality of public spheres, both democratic theorists and media scholars have provided ambivalent interpretations of what the pluralization of public spheres actually means for democracy. Thus, there remains a fundamental difference of opinion (or perhaps emphasis) between those who emphasize the democratic benefits of the media that afford a universal public address and those who advocate a media system that enables maximum dispersal of power and resources among multiple, competing publics or counterpublics.

THE ETHOS OF PLURALISM IN MEDIA POLITICS

The intellectual trends in media and communication studies largely reflect the general renaissance of pluralism in social and political theory. The emphasis on the plurality of public spheres, the politics of difference and the multiplicity of ways in which the media can contribute to democracy are highly prominent in contemporary debates on media and democracy.

The pluralistic turn in thinking about the media is exemplified in Brian McNair's (2006) argument for a fundamental shift where the idea of the media as mechanisms of social control and political consensus has given way to a hyper-adversarial, decentralized, and demand-driven media environment. Written as a critique of scholars who see the media as a vehicle of elite power, the book seeks to replace the terminology and conceptual apparatus of the pessimistic "control paradigm" with what McNair calls the "chaos paradigm." While the control paradigm saw the media as functional for social stability and control and stressed the importance of political economy, hierarchy, structure, and their role in maintaining ideological control and domination, the chaos paradigm shifts the attention to the diverse, often anarchic developments in contemporary media culture.

Similarly, John Keane (2009) has recently argued that democracy has started to morph into a new historical form of postrepresentative democracy that is defined by the multiplication and dispersal of many different power-monitoring and power-contesting mechanisms, many of which are closely tied to the new communication media and the communicative abundance they afford.

The common denominator for these and many other recent visions of the new media is that rather than working with any universal normative criteria, they increasingly understand the relationship between media and democracy in a way that takes into account the plurality of communication media and the various modes in which they can contribute to democracy. Such a pluralist approach is then inclusive of different genres of media texts and different forms of media organization, not privileging "high modern journalism" or any other media form as an inherently superior form of rational communication (see Jacka 2003).

The erosion of faith in the rational public sphere model has also given rise to arguments that emphasize the democratic and emancipatory functions of popular culture and entertainment. While critical scholars have traditionally debated phenomena such as tabloidization and commercialization in terms of the decaying rationality of the public sphere, others have argued that the inclusion of the seemingly trivial and personal is actually providing a more inclusive, representative and empowering perspective of society. As McNair (2006, vii) puts it, the proliferation of channels and the erosion of taste hierarchies used to police cultural consumption have radically increased "the possibilities . . . for dissent, openness and diversity rather than closure, exclusivity and ideological homogeneity." In this sense, there are some clear parallels between the intellectual trends in media studies and the pluralistic turn in democratic theory.

However, the replacement of the unitary model of a rational public sphere with the plurality of public spheres and different modes of communication has hardly produced a consensus on what this means for media policy and the structure and organization of the media—other than that anything goes. While the Habermasian public sphere approach has long been mobilized as a normative backbone in debates on media structure and policy, for example in defense of public service broadcasting, the political and policy implications of various postmodern and radical pluralist perspectives have been much less debated. Often these perspectives have found most of their resonance as a critique of the biases and flaws of existing normative frameworks, rather than as coherent normative theories that would pertain to questions of media structure and policy. In fact, it seems that the lack of institutional proposals or interest in concrete political questions is a more widespread feature of postmodern theories of new pluralism and complexity (McLennan 1995, 85).

The shift away from institutional politics can be illustrated by examining some of the recent debates on media and democracy. According to John Hartley (2004, 386), the purpose of critical media studies, particularly perspectives that have been based on the public sphere approach, has been "not to understand but to discipline" existing media practices. The normative perspectives derived from the Habermasian notion of the public sphere, in particular, are seen as unnecessarily pessimistic and one-dimensional. In the words of Elizabeth Jacka (2003), they impose a theoretical frame of "democracy as defeat." The need for fresher theoretical perspectives is thus accentuated by the fact that in media and communication studies, Habermas is often considered to defend an outdated ideal of a unitary public sphere which has little relevance in contemporary societies.

Jacka (2003) draws explicitly on Chantal Mouffe to argue that the dominant arguments in media policy and especially those defending public service broadcasting are based on an indefensible theoretical ideal of a universal, rationalist, and unitary public sphere. Following Mouffe's critique of deliberative democracy, Jacka calls for rejecting the utopia of a rationally based common public sphere, and argues that democracy needs to be seen as pluralized, as marked by new kinds of communities of identity that break the traditional public-private divide and ditch universal visions of the common good. In particular, her criticism is targeted at the elitism and paternalism of the criteria of quality and rationality inherent in the ideals of public service broadcasting, which she sees as leading to the exclusion of certain modes of expression in the public sphere.

Instead, Jacka (2003, 183) maintains that the relationship between media and democracy ought to countenance a plurality of communication media and modes provided by the contemporary media landscape. Rather than cultural policing, the key development in making possible a more pluralist media system is thus the growth of channel availability that allows for ever greater diversity and choice, catering to more and more specialized tastes and needs (ibid., 188). In other words, pluralistic democracy is then seen to be realized when people can freely construct their identities by choosing from the ever expanding options in the public sphere.

Following this line of reasoning, scholars in cultural studies have coined the notion of *semiotic democracy* to separate democracy from the tediousness of collective action and to rearticulate it with questions of self-realization and choices that people make for themselves.[1] Interpreting citizenship primarily in terms of identity and difference, John Hartley (1999, 178), for instance, defines the concept of "do-it-yourself citizenship" as "the practice of putting together an identity from the available choices, patterns and opportunities on offer in the semiosphere and the mediasphere." In this formulation, then, "citizenship is no longer simply a matter of a social contract between state and subject, no longer even a matter of acculturation to the heritage of a given community; DIY citizenship is a choice people can make for themselves" (ibid.). It is thus claimed that a shift is taking place in postmodern democracy from politics to ethics. Seeking "democratization without politicization," writers such as Jacka and Hartley envisage a shift from political democracy to semiotic democracy, a future of postpolitical citizenship that is based on semiotic self-determination, not state coercion, paternalism or social engineering.

---

[1]The term was first introduced by John Fiske (1987), who argued in the 1980s that we now live in "a semiotic democracy," where the power to produce meanings, pleasures, and social identities from media texts lies with audiences and not some abstract structures of domination.

The same kinds of arguments are often associated with many other views in cultural studies that perceive popular media as providing pleasures and expressions of protest (see Curran 2002, 201). Presuming that the public is capable of generating its own meanings, it can be argued that pluralism is not produced by institutions or programs but by audiences: homogeneous programming does not necessarily produce a homogeneous range of readings among the audience. Instead, popular media are regarded as open, generative resources for growing popular self-realization and emancipation, to which new forms of social media have further added a dialogic and demotic "do it with others" mode (Hartley 2009, 69–70).

For critics of such postmodern perspectives, this kind of complacency with the current media landscape only affirms the evasiveness and vacuity of these perspectives. As a consequence, postmodern theories of radical difference and pluralism are often seen to celebrate complexity, heterogeneity, and "the end of reason"—to the extent that they have given up on the capacity to understand and make sense of social reality, let alone regulate it. In this sense, they reflect the postmodern antipathy towards "cultural policing" of all kinds, which they see as attempts to stabilize or stifle difference, create political closure, or otherwise define the acceptable limits of pluralism from above.

Such postmodern antipaternalism, which leans on the recognition (and praise) of complexity and plurality, also reflects a broader denial of any systematic or integrative meta-theories. In this sense, the arguments of Hartley, Jacka, and others resemble the perspective of radical pluralism and its denial of the universal criteria of rationality. Given their praise for individual cultural autonomy and choice, however, it is no surprise that the emphasis on popular consumption, active audiences, and individual creation of meaning has often been criticized for simplistic celebration of all multiplicity, which all too easily converges with cultural relativism and the neoliberal illusion of free choice (Garnham 2000; Gitlin 1997; McGuigan 1997).

Nicholas Garnham (2000, 98) has argued against current tendencies of postmodern and relativist thought precisely because of their discomfort with any evaluative or critical judgment of media performance on the basis truth, beauty, or right. In many ways, such evasiveness and vacuity is central to contemporary debates in media studies and media policy. If promoting pluralism and diversity in the media is to say nothing about the quality or responsibility of the media, how can it be used in any critical sense, without slipping into indifference and an unquestioning acceptance of consumer sovereignty and market-driven diversity. In its refusal to acknowledge old hierarchies of taste, the postmodern praise of pluralism can be celebrated as liberating and even democratizing. However, it can also be argued that the question is not whether these judgments are made, but who makes them and what are the criteria against which such judgments are made and validated. In this sense, as Garnham (2000, 107) argues, denying all claims of truth, beauty, or right leaves the field free either to consumption choices in the market as the only test of value, or to the unquestioned exercise of judgment for cultural producers themselves. Particularly for those concerned with institutional politics and media structures, postmodern pluralism and multiplicity thus often represents an irrational threat to modern democratic ideals. If there is no rational basis or if there are no common standards of evaluation, it is feared that relativism will take over and the politics of difference will lead to the politics of indifference.

This criticism also applies more generally to radical pluralist perspectives. While many acknowledge the value of their critiques, radical pluralists such as Mouffe are easily criticized for their refusal to develop any substantive normative positions (see Crowder 2006; Knops 2007). This has led some critics to argue that with all the emphasis on pluralism, difference, and the proliferation of identity movements, politics is becoming pluralized to the point of being trivialized (see Fraser 1997, 11). Although the pluralistic emphasis on complexity, difference and conflict has an attractive purchase in terms of immediate experience, it can become myopic. As McLennan (1995, 98) argues, critical social science and radical politics cannot do without some kind of long-term ideal visions or substantive values that inevitably stand as counterpoints to the deconstructive aspects of pluralism.

AGAINST NAÏVE PLURALISM

Although the critics of the public sphere approach in media and cultural studies have cited Mouffe and other radical pluralist critics of deliberative democracy, I argue that these self-proclaimed "postpolitical" perspectives are in many key respects actually rather antithetical to the main arguments of Mouffe's radical pluralism.

My main argument here is that in order to have any critical potential, radical-democratic pluralism must be distinguished from the celebration of all multiplicity and difference. While Mouffe and other radical pluralists criticize the essentialism of unitary and universal-rationalist forms of political theory that tend to fix social identities in a closed political community, Mouffe also criticizes its opposite: a type of extreme postmodern fragmentation that puts exclusive emphasis on all kinds of heterogeneity and incommensurability. This latter criticism has so far largely been overlooked in media and cultural studies.

Contrary to the postmodern celebration of all plurality, Mouffe has argued that radical democratic pluralism must be distinguished from the forms of postmodern politics that emphasize heterogeneity and incommensurability to the extent of valorizing all differences. This is not because they are in conflict with some abstract idea of the common good, but because what such pluralism misses are the dimensions of power and the political. The political, for Mouffe, here refers to the dimension of antagonism that characterizes all societies, while relations of power refer to the struggle between hegemonic projects around which a given social order is structured. Because every social order is thus based on power relations and entrenched hegemonic practices, even claims for pluralism always involve some form of exclusion.

Because of its refusal to acknowledge the relations of power involved in "constructions of differences," such naïve pluralism, Mouffe (2000, 20) argues, is compatible with the liberal evasion of politics, and converges with the typical liberal illusion of pluralism without antagonism. Instead, for radical pluralism to be compatible with the struggle against inequality, one must also acknowledge that there are limits to pluralism, and that drawing those limits always entails political choices.

Equally critical of ideas such as life politics or subpolitics—ideas that the notion of semiotic democracy seem to reflect—Mouffe (2005, 54) has stressed the need to acknowledge the crucial role played by economic and political power in the structuring of the hegemonic order. Instead of standing for dissolution of politics into semiotic democracy, personal therapy, or individual do-it-yourself citizenship, she has stressed that the democratization of any social institution is above all a political task. According to Mouffe, "without grasping the structure of the current hegemonic order and the type of power relations through which it is constituted, no real democratization can ever get off the ground" (ibid., 51).

The fundamental role of power is thus central to Mouffe's conception of radical democratic pluralism. Relations of power are seen as constitutive of the social order, and thus ineradicable. In this sense, Mouffe's position here would seem to complement the criticism of cultural politics of difference that override political-economic considerations and valorize agency within communicative practices without providing adequate attention to structural constraints (see Fraser 1997, 1–2). In this sense, I argue that the radical pluralist approach can also be used as a critique against the strands of cultural studies that emphasize individual agency and downplay the structural constraints posed by the political economy of the media.

It is by emphasizing the fundamental role of power that radical pluralism also takes distance from both the liberal notion of the free marketplace of ideas and the postmodern praise of all differences. Consequently, I argue that in media studies, the radical-pluralist approach is best interpreted not as praise of multiplicity as such, but as a call to recognize the aspects of power, exclusion, and control inherent in all conceptions of the public space. The structures and the practices of the media undeniably affect the balance between different social forces and the opportunities of different groups to enter the public sphere. Therefore, from the radical-pluralist perspective, the media are viewed above all as a battleground of contending social forces, rather than as resources for some kind of individualized semiotic democracy.

To summarize my main argument, radical democratic pluralism is more about social and power relations than about defining or defending diversity as such. Departing from the political minimalism of liberal pluralism, this implies that pluralism is not only to be treated as a fact, but that spaces in which differences may turn into agonistic political projects must also be established by political means (see Connolly 1991, xi). In the context of the media, this means that it is not enough to celebrate the proliferation of channels as an expression of pluralism. Instead, what radical pluralist perspectives emphasize is the need to examine the changing relations of power both within the media and between the media institutions and other powerful social forces. In this sense, even though Connolly, Mouffe or other theorists of radical pluralism themselves have not shown much interest in elaborating on the concrete political implications of their philosophy, there is no reason in principle why the radical-pluralist perspective would be incompatible with concrete questions of media policy or the political economy of the media. Indeed, if the critical political economy approach is defined as interested "in the ways that communicative activity is structured by the unequal distribution of material and symbolic resources" (Golding and Murdock 2000, 73), then it would seem that there is much it can draw from radical pluralist perspectives in political philosophy. The implications of this kind of thinking for media policy, however, have so far not been adequately developed in media studies.

CHAPTER 3

Toward a Critical Concept of Media Pluralism

The argument developed so far has stressed that while it is easy to subscribe to the concept of media pluralism, it does not offer an unambiguous basis for democratic media politics. The notion itself does not seem to constitute a coherent, substantive ideology, and there will always be controversy over its proper institutionalization or realization. Moreover, given its vague uses in contemporary media policy, it is fair to ask whether the concept of pluralism retains any critical potential at all. As suggested in Chapter 2, it can even be argued that appeals to the complexity and pluralism of contemporary media cultures may sometimes reflect the inability of researchers to properly tackle the politically sensitive issue of evaluating media performance.

However, this is not to suggest that the concept of media pluralism should be abandoned. Because of its ambiguity and amorphous nature, there is little sense in saying that pluralism is good or bad. Instead, following McLennan (1995), I take the view in this book that the notion of pluralism is best seen as a critical or oppositional value rather than as a positive finality. Therefore, its value lies above all in generating a series of challenging dilemmas or in problematizing monistic orthodoxies of all types. In this respect, the critical conception of media pluralism that I sketch below draws on the radical pluralist ethos of dislocation and deconstruction, rather than on the aim of constructing new universal principles. In substance, however, it can be argued that the perspectives of radical pluralism and deliberative democracy are not necessarily fully incompatible.[1] Instead, I assume a certain theoretical eclecticism in using both approaches as critical perspectives that help reflect on the ideals of democratic public communication.

In the context of media studies and media policy, I argue against those who see pluralism as a linear variable or as an end-all value of media policy, yet I remain sympathetic to the core aspects of pluralism, and particularly to its tendency to constantly challenge prevailing truths and concentrations of power. The main argument advanced in this chapter is that in order not to lapse into unquestioning praise of multiplicity and choice, media pluralism needs to be understood in terms of power relations between different social actors, and not in terms of diversity or variety as such. A critical concept of media pluralism must thus be distinguished from the forms of postmodern politics discussed earlier that emphasize heterogeneity and incommensurability to the extent that they valorize all differences.

Another key argument presented in this chapter is that pluralism need not displace critical judgments about media performance and media quality. As Garnham (2000, 35) has argued, one cannot avoid normative judgments or the critique of mass culture simply on the grounds of defending pluralism or avoiding elitism or paternalism, because that leaves unanswered the problems of unequal cultural and economic power that arise from the cultural forms produced by a minority for large, dispersed audiences (unless it is claimed, as some do, that all this has changed with new participatory media platforms).

Instead of renouncing media pluralism as an anachronistic objective, this chapter aims to build on recent discussions in democratic theory to reclaim the notion of media pluralism from complacent celebration of increasing diversity and consumer choice to the critical purpose of identifying old and new forms of power asymmetries in the contemporary media environment.

ASYMMETRIES OF COMMUNICATIVE POWER

The starting point for understating media pluralism as a critical concept is to acknowledge that all media institutions are necessarily marked by asymmetries of communicative power. Because of their mediated nature, the mass media have always raised the question of social power. As Nicholas Garnham (1999b, 78) explains, once communication expanded beyond face-to-face interaction, the question of who commanded the cultural and material resources for communication and for what purposes became central to an understanding of the social order. For Garnham, it is this distribution

---

[1] This argument has been further developed in Karppinen, Moe, and Svensson (2008).

of communicative power that forms the essence of "information politics." Unequal opportunities to access the mediated public sphere and to mobilize communicative power thus inevitably reveal a power structure. However the media are organized, they always influence the distribution of communicative resources in the public sphere. Asymmetries of communicative power thus refer to the simple fact that some social actors are always better placed than others, both materially and culturally, to express their views and participate in public life through the media.[2]

The media institutions themselves, of course, can be understood to have power in many different forms. The media can be understood as powerful social actors in their own right, but also as gatekeepers on which other powerful social actors depend to a lesser or greater extent (see Couldry and Curran 2003). Even when guided by norms of balance or objectivity, all media institutions act selectively as filters of topics and voices, which endows them with the power to define problems, set agendas and mark the limits of legitimate public discussion. Furthermore, as the media are never completely independent from other powerful influences, such as pressures from government, interest groups and media owners, that power will always be strategically used to influence the agendas and framing of public issues. The point here, however, is not to assess where exactly media power resides or which of these actors are the most powerful. Instead, the point is that all forms of mediated communication are necessarily interwoven with broader social relations of power.

As Habermas (2006, 421) puts it, the problem from the perspective of public sphere theory is "the incomplete differentiation of the media from political and economic systems." In much of normative democratic theory, this is seen to undermine the quality of mediated communication because it introduces distortion and manipulation in public communication. The role of the media seems particularly problematic when considered from the point of view of more demanding conceptions of democracy, such as deliberative democracy, and their norms of equal participation, rationality and the discursive quality of public debates. Given that mediated communication lacks many of the defining features of rational deliberation, the capacity of the media to generate considered public opinions is often viewed somewhat

---

[2]Power can here be provisionally defined as "the relational capacity that enables a social actor to influence asymmetrically the decisions of other social actor(s) in ways that favor the empowered actor's will, interests, and values" (Castells 2009, 10). Communicative power can thus be defined as the capacity of a social actor to mobilize means of communication in order to exert such influence. This includes political and economic as well as symbolic and discursive influence. For a review of alternative approaches to power, see, for example, Scott 2001.

pessimistically. It is this very pessimism that has led many scholars in media and cultural studies to criticize the normative ideals of the public sphere for producing a defeatist attitude that has nothing positive to say about the contribution of media to democracy (see Jacka 2003; McNair 2006).

The traditional liberal solution to the problems of media power has been to establish a free marketplace of ideas through a diversity of competing communication channels and through professional standards of balance and objectivity pursued by media professionals. Yet, as noted in the discussion above, the metaphor of the free marketplace of ideas evades questions about the structure and political economy of the media and the relations of power intrinsic to media markets and media ownership. In short, a plurality of channels is not in itself enough if all those channels are structured by the same structural patterns of influence, such as advertising and profit pressures.

Although adopted by many critical political economists of the media, the Habermasian ideal of the public sphere is in fact subject to this same criticism. The metaphors of the free marketplace of ideas and the public sphere both tend to assume a sphere of action that is somehow immune to the structural inequalities and power relations of society. In this sense, both employ idealized models that only become counterproductive when applied to real life institutions characterized by pervasive inequality. It is exactly because of the separation of the communicative realm from the systemic spheres of money and power that John Dryzek (2000, 26) has concluded that, if it provides no sense of how political and economic structures themselves should be further democratized, it is difficult to regard Habermas's theory of democracy as a contribution to critical theory.

James Bohman (2000) has emphasized that, given the variety of possible topics of public discussion in a heterogeneous citizenry, some kind of communicative division of labor is inevitable in large, complex societies. In modern societies, the existence of the public sphere is dependent on some form of technological mediation in that it requires expanding dialogue beyond face-to-face encounters. As most media are large-scale organizations and corporations characterized by a highly uneven distribution of power and resources, the public sphere inevitably involves asymmetries in competence and access to information. Instead of a dialogic conception of the public sphere or an idealized free marketplace, it is better then to understand all media as institutions that are subject to these asymmetries of power. Or as Keane (1992, 118) puts it, all media are essentially institutions that distribute entitlements to speak and to be heard and seen unevenly.

If structural inequalities are inevitable, as radical pluralist theories say they are, then the main question regarding the public sphere is not how to bracket out or even eradicate the aspect of power, but rather how to recognize it and make it visible so that it can enter the terrain of political contestation. In conditions of enduring unequal distribution of communicative power, media pluralism is thus best conceptualized in terms of leveling the unequal opportunities to exert political influence and the inclusion of new social perspectives and alternative political voices in the public sphere.

Following Nancy Fraser's (1992, 122) conception of democratizing the public sphere, a crucial question for media policy informed by radical pluralism is then: what institutional arrangements will best help narrow the gap in participatory parity between dominant and subordinate social actors and create a plurality of power structures that are maximally open to different social perspectives and democratic contestation?

From this perspective, radical pluralism in media politics can be understood not as a positive finality or as postmodern celebration of spontaneous multiplicity, but as a call for attention to institutional restructuring and macropolitical concerns that also pertain to the political economy of the media. The conceptualization of media pluralism thus does not have to derive from a contrafactual model of an ideal communicative situation or a free marketplace of ideas that is unaffected by unequal power relations. Instead, it would be guided by the more oppositional and critical aim of leveling out and exposing existing asymmetries of power. Understood this way, the abstract ideal of media pluralism need not be identified with any particular institutions, but rather with a normative ideal that can be realized in a variety of structures under a wide range of conditions. Like radical pluralist theories of democracy, it is best conceived as an ongoing project with no final solution or perfect equilibrium in sight.

BEYOND FREE CHOICE

The first consequence of conceptualizing media pluralism in terms of the distribution of communicative power and influence is that it becomes misleading to associate pluralism with individual consumer choice only. The rhetoric of "free choice" is one of the basic notions of neoliberal media policy and has become increasingly dominant in contemporary media policy. In the same vein, arguments for media pluralism and diversity are often presented in terms of increasing the choice of the citizen-consumer. However, as many political economists of the media have argued, the concept of "increasing choice" is problematic in itself. From the perspective outlined above, the problem with the association of pluralism with individual consumer choice is, above all, that it often fails to address the broader structures of power within which the media operate.

The emergence of the idea of consumer choice in media policy discussions is often associated with the recent deregulatory trends in European media policy. Secondly, as many critical scholars have noted, the rise of cultural audience studies since the 1980s has also provided empirical and theoretical support to the principle of consumer choice by portraying audiences as active and reflexive agents (Pauwels and Bauwens 2007, 149). As noted above, it can be argued that in emphasizing individual agency and autonomy instead of structural constraints, the dominant postmodern perspectives of cultural and media studies are actually rather complacent with the ontological premises of market liberalism (see also McGuigan 1997).

Often portrayed in cultural studies as a counter-narrative to the "vision of enslavement" that dominated critical media studies and media criticism in the 1960s and 1970s, the active audience thesis has involved a shift from a paternalistic and a disapproving attitude to a more empathetic and celebrating attitude towards the public and their media consumption (McNair 2006; Pauwels and Bauwens 2007). Audiences are no longer regarded as soulless, powerless recipients of ideological manipulation, but as conscious and critical users who are able to decode media texts in creative and critical ways and whose consumption choices can be taken as genuine expressions of identity politics. When combined with the current discourse on the blurring relationship between the producers and consumers of information, pluralism is hence increasingly associated with individual media use rather than with the broader social structures of which the media are part.

Together with ongoing technological advances, ideological changes in media policy and changes in conceptualizations of the audience have thus created a new antipaternalistic discourse of free choice and consumer sovereignty that dominates contemporary media policy debates. Consumer choice has become an important criterion for decisions on broadcasting licenses, assessments of media performance, and norms of regulation in general (see Hellman 1999; Pauwels 1998; van Cuilenburg and McQuail 2003). Indeed, as I argue in the second part of this book, the discourse of consumer choice has become so pervasive that it is adopted even by advocates of public service media as they reframe their arguments in terms of consumer satisfaction rather than public interest and social benefits.

In line with this, Des Freedman (2008, 74) argues that pluralism and diversity are increasingly conceived in terms of "a smorgasbord of companies, formats, styles, niches, and narratives from which audiences are free to pick and choose." Pluralism thus refers not so much to what distinguishes one choice from another, but to the size of the menu as a whole. The problem with this, as Freedman acknowledges, is that it produces a consumerist construction which privileges satisfaction of individual preferences over the broader objectives of public debate and antagonistic viewpoints.

Of course, consumer choice does not necessarily have to be only about pleasure seeking and the satisfaction of immediate preferences. Increasing choice is not a bad thing and the point here is not to argue that audiences should be seen paternalistically as passive recipients of media influence. Regardless of how creative or critical audiences are, the belief that consumer choice directs the media in accordance with the general will of the people misses the point that the set of alternatives for choice is always limited by structural effects, such as the concentration of ownership, high costs for market entry, advertising, unequal representations and political influences, and other asymmetries of power that characterize any media market (Curran 2002, 227–30).

Pauwels and Bauwens (2007, 153) argue that in reality it is "self-evident that audiences' power to do anything fundamental with what the institutions offer remains subordinate to the economic, political and discursive power of media enterprises." For them, consumer sovereignty is therefore above all a myth perpetuated by large media corporations to encourage consumer individualism and to justify and defend their business models (ibid., 149). Similarly, Slavko Splichal (1999, 291) contends that the diversity of outlets and channels creates only an illusion of pluralism by hiding the fact that all media are restrained by some kind of self-censorship and indirect control exercised by both the state and private corporations, ranging from formal regulation to pressures from advertisers and sponsors.

Furthermore, despite its rhetorical appeal, it can be questioned whether choice itself has much intrinsic value even from the individual consumer's point of view. As Keith Dowding (1992) argues, the very notion of increasing, let alone maximizing, choice is inherently problematic. According to Dowding (1992, 312), advocating markets on the basis that they increase consumers' choice is doubly wrong. The market is a preference-revealing machine; it provides consumers with what they want and where it fails to do so, it is replaced with something else. Where preferences are diverse, the market often gives us a range of alternatives. However, it is not clear whether greater choice actually gives consumers greater control over the type of products (or media contents) that are made available, and indeed whether greater choice is something to be valued in the first place. The market does not inherently provide for more or for better alternatives.

From a critical perspective, it is more useful to think that all media are regulated in one way or another, and that despite the rhetorical appeal of deregulation and free markets, the market itself is hardly free from the effects of unequal social power and control. As Stuart Hall (1997, 22) argues, there are at least two reasons to resist the articulation of markets with freedom. First, markets do not operate on their own. Contrary to the language of the free marketplace of ideas where the market is seen as a self-regulating and spontaneous mediator, the market is a politically designed institution, not a homogenous, unstructured, and unregulated natural entity that emerges spontaneously from civil society. The "liberalization" of the market has therefore often meant a reregulation and proliferation of rules and regulatory cultures that aim to safeguard the "freedom" of the market. Secondly, and more importantly, the market itself regulates. It allocates resources, rewards certain modes of action, and creates winners and losers. In effect, the market creates incentives that induce certain forms of conduct and discourage others. Any market imposes its own criteria of preselection and censorship. In other words, all markets necessarily limit the range of public choices, yet all of them have a tendency to present this process of preselection as neutral or natural, while in truth their criteria are inevitably political, in the broad sense of the word.

Zygmunt Bauman (1999, 73–78) explains that throughout modernity, the principal tool of "setting the agenda for choice" or pre-selection has been legislation. The fact that political institutions are now increasingly abandoning this tool does not necessarily mean that freedom of choice is expanding, but that the power of preselection is being ceded to other than political institutions, above all to the markets themselves. Consequently, the code or criteria of preselection are changing, and among the values toward which choosers are trained to orient their choices, short-term pleasure, hedonism, entertainment, and other market-generated needs come to occupy a superior place. According to Bauman, the late-modern emphasis on freedom of choice and individual autonomy has not really increased individual freedom, but led instead to "unfreedom," to the transformation of a political citizen into a consumer of market goods.

Similarly, many critical political economists of the media hold that a more realistic question is not whether there will be forms of intervention or regulation in the future, but rather what form they should take, what values they are based on, and how these decisions are arrived at. Shifts in media policy are thus best conceptualized as shifts from one mode of regulation and one form of power structure to another, not as a dichotomy between freedom and constraint, as the discourse of liberalization or deregulation would let believe.

Overall, despite the universalistic and ideal character of concepts such as the public sphere or the free marketplace of ideas, in practice the public sphere always involves the practice of selection at its very core. This includes: the selection of actors who gain access to the public sphere; the selection of the topics or themes to be addressed in the public sphere; and the procedures followed in the selection process (Nieminen 2000, 54). While there are different types of regulation, set by market rules, cultural and moral norms, political regulation or bureaucratic/administrative control, none of these sets of rules are inherently natural or free in their logic.

Even when individual consumers make relatively autonomous choices and actively give meaning to media content, this does not mean that these broader structures of power and influence on the level of media production become irrelevant. Consequently, it can be argued that, in the context of continuing structural power, the main emphasis should be placed on the inclusiveness of the public sphere, access to alternative voices, and the contestability of all hegemonic structures instead of any tangible criteria for the quantitative number of choices. As Freedman (2008, 78) argues, pluralism should not be simply about expanding the number of media outlets or celebrating existing differences, but about acting on these differences and using the media to articulate them. Instead of a diversity of options as such, a critical notion of pluralism must refer to a system of representation within a given society for different political viewpoints and different forms of cultural expression. If pluralism is valued on the basis that it expands viewpoints and increases engagement between social perspectives rather than on the basis of increased choice per se, then it must also rely on some other justification than mere consumer satisfaction.

Cass Sunstein (2002, 285) has argued that another reason why individual choice is problematic as a normative principle in media policy is that citizens should also be exposed to materials and information that they would not have chosen in advance. This has, of course, traditionally been the goal of public cultural policy, whose purpose according to Nielsen (2003, 243) is to "create activities that challenge these immediate private preferences, and a central criterion for success and for quality, will be precisely whether these activities are capable of facilitating experimental processes that open the mind and senses of the public to something they didn't know they wanted."

While the capacity of public media policy to create such activities is debatable, what all of these concerns clearly illustrate is that the various values associated with pluralism cannot be reduced only to consumer choice and to the satisfaction of individual preferences. Even though the number of outlets and channels has proliferated, the processes of political and social representation are still central to the justification of media policies and still bear relevance to the discussion of media pluralism. It may well be that in some cases the market remains the most efficient mechanism for ensuring pluralistic media output. However, it needs to be noted that there is nothing natural, neutral or inherently free about the market or the range of choices it offers. Therefore, I argue that instead of the rhetoric of individual choice, any analytical debate on media pluralism should focus on the structural level of media systems and the distribution of communicative power within those systems.

THE PROBLEM OF REPRESENTATION

Pluralism can be defined from a number of different perspectives, including the interests of different speakers, the interests of individual consumers, and the interests of society as a whole. While current debates are dominated by the normative framework of consumer choice, this perspective is often criticized for producing an unrepresentative media system that excludes broad social interests from the control of mainstream media and narrows ideological diversity by encouraging bland, common denominator provision for mass audiences.

Consequently, critical views of the media often tend to approach pluralism in terms of how different media enable the full and equal representation of divergent interests and social perspectives in the public sphere. As John Durham Peters (2001, 85) emphasizes, as long as political life is not centered on a single place where people can assemble as a single body, the expression of the people's voice(s) will always be inseparable from various techniques of representation. In this sense, the public sphere is not simply an open space of free-floating discourse; it is always constituted as a representative order linked to particular institutions that confine public discourse in various ways (see Trenz 2009, 2). However, the perspective on pluralism that starts from the ideals of reflection, equality or balance, which are often raised to justify a more interventionist media policy, is not without its problems either. The idea of media as representative institutions inevitably raises questions about who is entitled to speak for others and how one is to define the different constituencies or *publics* that the media should represent or that should have access to the media.

Another problem with defining pluralism in terms of representation is whether the media should reflect the prevailing balance of forces in society (implying an implicit definition of a representative media system in terms of existing identities and existing structures of power), or whether it is the task of the media to introduce new perspectives and to seek to redress the existing imbalances of power (see Curran 1991, 30). In either case, further problems arise from the question of how to identify relevant groups or perspectives that require representation and how to make decisions on which groups or perspectives are considered underrepresented or underprivileged.

Pluralism usually signifies the incorporation of an increasing number of social and cultural perspectives into the political arena. The idea of reflecting different perspectives, however, is only intelligible in relation to some criteria for the differentiation of these perspectives. However the possible differences that the media ought to reflect are virtually endless. A common criticism against many theories of the public sphere, for instance, is that they conceive diversity only in terms of opinions or ideas and the discovery of truth, which leaves out the more affective and expressive aspects of political and cultural identification. Consequently, it can be argued that many accounts of pluralism lean on problematic assumptions about the role of ideas and interests in politics, ignoring other sorts of diversity than that of political opinions (see Phillips 1996, 139).

The forms of identity politics that conceptualize pluralism beyond opinions or ideas and emphasize the specific situations of differentiated social groups in society, are not without problems either. Seyla Benhabib (2002) argues that the problem with much of the discourse on multiculturalism or cultural diversity is the assumption that each human group has some kind of culture that is clearly demarcated from the cultures of other groups. According to Benhabib (2002, 4), a "reductionist sociology of culture" that assumes that cultures or social groups are clearly delineable wholes and congruent with population groups only reifies existing categories by overemphasizing their boundaries and distinctiveness. This leads to a static, preservationist model of pluralism that draws too rigid boundaries, accepts the drive to police or regulate their authenticity, privileges cultural preservation and continuity and legitimates culture-controlling elites (Benhabib 2002, 68). Similarly, William Connolly (1995, xiv) claims that contemporary advocacy of pluralism is plagued by the conservative element of preserving current established identities, which resists the possibilities of new bases for pluralization.

For many critics, the forms of identity politics that have not examined their own essentialist notions of identity and difference also nourish confrontation and separation around various essential and oppositional identities. According to Young (1997, 383), the result of this is the evacuation of the public sphere of coalition and cooperation, and the decreasing motivation and capacity of citizens to talk to one another and solve problems together.

Cultures, identities, or even social perspectives, however, are not static wholes, but dynamic processes, entailing many contradictions and antagonisms. Therefore, a faulty epistemology in conceptualizing these differences has normative consequences for how we think about diversity, pluralism, and inclusion in the context of the media and the public sphere, too. This is especially pertinent if the principle of media pluralism is linked to the idea of balanced or equal reflection of existing difference in society. If we accept that identities are never pre-given but that they are always discursively constructed, the question that inevitably arises is the type of identities that the media should then aim at fostering.

Public service broadcasting institutions, for instance, have often coped with pluralism through a system that devolves control over programming and scheduling to certain established social, political, and religious groups. While blunting the criticism that public service broadcasting represents a centralized, paternalist force in society, such arrangements can equally be criticized for stabilizing differences based on established power relations. The extension of such formal rights to certain minorities, for instance, inevitably raises the question as to why other minorities don't get the same privileges.

More generally, claims of balance and representation embodied by institutions such as public service broadcasting are always problematic from the point of view of genuine pluralism. John Keane (1991, 123) asserts that it is self-evident that the repertoire of public service programming (or any other institutions) cannot exhaust the multitude of publics and voices in a complex pluralist society in motion. The complacent idea of informing all the people all the time thus clearly involves a certain paternalistic attitude. As Keane notes, the typical public service claim to balance is necessarily a defense of virtual representation of a fictive whole, a resort to programming that stimulates the actual opinions and tastes of some of those to whom it is directed. In reality, the commitment to balance will inevitably in some cases close off contentious, unbalanced views, favor representatives of established social groups, and in effect stabilize existing lines of difference. Public service institutions or subsidized media are therefore also subject to existing power relations and the unequal opportunities of groups and individuals to access the public sphere.

On the other hand, the alternative of conceptualizing pluralism in terms of openness to any and all ideas and in terms of unquestioning praise of all multiplicity raises equally difficult questions. It seems then that the conceptualization of pluralism runs into a double pathology of either affirming existing power arrangements (or the policy makers' view of the desirable distribution of communicative power) or naïvely celebrating all differences in a way that fails to account for any institutional structures.

From the vantage point of radical democratic pluralism, one answer to such problems is to argue that pluralism in media politics is best conceptualized in terms of the contestation of hegemonic discourses and structures rather than either as an ultimate solution or as some kind of postmodern play of identity and difference. It is much in this sense that James Curran (2002, 236–37) argues that rather than relying on the traditional justification that truth will automatically arise from either free competition of ideas or open rational-critical debate, pluralism in the media should be conceived from the viewpoint of contestation of power that different social groups can openly enter.

In fact, it can be argued that such a conception could also be derived from J. S. Mill. As noted in Chapter 2, Mill emphasized the value of minority opinions as a counterforce to the tyranny of the majority. This is evident in the following quote: "If all mankind minus one were of one opinion, and only one person were of the contrary opinion, mankind would be no more justified in silencing that person, than he, if he had the power, would be justified in silencing mankind" (Mill 1948, 14).

In this sense Mill's argument comes rather close to Mouffe's agonistic pluralism. As Mouffe puts it in a recent interview, the role of the media should be to contribute to the creation of an agonistic public space in which there is the possibility for dissensus to be expressed or different alternatives to be put forward (Carpentier and Cammaerts 2006, 974). Rather than idealizations of balance or representativeness, the primary value guiding the evaluation of the media would then be their ability to give voice to all those who are silenced within the existing hegemony and make visible what the dominant consensus tends to obscure (see Mouffe 2007). Similarly, Cass Sunstein (2003, 95) points out that while it will never be possible to hear all arguments, the public sphere is above all a domain where multiple perspectives should be presented and prevailing truths challenged. The media should therefore level out the existing asymmetries of power and seek to broaden access to the public sphere, especially for subordinate and underprivileged groups.

In line with this, James Bohman argues that pluralism is to be valued primarily because of its epistemic benefits. Like Habermas, Bohman values pluralism because it produces better public deliberation. However, departing from Habermas's arguments about "truth tracking," Bohman (2007) prefers to interpret this epistemic dimension in terms of error avoidance. Rather than the ideal of rational consensus or truth tracking, the availability of different social perspectives can be valued simply because it reduces the cognitive errors and deliberative biases that arise from discussions among the like-minded.

Without ever claiming to equally represent all groups in society, pluralism and its promotion in the public sphere can be guided by the aim of questioning prevailing truths and including as many social perspectives as possible. Social perspectives in this sense are understood as something broader than association with a particular group or subculture. As Young (1997, 394–5) explains, each perspective offers "situated knowledge," possible ways of looking at social processes, rather than any determinate, specific content. Contrary to Millian liberalism or Habermasian rationalism, pluralism would thus not be conceived solely in terms of opinions and interests, but neither would it be conceived solely in terms of recognizing different group identities, as prescribed by some forms of multiculturalism or identity politics. In this sense, then, social perspectives are not reducible to any particular set of values and opinions, but rather to different social positions and the range and type of experiences that different individuals and groups can contribute to the public sphere (Bohman 2007, 350; Young 1997). This approach can include expressions of ethnic identity, for instance, as a valid part of a social perspective, but it would not privilege or valorize any expressions of identity politics as inherently emancipatory.

Furthermore, pluralism does not necessarily imply designing institutional structures that are perfectly balanced or equally open to all views. Instead, pluralism is best conceived not as ultimate goal of media policy, but as a critical concept that refers to the recognition and challenging of existing power relations. In this sense media pluralism is not a state of affairs that can be achieved in a definitive or perfect sense. Rather it denotes an ongoing project that has no ultimate solution and that constantly throws up new contradictions and dilemmas.

RECONCILING PLURALISM AND CONSENSUS

Aside from proper models for the conceptualization of pluralism, another crucial question in grounding the value of pluralism in democratic theories is whether more pluralism and diversity is always desirable. Although it may seem that all things plural, diverse, and open-ended should be regarded as inherently good, in any practical situation we are inevitably faced with questions about the limits of pluralism (McLennan 1995, 8). Does pluralism then mean that anything goes? And what exactly are the criteria for stopping the potentially endless multiplication of perspectives?

As discussed above, one of the central tensions in contemporary political philosophy concerns the relationship between pluralism and the necessary commonalities assumed by democratic theories. In this sense, the approaches of deliberative democracy and radical pluralism are often considered to represent opposite poles of contemporary political philosophy. Whereas deliberative democrats such as Habermas are often seen to rely too heavily on the ideal of consensus, radical pluralists such as Mouffe tend to be seen as valorizing dissent, contestation, and conflict almost to the point of anarchy (see Karppinen et al., 2008).

There are reasons, however, why we should not too readily accept these polarized readings. As Dryzek and Niemeyer (2006) have recently argued, unbridled pluralism and absolute consensus both have very few advocates or defenders in contemporary political philosophy. As the discussion above indicates, almost all political theories view pluralism as a potential challenge as well as a value. Although they differ in their conceptualizations of what pluralism actually means, in one sense or another, all of them see communication and engagement across difference as a key value. In short, it makes little sense to argue for or against pluralism or consensus in any absolute sense.

Many of the polarized views of Habermas and Mouffe are arguably based on a rather simplified reading of current debates in democratic theory. Habermas's later work, for instance, can be seen as advocating a much more plural conception of public spheres than his critics would concede (see Brady 2004; Dahlberg 2005b; Karppinen et al. 2008; Moe 2008). Similarly, as was pointed out above, Mouffe is often accused of postmodern relativism that does not fully reflect her work. Mouffe does not want to abolish communication in the name of conflict and difference, and in denying "anything goes" relativism she has also criticized the type of extreme postmodern fragmentation that puts exclusive emphasis on all kinds of heterogeneity and incommensurability.

There is also no necessary reason to treat the logics of consensus and contestation as fully incompatible. The question is therefore not which one is the essence of democracy. Instead, they can be seen as two necessary perspectives on the democratization of any social institution. As Bonnie Honig (1993, 205) has noted, democratic politics consists of practices of both settlement and unsettlement, and of both disruption and administration. Ultimately, these are perhaps best understood as coexisting impulses of political life and political communication. Similarly, William Connolly (1991, 94) has argued that while a common institutional setting and a political forum for articulating public purposes are indispensable to political life, every form of social order also contains subjugations within it. Politics, then, is the medium through which these ambiguities can be engaged and confronted. It is a medium through which common purposes are crystallized, but also a medium through which they can be contested, exposed and unsettled.

The argument here is that in conceptualizing the democratic role of the media, we need to move beyond the simplistic opposition between consensus and contestation and examine more closely the various modes of critique enabled by different theories. While consensus was a significant component of early theories of deliberative democracy, more recent contributions have moved beyond the purely reason-centered and consensus-oriented emphasis to appreciate the role of contestation and conflict (Bohman 2000; Dryzek 2000; Young 2000). In contrast to what many critics argue, Habermas himself has in his later work emphasized the richness and openness of less rigidly structured communication as the "wild" social background of formal democratic decision making (Habermas 1996; 2006). Instead of a unified public sphere, he talks of a complex, multilayered notion of the public sphere as "a network of communicating information and points of view" which connects the private world of everyday experience to the political system (Habermas 1996, 360) and "branches out into a multitude of overlapping international, national, regional, local, and subcultural arenas" (ibid., 379). These "networks for wild flows of messages" can have "an informative, polemic, educative, or entertaining content" and they "originate from various actors—politicians, lobbyists, experts, intellectuals, civil society actors" (ibid., 415–16).

Rather than producing consensus or rational decisions, Habermas (2006, 416) says, "the deliberative model expects the political public sphere to ensure the formation of a plurality of considered public opinions." Furthermore, many recent theories of deliberative democracy maintain that the theory of the public sphere should not draw any sharp distinction between discursive forms that are rational and communicative and those that are merely manipulative or rhetorical. Instead, it should value different alternative forms of speech, particularly those originating from excluded social perspectives (Benhabib 2002; Fraser 1992; Young 2000).

The conception of the public sphere as a "public of publics" (Bohman 2007, 354), rather than as a unified, all-encompassing public sphere in which all commentators participate, thus seems to provide some common ground for the agonistic model and for more recent theories of deliberative democracy.

Even though theories of radical democratic pluralism can easily be criticized for their one-sided emphasis on the democratic value of conflict and lack of interest in the cooperative aspects of democracy, I have argued so far that the emphasis on democratic dissent and contestation are in many ways valuable for retheorizing the relationship between media and democracy in conditions of ongoing, structurally unequal power relations. As Nancy Fraser (1992, 122–24) has argued, a plurality of competing publics and the widening of discursive contestation that they bring about often promote the ideal of participatory parity better than a single, overarching public. Counterpublics and various alternative media can expand the topics and issues of public debate, enable the entry of excluded groups and perspectives into a public arena so that they can be taken into account and included in deliberation. Furthermore, the "enclave deliberation" of multiple smaller public spheres is thought to promote the development of positions that would otherwise be silenced or marginalized in the wider public sphere.

However, as argued in Chapter 2, despite the apparent convergence around the model of multiple publics, it can still be argued that from the viewpoints of democratic theory and self-government, unless these different publics are brought to bear on one another, they remain only parochial enclaves with little ability to address issues across and between different social groups. Disagreement is central to democratic politics, yet disruption for the sake of disruption can hardly be its primary purpose. Democracy also requires common forums where people are exposed to different views. In this sense, the mass media also serve the function of focusing and coordinating public debate in such a way that it can influence the political system.

Even Fraser (1997, 85), who is often regarded as one of the main advocates of the plurality of subaltern public spheres, acknowledges that the plurality of public arenas need not preclude the possibility of an additional, more comprehensive arena in which "participants can deliberate as peers across line of difference about policy that concerns them all." While it is important to ensure that there exist public sphere enclaves for deliberation by like-minded people, it is crucial that members of the relevant groups are not isolated from other views in society. In addition to the availability of a wide range of social perspectives, a democratic public sphere thus also requires that participants are prepared to cross and transcend their partial social perspectives and engage in communication across group-differentiated perspectives (see also Young 1997, 385). Even radical pluralists who deny the search for mutual understanding or common good thus tend to use notions such as "agonistic respect" and "critical responsiveness" which imply some form of commonality (Connolly 2005, 126).

It is somewhat revealing that both Habermas and Mouffe have expressed similar concerns regarding the development of the mass media. Habermas (2006, 422) acknowledges these fears in a brief note on the implications of the Internet to the public sphere by arguing that in liberal-democratic regimes, the Internet serves only to fragment focused audiences into "a huge number of isolated publics." Mouffe, on the other hand, expresses very similar skepticism in an interview dealing with the implications of her ideas on media and journalism. According to Muffle, the new media "perversely allows people to just live in their little worlds, and not being exposed anymore to the conflicting ideas that characterize the agonistic public space [. . .] making it possible to only read and listen to things that completely reinforce what you believe in" (Carpentier and Cammaerts 2006, 968).

Encouraging encounters between conflicting ideas thus seems to be a goal shared by both Habermas and Mouffe. Similarly, in the context of media institutions and programming, Graham Murdock (1999, 16) argues that rather than parceling out specially demarcated "minority" programs or narrow-casting that serves self-defined groups, we must also challenge the accepted divisions between mass and minority, mainstream and margins, and "develop forms of representation, participation and scheduling that promote encounters and debates between the widest possible range of identities and positions."

To summarize these strands of debate, it can be concluded that differences, both among participants and among possible opinions, are at the heart of a democratic public sphere. If people share the same views, there is no need for a public sphere, beyond the ritual celebration of unity. On the other hand, a democratic public sphere will always require a certain amount of commonality and unity, as is readily accepted even by radical pluralists such as Mouffe. Along with various mini-publics and marginal media, there is also a need for common public spheres that bring together different voices and social perspectives, and where antagonistic perspectives meet and people are exposed to views and perspectives that differ from their own. As Georgina Born (2006) argues, the point is that contemporary media politics cannot only be about a proliferation of micro-publics, but it should be about achieving a space in which differences are displayed and in which mutual encounters take place between expressions of diverse and apparently incommensurable perspectives and worldviews. In a broad sense, this is a position that can be justified from the perspectives of both deliberative and agonistic models.

SOME IMPLICATIONS FOR MEDIA POLICY

What, then, are the implications of these observations for media policy, and what do they add to the broader question of evaluating media institutions and structures in society? Most of the theories discussed above remain on the level of ideal theory and avoid engaging with questions of institutional design. While the purpose here is not to provide a blueprint for a democratic media system, this book can only hope to accomplish its stated purposes if its theoretical reflection offers some useful perspectives from which to challenge the prevailing assumptions in media policy.

Because of the opportunities opened up by new technologies, the search for answers to democratizing the media nowadays often turns to the interaction between professional media and their audiences. As Bohman (2000, 56) argues, while some communicative division of labor may be inevitable, the public must be able to challenge the credibility of professional communicators, especially as regards their capacity to set the agendas and frames for discussing issues. In some ways, this is what the various forms of social media and citizen journalism are already doing today. They are holding media institutions accountable by contesting their claims and challenging their monopoly over producing journalism. In other words, it is the public who must provide the critical reflexivity with which to hold the media accountable for their structural limitations. Similar conclusions have recently been drawn by Habermas (2006), who argues that inclusive civil society must empower citizens to participate and respond to public discourse, acknowledging a feedback between informed elite discourse and a responsive civil society.

Yet opportunities to participate in the public sphere are far from equal, and the framing of the terms of public debate is still largely controlled by mass media institutions. For most critical scholars, the ideal of a fair distribution of communicative power continues to require some normative regulation to limit structural inequalities and enhance the opportunities of underprivileged or marginalized social perspectives to influence public spheres. If existing media systems are not regarded as inevitable or as the only possible institutional arrangements, then the question of democratizing the media must also have consequences for institutional design. While the discussion above has remained on an abstract level, contemporary discussions in democratic theory provide at least some normative criteria for a democratic and pluralist media system.

One of the main implications of recent theorization on public spheres for the project of democratizing the media is that media power must be exercised in a differentiated way (see Bohman 2007). This means overall institutional pluralism: rather than a single institutional ideal or an organizing principle (such as public service institutions or free market competition), media systems should involve a variety of overlapping and mutually checking systems or logics. As James Curran (2002, 239) notes, "the media are not a single institution with a common democratic purpose. Rather, different media should be viewed as having different functions within the democratic system, calling for different kinds of structure and styles of journalism." Therefore, we should always be suspicious of any totalizing claims of genuine pluralism or unrestricted communication.

According to Curran, a democratic media system should enable the expression of conflict and difference and allow opposed or separate groups to express themselves; yet it should also support social conciliation and the process of reaching equitable compromise (see also Curran 2011). Recognizing that different types of media may have different functions means that public service broadcasting and other similar institutions may be best defended on the grounds that they provide unifying, regulated spaces which bring together various divergent perspectives (see Born 2006). Yet it needs to be acknowledged that no public communication system will ever achieve social objectivity or balance between all social perspectives. Other media, such as online community media or activist networks, serve the function of self-expression for diverse groups, allowing them to articulate their needs and strategies in their own voice, and may thus be better conceived as serving the purpose of mobilizing counterpublics. Similarly, public support for marginal media may be justified by the aim of supporting these groups' expressive resources and their ability to challenge and contest prevailing views and cultural codes. Furthermore, there are countless other forms of public communication that clearly take place outside the scope of formal institutions and regulation, such as street demonstrations, graffiti, or online discussion forums and that enable spontaneous expression of conflict and resistance.

Normative theories of democracy provide some tools for conceptualizing these different aspects. The Habermasian public sphere thesis has long served as the normative basis for justifying institutions such as public service broadcasting as a space for rational, cohesive debate. It would obviously be too exclusive and restrictive to apply the same normative criteria to all media. However, there is no reason why radical-pluralist arguments could not be used to defend concrete institutional arrangements in media policy as well.[3] Support for alternative and minority media, for instance, can be seen as an important media policy tool in creating institutional plurality that is open to democratic contestation and that can disrupt existing power structures.

More generally, the key task for media policy from the radical-pluralist perspective is to support and enlarge the opportunities of structurally underprivileged actors and create space for the critical voices and social perspectives excluded from the systemic structures of the market or state bureaucracy. These aims can be justified by the principled goal of increasing the inclusiveness and openness of the public sphere to differing social perspectives, but also by the more diffuse aim of fostering a culture of dissent and contestation.

---

[3]For one of the few attempts to theorize the implications of the radical-pluralist theories for media policy and public service broadcasting, see Craig (2000).

On a general level, these aims are already reflected in some critical theories of the media and democracy. One of the most prominent outlines for a media system has been developed by James Curran (2002, 240). In Curran's working model for a democratic media system, general interest media retain an important role as a source of social cohesion. This is where different individuals and groups come together to engage in a reciprocal debate about the management of society. In the European context this refers primarily to public service broadcasting and other socially accountable mass-audience media. This core sector, however, needs to be complemented and challenged by various peripheral media sectors, some of which specifically facilitate dissenting and minority views. For Curran (2002, 241), these include a civic media sector, which will provide channels of communication linked to organized groups and networks, and social movements within civil society; a professional media sector that allows professional communicators to relate to the public on their own terms with a minimum of government constraint; a social market sector, where the state subsidizes minority media to promote greater market diversity; and finally a conventional private sector, which relates to the public as consumers and acts as a restraint on the over-entrenchment of minority concerns to the exclusion of majority pleasures.

This of course is just one institutional model and it is not intended to be exhaustive of different media structures and styles of journalism. In the current media environment, it might be apposite, for instance, to add new social and participatory media as a further sector with its own operating logic and functions (see Chapter 5). Furthermore, the constitution of all these sectors, their structure, respective importance, and internal norms will remain debated. The main strengths of Curran's model, however, lie in its acknowledgment of different operating logics and institutional pluralism, as well as in the assertion that a democratic media system should create spaces for the communication of opposed viewpoints and a common space for their mediation (Curran 2011, 79–80).

Similarly, John Keane (1991) maintains that a nonfoundational account of media and democracy must be based on the plurality of nonstate media institutions, which facilitate a wide variety of communicative forms, combined with measures to curb the self-paralyzing effects of market-driven media and to reduce corporate power over the means of communication. Therefore, rather than clinging to a universal, naturalized model of a free marketplace or an idealized rational public sphere, we need to have a more differentiated model that acknowledges the many, often contradictory, functions that the media serve, reflected in different institutional designs and operating logics.

The realization of such a media system will of course be politically contested—the distribution of resources, subsidies, and regulations will always be contested, but that is what media policy is all about. As Nicholas Garnham (2003) has noted, while one form of pluralism emphasizes toleration and recognition of differences, another aspect of it inevitably concerns the distribution of scarce resources, such as access to the media, cultural subsidies or production resources. Yet, "too often there is an attempt to combine a request for recognition and a share of public resources that such recognition brings with it and, at the same time, demonize the very common decision making, the politics, that must inevitably go with such resource distribution" (ibid., 198). This is another way of saying that pluralism does not mean that value judgments can be averted in policy making.

The argument I have elaborated here by applying the idea of radical pluralism to the context of media politics is that it is not enough to conceive media pluralism in terms of heterogeneity and a more diverse range of options for choice. Rather than simply counting the number of different companies, channels, or formats, any serious analysis of media pluralism must be conducted on the level of structural relations of power that the media are part of. This includes struggles over the framing and agenda of public discussion, but also more concretely, political and corporate decisions about the architecture and ownership of media systems.

Proposed as an alternative to both liberal minimalism and to rationalistic idealizations of deliberative democracy, my argument has been that a radical-pluralist approach can be understood as an argument for the continuing centrality of the question of power in media politics. The danger of what I have called naïve pluralism is that such questions are veiled or ignored under the illusion of communicative abundance or limitless choice. Unequal relations of power remain crucial in the field of media policy and media institutions and, as I argue in more detail in Chapter 5, there is no reason to think that technological or any other developments will lead to spontaneous harmony.

This perspective points to the continued relevance of the critical political economy of communication and its attempts to reveal and analyze structural hierarchies of power that influence and shape our media environment. However, given that the definition of what constitutes a fair distribution of power usually leads to difficult normative questions, this also requires that the normative ideal models and assumptions are continually questioned and not taken for granted.

The purpose of this chapter has been to bring some new intellectual resources to the debate on the democratic roles of the media and the ideal of media pluralism, which often revolves around worn-out metaphors such as the marketplace of ideas or the rational public sphere. Yet in the end, the values and meanings associated with pluralism and diversity are open-ended and subject to a continuous process of social negation, and it is not feasible to invoke an absolute final value or an authority to establish the relevant norms and criteria for their assessment. Media pluralism, as a policy principle, does not signify any absolute core value. Instead, I have argued, it signifies a critical attitude that involves a continuous questioning and challenging of existing structures of communicative power.

PART II

The Politics of Media Pluralism

This part shifts focus from theoretical debates on pluralism and the public sphere to the actual uses and definitions of media pluralism in contemporary media policy practice and research. So far I have argued that the value of media pluralism as a policy objective derives from explicit and implicit assumptions about the nature of a democratic public sphere. Instead of being premised on some coherent ideology or theory, however, concepts and principles often guide policy debates in a more mundane way, in the form of background assumptions and discursive frames. The purpose in this part is to examine the variety of ways in which the concept of media pluralism is employed in contemporary media policy debates and to analyze the normative assumptions and political rationalities in which different uses are grounded.

Chapters 4 and 5 deal with existing definitions of media pluralism and diversity in contemporary media (policy) research. Based on the substantial literature around these notions, Chapter 4 first illustrates and problematizes the dominant ways in which these concepts have been used and interpreted. Chapter 5 then proceeds to recent technological changes and their impact on debates about media pluralism. After reviewing different arguments about the present "communicative abundance" and its implications for the debate on media pluralism, I argue that technological changes have only amplified the need for a more holistic conception of media pluralism that is concerned not only with measuring media content or market structures, but with the distribution of communicative power in a broader sense.

Chapter 6 then turns to uses of media pluralism in recent European media policy, focusing particularly on debates surrounding media concentration and the role of public service media. Finally, Chapter 7 focuses on what I call "the politics of criteria" and analyzes how various empirical objectifications and indicators of pluralism and diversity are becoming more and more important in media policy.

CHAPTER 4

Aspects and Scope of Media Pluralism

There have been many attempts to define, deconstruct, and classify conceptions of media pluralism and diversity, their relations to other concepts, and their various aspects and components in media research. It is beyond the scope of this book to review all the various classifications and categorizations, but despite the complexity of the concepts, media scholars and policy analysts have articulated some more or less established dimensions on which pluralism and diversity can be discussed and even measured. This chapter introduces some of the main lines of argument in the contemporary debates and points to the main problems they involve.

Given the abstract nature of the concepts, it is obvious that any meaningful empirical analysis of media pluralism and diversity requires that we first specify the different levels and contexts in which these values can be discussed. The main argument put forward here, however, is that it is also important to reflect on such analytical and practical distinctions from a broader normative perspective. Otherwise, there is a danger that the conceptual classification made for empirical and practical purposes will also start to guide our understanding of media pluralism as a political and normative value.

ON TERMINOLOGY: PLURALISM AND DIVERSITY

While the concepts of media pluralism and media diversity are often used more or less interchangeably in both political and analytical discourses, there is some confusion about the distinction, or a possible hierarchy, between the two concepts. As noted in the introduction, it seems that media diversity is more commonly used in American media policy debates, while media pluralism has become the main term used in European debates.

There have also been some attempts in media studies and in the media policy literature to distinguish the two and define them more precisely. Lesley Hitchens (2006, 9), for instance, takes media pluralism to relate to the way in which the media environment is structured, while diversity refers to media content. Similarly, Des Freedman (2008, 72) says that pluralism is associated with the wider political context in which the media operate, while diversity refers to the ability of the media to reflect existing social differences and maximize the choices offered to audiences. However, since both these concepts have multiple meanings and are used in a variety of contexts, these distinctions have not become firmly established.

Another difficulty in grasping the different meanings of media pluralism and diversity is that they are often used in separate but interlinked debates that reflect different areas of academic interest. As noted above, some associate the terms above all with cultural identities, minorities and linguistic diversity and ground their discussions in larger debates on multiculturalism. Others, who are more concerned with the diversity of political opinion and the conditions of public debate, tend to ground their approach in democratic theory and the metaphors of the free marketplace of ideas or the public sphere. Accordingly, a distinction is often made between *political pluralism*, which is about the need, in the interest of democracy, for a range of political views represented in the media, and *cultural pluralism*, which refers to the reflection of cultural diversity within society (Doyle 2002, 12).

Again, such a distinction might sometimes be useful, but sometimes it may only create more confusion. On a manifest level, the focus of this book is on political pluralism and the justification of media pluralism from the perspective of democratic theory. However, it is in practice often impossible to separate the relevance of political pluralism from cultural concerns, which makes the distinction very fluid.

Although I have mainly used the concept of media pluralism instead of diversity, both these terms are contested umbrella concepts whose flexibility and ambiguity is at the center of my research. Understanding media pluralism as a broader category or an umbrella term does not remove the ambiguity that arises from the fact that both terms are often used in a normative as well as a descriptive sense, as both justifications for policies and as empirically measurable and assessable constructs.

It is clear by now that there is no commonly agreed definition of either media pluralism or media diversity, let alone their relationship to each other. The elusiveness of definitions, however, is not confined to these concepts only. As Philip Napoli (2001) has noted, the use of normative guiding principles in media policy has historically been plagued by tendencies towards ambiguity, inconsistency and manipulation:

> Terms such as the public interest, diversity, and the marketplace of ideas, are used rather casually and, sometimes, carelessly, with little sense of what these terms might actually mean and even less sense of how individual policy decisions actually contribute to the fulfillment of these principles . . . too often, these foundation principles function primarily as rhetorical tools for advocating particular policy actions, as opposed to analytical tools for the rigorous assessment of these actions. (Napoli 2001, 3)

Apart from different political uses of these concepts, which are analyzed in more detail in Chapter 6, there are also a number of genuine conceptual obstacles to defining and clarifying the concept of pluralism in media studies and media policy. Partly this has to do with its different contexts of use: some definitions reflect different political philosophies and theoretical models of media and democracy, others are formulated in legal standards and regulatory decisions, and yet another set of definitions is needed for the empirical measurement or assessment of media performance.

While this book has mainly dealt with media pluralism as an abstract theoretical value, contemporary media policy takes it often as a more tangible goal that should be somehow measurable. The first problem with any measurable definition is that while pluralism clearly denotes heterogeneity on some level, it can refer to almost any aspect of the media. Beata Klimkiewicz (2008, 82) distinguishes three levels on which media pluralism can be conceptualized: a *macro-level of media systems* (media ownership, structures and entry conditions), a *meso-level of media institutions* (media performance, professional practices and user access), and a *micro level of media contents*. Within and beyond these categories, concepts of pluralism and diversity have been broken down to an almost endless number of different aspects and dimensions, from ideological, demographic or geographic diversity to the diversity of media outlets, sources, types, genres, representations, or issues covered (see, for example, Hitchens 2006; Klimkiewicz 2008; McQuail 2007b; Napoli 1999; Napoli 2011). All these aspects can furthermore be considered in the context of local, national, or even global media markets, and within one sector of the media (for example, broadcasting or newspapers) or on the level of the media system as a whole.

Media pluralism can refer to the extent that media contents reflect and serve the demands and opinions of the public, or it can refer to the general diffusion of media power in society on the level of ownership, economic structures and political influence. In addition to its various political and cultural connotations, pluralism can also be seen as an economic value, as an impulse to invention, competition and choice. Consequently, it appears clear that there is no absolute means for defining or measuring plurality or diversity, but they are only intelligible in relation to some criteria and definitions that are deemed more important than others. As Jan van Cuilenburg (1998) puts it, they always have to be gauged in some way in relation to variations in social reality. The question then arises, how to conceptualize this relationship: Which aspects are considered the most relevant, and how to institutionalize and operationalize the differences against which plurality is examined?

In addition to determining the relevant aspects, we also need to have some kind of normative framework in order to be able to assess what is meant by *more* or *less* plurality. In other words, the discourse through which media pluralism is conceptualized and operationalized as a policy rationale depends on the way that the relationship of media with the political system and larger society is conceived. Although often presented as an end in itself, speaking of pluralism and diversity in any political context always requires a frame of reference in which it makes sense.

Denis McQuail (2007b, 49) distinguishes four normative frameworks within which media diversity is commonly assessed: the norm of *reflection* means that the media are expected to reflect proportionately the existing political, cultural and other social variations in society in a proportionate way; *equality*, on the other hand, means that the media should strive to give equal access to any different points of view or any groups in society, regardless of their popularity; *choice* conceptualizes diversity from the perspective of an individual consumer and equals it with the amount and range of available choices for consumers in any given market (between channels, programs, etc.); and finally, *openness* places emphasis on innovation and difference, valuing new ideas and voices for their own sake.

These categories, whose conceptual ambiguities I also discuss in the Chapter 3, illustrate the different perspectives from which pluralism and diversity can be analyzed: the interests of different speakers, the audience or individual consumers, or the interests of society as a whole. Each framework implies a different interpretation of the meaning of pluralism and the standard by which it should be assessed.

Different frameworks may often be in contradiction with one another. According to van Cuilenburg (1998, 41), for instance, reflective diversity usually goes with less diversity in terms of equality or openness. As noted above, this is because the idea of representation is usually based on the existing balance of forces in society and thus tends to reinforce the status quo in terms of marginalized and excluded voices.

Similarly, an increase in the choices available to consumers does not necessarily mean that the media better serve minorities or provide access for alternative and innovative voices. Van Cuilenburg (1998, 42, 45) goes so far as to claim that these paradoxes make diversity in information and opinion a completely fictitious concept with no practical meaning. Instead, he argues, the real issue for media policy is not lack of information as such, but information accessibility, particularly access to the new and innovative ideas and opinions of small minority groups. Given the proliferation of media outlets and the shift from a supply to a demand driven environment, it can be argued that reflective or representative diversity—the idea that individual media institutions or even the media system as a whole should somehow proportionately correspond to existing differences in society—is thus bound to lose its prominence in favor of access and openness as more general communication policy objectives.

Traces of all these perspectives, however, are still present in contemporary media policy. Most quantitative empirical approaches, for example, are based on measuring the number of choices available to consumers, while theoretical and normative arguments often rely on the broader conceptions of reflection, equality or openness. Accordingly, consumer choice is often discussed in terms of the free marketplace of ideas metaphor, while critical media scholars tend to privilege the perspective of the public sphere and its underlying norms of universal access and openness.

Given these different assumptions, differences over the meanings of media pluralism are not only a matter of technical clarification, but they go to the very heart of the concept. Because there are so many different conceptions of why pluralism is desirable, it is difficult to agree not only on the relevant aspects of pluralism, but also on what is considered more or less pluralistic.

LEVELS OF ANALYSIS

In theoretical discourses, pluralism is often discussed as a highly abstract value whose meaning is continuously debated and discussed without even trying to give it any specific, empirical substance. In this sense, pluralism is similar to the concept of freedom, which is almost universally valued as an abstract principle but hardly ever unambiguously defined or measured. As

I have argued above, there are some good reasons for treating pluralism in this way, without reducing it to any specific indicators.

In this broad sense, Gillian Doyle (2002, 11–12) defines pluralism simply as "the presence of a number of different and independent voices, and of different political opinions and representations of culture within the media." Similarly, a broad working definition suggested by the Council of Europe describes pluralism as "the scope for a wide range of social, political and cultural values, opinions, information and interests to find expression through the media" (Council of Europe 1999; 2007b). While no definition will cover all meanings of the concept, or be agreed upon by everyone, such broad and sweeping definitions seem to capture the underlying value of media pluralism in a rather uncontroversial manner without specifying its institutional preconditions. As is the case with other broad values such as media freedom or communication rights, any attempt to transfer them into concrete policies, institutional arrangements, or indicators will remain contested.

Developments in the nature of media policy making itself, and particularly the shift from ideological considerations towards pragmatic cost-benefit calculation (see van Cuilenburg and McQuail 2003), have also heightened the need for further conceptual clarifications of the different aspects and components of pluralism. A number of media policy scholars have argued that to serve as meaningful and effective tools for designing and analyzing actual policies, concepts such as pluralism and diversity need to be infused with a more specific and concrete meaning (see Napoli 1999; 2007; Valcke 2011).

The most established framework for an operational definition of media pluralism is based on a dichotomy between media structures and content. The Council of Europe (1999) defines media pluralism as diversity of media supply, reflected, for example, in the existence of a plurality of independent and autonomous media (generally called *structural pluralism*) and in a diversity of media types and contents made available to the public. A related dichotomy is often drawn in policy debates between external and internal pluralism. This distinction has been frequently used by the Council of Europe, too, whose expert committee has applied the following definition: "Pluralism may be internal in nature, with a wide range of social, political and cultural values, opinions, information and interests finding expression within one media organisation, or external in nature through a number of such organisations, each expressing a particular point of view" (Council of Europe 1994a).

In European media policy debates, the dichotomy of external and internal pluralism has parallels with the notions of structural and behavioral regulation, respectively (see Ward 2001). This is because the concept of internal pluralism has been considered particularly relevant regarding public service broadcasting and its objective of offering a comprehensive service for all citizens (see Gibbons 2000, 306–7; Hallin and Mancini 2004, 29–30; Ward 2001), while external pluralism refers more to efforts to maintain competition between different outlets.

In one of the most frequently cited classifications of media diversity, Philip Napoli (1999) adds a third component and breaks down the principle of diversity into the components of source, content, and exposure diversity, each having multiple subcomponents (see Table 1).

TABLE 1. COMPONENTS OF DIVERSITY AND THEIR ASSUMED RELATIONSHIPS

Source Diversity →	Content Diversity →	Exposure Diversity
Ownership	Format/Program	Horizontal
Outlets	Type	Vertical
Workforce	Demographic	
	Ideas/viewpoints	

Source: Napoli 1999, 10.

Source diversity, for Napoli, reflects the established policy goal of promoting a diverse range of information sources or content providers. This includes questions of ownership, number of outlets, and various dimensions of organizational or economic structures (public, private, non-profit). Source diversity can also be conceptualized in terms of recruitment and people working within media outlets (again categorized by some criteria, such as gender or ethnicity).[1] *Content diversity* refers to another established policy goal, namely the diversity of ideas, viewpoints, or content options in the actual output of either the media system or one channel/medium, which can again be measured on almost any criteria, such as formats, genres, subjects, or viewpoints.

The third aspect identified by Napoli is that of *exposure diversity*, or user-focused diversity, which refers to the range of content that people actually use (see also Napoli 2011). As discussed in Chapter 1, political theorists from Mill to Mouffe have emphasized the democratic value of exposure to conflicting viewpoints. While traditionally the focus in media policy has been on the diversity of sources or contents available or their relationship

---

[1]In Europe the debate on the diversity of the journalistic workforce is only just beginning, whereas in the United States this debate has been going on much longer (see Kretzschmar 2007).

to one another, questions around exposure diversity have recently attracted increasing debate. Yet the aspect of what the public actually consumes and what they do with the options open to them has until now been largely ignored by media policy makers (see also Hargittai 2007; Hindman 2007; Webster 2007).

Traditionally the assumption has been that greater source diversity will lead to enhanced content diversity, which in turn is thought to promote diversity of exposure as audiences have a greater range of options to choose from. However, despite the common assertion of a causal relationship, there is little systematic evidence to back this up. Recently, the linear relationship has increasingly been called into question, and it has been suggested that greater choice, and the ability of people to filter what they see, may actually narrow the range of media and different viewpoints to which people are exposed (Prior 2007; Sunstein 2007). If the ultimate value behind media pluralism is taken to be citizens' exposure to diverse perspectives and antagonistic viewpoints, then understanding the dynamics of how source and content diversity impact the diversity of exposure in the current media environment will have to be one of the crucial questions for future research.

There are multiple factors that influence the way that citizens find and are exposed to different opinions in general. These include the concentration of media ownership, general social and residential segregation, ideologically exclusive media outlets, and not least the recent technological advances that allow the filtering of online news (see Sack, Kelly, and Dale 2009). In Chapter 5 I will return to the problems that new media technologies raise regarding the relationship between availability and actual use. In the meantime it is easy to see that from the perspective of the democratic values that underlie the notion of media pluralism, exposure diversity raises some fundamental normative questions about the ideal of a public sphere where different perspectives meet and everyone attends to issues of general interest.

In particular, the exponential growth of the availability of information combined with the fragmentation of audiences into smaller enclaves or *sphericules* has raised the question as to whether there are contents that everyone should see, regardless of their individual preferences or tastes. As I note in the discussion of different democratic theories in Chapter 1, pluralism entails that citizens are exposed to different views, not only to those that reflect their preexisting tastes and opinions. While exposure is the aspect that is closest to the normative theories behind the concept, it is also the one aspect that is most difficult to regulate, since the public cannot be forced to consume pluralistic content. Although exposure diversity has so far remained on the fringes of media policy discussions, it seems inevitable that with the continued growth of choices available to audiences, and the increasing ability of users to also take part in their production, this aspect will receive increasing emphasis. Reflecting this is the fact that questions of user competencies and media literacy, for instance, are clearly gaining increasing currency in debates on media pluralism.

SEEKING CAUSALITY: CONCENTRATION, COMPETITION, AND CONTENT

One of the most controversial aspects in the debate on media pluralism concerns the assumed relationships between its different components. Although the fundamental purpose of fostering media pluralism is usually associated with media content, and ultimately with ensuring that individual citizens have access to a broad range of opinions, knowledge, ideas, or cultural expressions, the aspects of media pluralism that have mostly preoccupied media policy makers are the structure and ownership of the media. This is explained by the difficulties involved in the direct regulation of media content, let alone the regulation of people's tastes and actual media use. Policies designed to enhance structural pluralism, however, are not implemented purely for the sake of themselves, but as Napoli (1999, 14) argues, they usually assume that a plurality of sources leads to a greater diversity of media content, which in turn has been presumed to lead to greater exposure diversity. This assumption makes it crucial to analyze how market structures and media ownership are related to the range of voices that have access to the public sphere and ultimately to what people actually see and hear.

Most prominently, the causal relationships have been debated in the context of media ownership concentration, which continues to be a topical issue with many governments as well as with the European Union, which is currently weighing competing concerns over the restructuring of media markets and the development of ever larger, transnational media conglomerates (see Doyle 2002; EC 2007a). Moreover, the question of media ownership often receives further prominence due to the power of individual media moguls such as Silvio Berlusconi and Rupert Murdoch, and the recurring scandals associated with their media empires.[2]

---

[2] The phone-hacking scandal, which resulted in a public outcry against News Corporation and its owner Rupert Murdoch in 2011, for instance, revealed many disturbing details about the close relations of UK politicians and media executives, and at least temporarily also resulted in closer scrutiny of media concentration in general (see Freedman 2012).

The underlying rationale for regulating media ownership generally lies in the fear that concentration may limit the number of voices that have access to the media (see Bagdikian 2004; Baker 2007; Horwitz 2007). Debates on media pluralism have often been so closely bound with the issue of media ownership that the concepts of concentration and pluralism have been defined as antonyms. This implies that free market entry and effective competition are naturally the best guarantees of pluralism, as assumed by the metaphor of the free marketplace of ideas. Reflecting this assumption, the Council of Europe Committee of Experts (1997, 5) has stated that "democracy is best served by a situation in which many media operate on the market by offering a wide range of ideas, information and types of culture" and that "a viable marketplace of ideas depends in large measure upon a competitive economic marketplace in the media field."

While the assumption that media pluralism is related to competitive markets is widely accepted in media policy-making, the exact nature of the relationship between market competition and media content is particularly contested. The empirical research is also less than unambiguous. Denis McQuail (2007b, 52) notes that much of the research on media pluralism and diversity has been descriptive, with reference to either the content supplied by the media (for instance, the range of formats or genres or the degree of linguistic or cultural diversity) or the structure of ownership and markets, and as such it has not contributed greatly to explaining the causes or consequences of more or less diversity or the relationships between its different aspects.

It is clear from the literature that does exist on the relationship between ownership concentration and content just how difficult it has been to empirically establish almost any kind of causal relationship (see, for example, Harcourt and Picard 2009; Horwitz 2007; Meier and Trappel 1998; van der Wurff 2005). Some critics have argued that consolidation is conducive to greater centralization and greater emphasis on profitability in newly enlarged companies. Some studies report a correlation between competition and diversity, while others suggest that increasing competition only leads to further homogenization and standardization of media content. Some believe that free markets will provide diversity irrespective of the ownership structure. Yet others argue that the root problem is not concentration per se, but market competition and commercialization. After all, even if they are not part of chains or large conglomerates, all media are increasingly guided by the same commercial logic that relies on the standardization of contents and formats. Finally, there are those who argue that not only is consolidation benign, but that in some cases, and particularly in the context of small markets or at times of economic uncertainty, it can have positive effects since it helps preserve the resources that are necessary for producing quality journalism and providing a variety of services (Barnett 2009, 2–3; Cavallin 1998; Harcourt and Picard 2009; Puppis 2009, Raycheva 2009, 84). Unsurprisingly, the latter view has been advocated particularly by media industry representatives.[3]

Recent technological and economic developments and the uncertainties surrounding their implications for the business models of traditional media companies have also undoubtedly recast the traditional concerns about ownership concentration. As Napoli (2011) notes, these uncertainties have clearly diminished policy makers' focus on media ownership as the central element of the conversation about media pluralism and diversity.

Given all these inconsistencies in the presumed link between ownership and content, does ownership then matter at all for media pluralism? As Jens Cavallin (1998) notes, those in positions of power within the media often tend to downplay the role of ownership in general, arguing that the real power belongs either to individual journalists, the market at large, or consumers. With the rise of the Internet, lower barriers of entry and the proliferation of different outlets, it is often argued that the dynamism of the media markets together with new technologies virtually guarantee that people get what they want—regardless of any possible concentration in some sectors of the media (Compaine 2001).

As much as by lacking empirical evidence, however, the ambiguity is also explained by the confusion stemming from the use of different conceptual approaches and normative frameworks. Considering the range of possible definitions of pluralism and diversity, it is hardly surprising that the empirical evidence is so ambiguous. For instance, it is entirely possible that competitive markets enhance the number and variety of program types and genres available to the public, but at the same time narrow the range of political views or even exclude some contentious issues altogether. Furthermore, there is the question of whether all media should be treated as equivalent, or whether concentration in the ownership of radio, newspapers, magazines, and television be treated somehow differently. Given these questions, it is obviously very difficult to design empirical studies that take into account all these aspects and that demonstrate any universal causality.

Market expansion and proliferation of channels does not necessarily mean "more of the same," as some critics maintain, but neither does it mean an

---

[3]In recent European policy debates this argument has also been put forward by media industry representatives like the European Newspaper Publishers' Association who are opposed to the harmonization of ownership rules.

automatic increase in pluralism. Television in most countries with mature, multichannel markets, for instance, has evolved to involve an enormous range of genre variety. Yet it is not necessarily accompanied by corresponding increase in the ideological range of perspectives. Despite all the empirical research and economic models, the question of whether free competition produces more pluralistic media thus remains a normative and not only an empirical issue.

A broader problem with the ownership-content debate is that it is largely premised on the models of the free marketplace of ideas and consumer choice that tend to neglect externalities that are not quantifiable and that do not fit well into the standard cost-benefit calculus (see Horwitz 2007, 39–42). The metaphor of the marketplace of ideas essentially conveys the idea that the marketplace itself is a natural and neutral mediator of various demands placed on the media, whereas for many critical scholars the market itself is the main threat to pluralism. The economic concepts used in competition policy and the political and cultural concepts employed by social scientists are thus fundamentally different in their premises. In the competition policy discourse, media pluralism, and concentration are approached purely from the perspective of potential market distortions and the consumers' freedom of choice, while the political concept of media pluralism is associated with the wider (and admittedly more abstract) notions of public interest and citizens' communication rights. For many critics of media concentration, the demand for "proof" of the evils of media concentration will thus inevitably beg the question of whether it is even possible to present proof that is uncontroversial or even remotely objective when dealing with normative questions (see Baker 2007; Cavallin 1998).

Ownership is only part of the picture in debates on media pluralism, as understood in this book. The question of media pluralism cannot be re-duced to market structure and ownership, as if all other values associated with media pluralism automatically followed from that. The ambiguity of empirical research alone shows that the link between ownership and content works in a variety of ways and is influenced by factors such as journalistic culture, creative work within media corporations, routines of news produc-tion, and the nature of different media technologies themselves. As David Hesmondhalgh (2001) has noted, one of the ironies of debates about media ownership is that leftist critiques of media concentration have often had the same one-dimensional concern with competition and market structure as neoclassical economists at the other end of the political spectrum.

It seems doubtful that it will ever be possible to establish any direct quantitative link between media concentration and content diversity. Yet media ownership still clearly matters, and it remains one of the key questions in contemporary media policy. As the examples of the News Corporation scandal in the United Kingdom or the chronic entanglement of political and media power in countries like Italy or Russia indicate, the prospect of powerful groups controlling the majority of information sources is itself worrying, even if there are no methods for actually measuring the concrete harm it causes. From this point of view, it is obviously problematic to argue that only actual and proven abuse of positions of power, not concentration itself, calls for media policy measures. Yet the lack of evidence is one of the reasons why in many places the existing barriers on media ownership are currently being dismantled, making the inconclusiveness of empirical studies somewhat disconcerting for media reformers.

From the normative perspective outlined in this book, the debate on media pluralism has in many ways been confused by the reductive focus on measuring the effects of competition and concentration. As Steven Barnett (2009, 5) notes in the context of the United Kingdom, policy approaches to media pluralism have so far been essentially means rather than ends based—having started with the assumption that plural ownership means diverse output, policy measures have mostly been reactive and lacking in well defined ends.

As a multidimensional issue, media pluralism cannot be reduced to any of its components, since an analysis of one aspect does not necessarily say anything about other aspects or their relationships. An examination focusing on media content alone says nothing about the underlying structures of influence, yet focusing on ownership alone as an indicator of the distribution of media power is equally reductive, for it fails to capture the actual dynamics of media production and the variety of factors that influence it. As many critics of media concentration argue, it is crucial for democracy and pluralism that different actors in society should be given equal opportunity to exercise influence (see Baker 2007; Cavallin 1998). From this perspective, the distribution of power itself is a central issue that requires examination rather than just allegations of abuses of such power. In this sense, ownership of the media is a central but by no means the only aspect that influences the distribution of media power.

While much can be done to clarify the relationship between different aspects of pluralism empirically, it is also relevant to ask how the debate itself and the questions posed for empirical research are framed. From the broader normative perspective, the problem is that the aspects that are easily measurable are not necessarily the most relevant normatively, while those aspects that feature in normative debates are not necessarily measurable at all.

THE MEANS OF REGULATION

It is often argued in critical media policy studies that policy debates have been wrongly cast as disputes over the extent of regulation, and that it would be more accurate to talk about different forms of regulation with different aims. Every media system is regulated, whether by public authorities, market laws, or other kinds of norms. Similarly, although the issue of media pluralism is often associated almost exclusively with questions of media ownership regulation, there are numerous different ways in which media pluralism is tied to different forms of regulation. Even arguments for free markets often presume various intrusive means, such as competition and copyright rules, which influence what information becomes available and how various communicative entitlements are distributed.

Hence, it is argued in this book that media pluralism is best conceived as an objective that always implies political and regulatory choices, even if these are not explicitly recognized as such. When discussing the manifest forms of regulation associated with media pluralism, the different types of regulation are commonly classified into the categories of structural regulation, which broadly addresses the architecture of the media environment, and direct content regulation (Hitchens 2006, 11).

Aside from specific rules or restrictions on media ownership, the means through which the structure of the media environment is regulated are numerous, including licensing, competition policy, subsidies and public service media. According to Jens Cavallin (1998), policies that aim to influence media pluralism can be categorized into five groups: restrictions, counterweights, economic interventions, transparency measures, and organizational measures. Roughly, these measures can be associated with the dual objectives of deconcentration of resources in media industries and support for various nonprofit media, including public service broadcasting.

Although media ownership restrictions have been removed or relaxed and replaced with competition law in many countries recently, many countries in Europe, as well as the United States, also have media-specific restrictions on media ownership concentration, based on either the number of channels or audience and market shares (Baker 2007; Council of Europe 2009; Doyle 2002; EC 2007a; Harcourt and Picard 2009; Hitchens 2006; Valcke 2009). These can include limits on the number of outlets one company can own within a certain type of media or across different types of media (cross-media ownership). General competition policy and merger control rules can also have a significant impact on the structure of the media market, although they mainly have to do with other economic motives. The (unsuccessful) attempts to develop a common EU policy on media ownership and pluralism are discussed in more detail in Chapter 6.

Another set of basic measures to promote media pluralism involves efforts to provide the public with alternatives to commercial and market-based media. In Europe at least, there has traditionally been a relatively broad consensus, reflected in a number of political declarations, that the markets alone cannot guarantee a pluralistic media landscape (see, for example, Council of Europe 2002, 17). Public service broadcasters are the most prominent examples of institutions that are consciously designed as a counterweight to the commercial media. Public service media are also an example of what can be called "sectoral pluralism," which refers to measures that seek to ensure the presence of differently constituted sectors within the media landscape. With different funding, structures, and sometimes different program mandates, the purpose is thereby to ensure that pluralism is built into the basic structure of the media system (Hitchens 2006, 11). The remit of public service broadcasting has changed and varies between countries, but the preservation of pluralism and diversity are today almost universally accepted and applied as fundamental values and justifications for the position of public service broadcasters—despite persistent attempts by commercial media to argue that public service media actually present a threat to pluralism by distorting fair competition.[4] In any case, public broadcasters are expected to provide pluralistic programming both within their services and as distinct a sector that contributes to the overall media system. Contemporary debates on the future of public service broadcasting are also discussed in Chapter 6.

In addition to public service broadcasting, there are of course other forms of nonprofit media, including various activist networks and local community media. The European Parliament (EP) and the Council of Europe have both recently emphasized the importance of nonprofit community media for media pluralism and called for more public funding to support such initiatives (EP 2008b; Lewis 2008).

Most European countries also have a tradition of allocating public funds to other sections of the media, including the film industry, press subsidies, and the development of network infrastructure. The European Union also supports schemes such as the MEDIA program that can be regarded as a

---

[4]Recently this view has been reiterated by commercial media corporations in both national and European contexts. One version of the argument can be found, for instance, in the contributions of the media industry associations to the European Commission's consultation processes regarding public service broadcasting and media pluralism, which will be analysed in more detail in Chapter 7.

means of economic intervention to influence the structure of the media market by means of professional training and promotion.[5] In a broad sense, counterweights to the market system also include other cultural policies that aim to support cultural institutions, such as libraries and museums that foster broad expression of values, opinions and criticism. Most countries also have various indirect forms of economic subventions to the media, such as tax breaks and postal subsidies that reflect the belief that the media serve a social function beyond its economic value. Direct and indirect subventions are also commonly used to support the development of new information infrastructure and for making technological requisites like broadband connections accessible to more people.

Pluralism and diversity can be promoted not only at the level of the overall structure of the media market, but also through measures that have to do with organizational issues. Employment, education, and recruitment issues, including gender and ethnic minority representation in the journalistic workforce, can also be conceived as means of promoting media pluralism (see ICRI et al. 2009, 56; Kretzschmar 2007).

All of the above are forms of structural regulation. Content regulation in a direct sense is usually considered less common, mainly because it involves the politically sensitive issue of government interference in what types of content are permissible.[6] In reality, however, governments all around the world are actively attempting to influence the media based on considerations of national security, indecency and various other reasons (see Freedman 2008, 122). Despite the fact that policy makers have often preferred structural measures that do not directly intervene in media contents, there are a number of ways in which media policy places direct or indirect demands on media content. In many countries broadcasting licenses and public service mandates, for instance, include specific programming requirements that seek to guarantee the diversity of program types or views. In the European Union, content regulation also includes a contentious quota system that aims to promote the use of independent producers and local or European content. Furthermore, there are various types of requirements for right of reply, fairness and equal airtime for political candidates or parties during election periods that qualify as content regulation (Hitchens 2006, 11).

---

[5] See http://ec.europa.eu/information_society/media/index_en.htm.

[6] This is not to say that ownership and structural regulation are not often interpreted by corporations as violations of their rights to free speech (Horwitz 2007, 38). Not surprisingly, however, free speech objections tend to apply only to certain forms of regulation, while others, such as copyright, subsidies, and tax breaks, are rarely mentioned in that context.

Finally, aside from formal intervention, various transparency measures are often counted among the regulatory means of promoting pluralism. These include transparency in the control and ownership of the media as well as monitoring aspects such as media contents or program supply. On the European level, the Council of Europe has long demonstrated its desire to take on this kind of role, and recently the need for monitoring media pluralism has also been raised by the European Commission (2007a). In addition, there are various other bodies and NGOs that have adopted a monitoring role. These transparency measures serve a double function: empirical data can be used as a basis for regulation, but public information regarding media control is also considered valuable in itself. In practice, the focus of European media policy has mainly been limited to monitoring instead of more formal regulation. However, as I will argue in Chapter 6, monitoring activities are not without relevance for they also determine the terms of debate and define which issues become politicized.

The means discussed above are all traditional measures that have been discussed in the context of media policy for several decades. However, it has been increasingly argued that the new media and changes in delivery methods and media uses are challenging existing regulatory means and creating a need for new regulatory approaches and method (see Goodman 2007). The shift from a supply- to a demand-driven media environment, for instance, has clearly had an effect on traditional policies that focus on creating a diverse supply of content. To some extent, it appears that the focus of regulation is shifting from traditional structural regulation to questions concerning access to infrastructure and content, information rights and various other issues raised by the new media environment (see Gibbons 2000, 310; Goodman 2007; Hitchens 2006; Verhulst 2007).

For instance, it is increasingly recognized that a controller of a delivery platform or a software producer can be in a monopoly position and act as a new kind of gatekeeper (Hitchens 2006, 214). Other new issues that raise concerns about pluralism include the regulation of search engines, digital rights management, network architecture, software interoperability, net neutrality, must-carry requirements, and electronic program guides (see also Council of Europe 2002; 2012). So far, many of these concerns have been played out, for instance, in the charges about abuse of dominant position or privacy violations against companies like Google, Microsoft, or Facebook.

The means of regulation listed above are by no means comprehensive and serve only to illustrate some of the many ways in which media policy influences the distribution of communicative power. New media in particular can be expected to give rise to a number of other issues that are not yet even properly acknowledged as potential media policy issues. However it is important to recognize that despite the rapid technological and market changes, not all of the old regulatory concerns have gone away. Although new technologies are often used as arguments for relaxing existing regulations on media ownership, questions around media ownership continue to remain central in media policy. Similarly, despite the rhetoric of an ongoing crisis, public service broadcasting has demonstrated considerable resilience and continues to figure centrally in contemporary European debates on media pluralism. As Hitchens (2006, v–vi) argues, the rhetoric of new media and its liberating effects is an attractive handle for policy makers to distance themselves from difficult decisions about media regulation. However, from a broader normative perspective, it is necessary to avoid simplistic "old" and "new" media distinctions, for in the end, both raise similar questions about the unequal distribution of communicative power.

Also, instead of dichotomies such as those between regulated and unregulated or public and private, it is more useful to think that there are varieties of regulatory modalities that influence the structure of the media landscape. In effect, all media are regulated, and rather than viewing regulation as a departure from the norm of "free markets," it is more useful to consider the market as simply another instrument of regulation, which is no more or less natural than others (see Hitchens 2006, 60–61). So despite the changes that are taking place in the means of regulation and the changing discourses about the aims of regulation, it is unlikely that basic questions about who gets what, how, and when, will lose their prominence in media policy.

This also implies that concerns about media pluralism cannot be limited to means of regulation specifically designed to protect one or more aspects of pluralism or diversity. If media pluralism is understood more broadly in terms of the distribution of communicative power, it is evident that it must be discussed on the level of the norms and values guiding the media system as a whole. In the following chapter, I demonstrate this point from the perspective of new media technologies and discuss more closely the various claims made about their intrinsic implications for media pluralism.

CHAPTER 5

Paradoxes of Communicative Abundance

The most obvious challenges to existing conceptions of media pluralism today arise from the Internet and the increasingly malleable roles of media producers, new kinds of intermediaries, and users. It is often claimed that the changes brought about by the Internet are making the traditional analytic, normative, and regulatory frameworks of media policy increasingly obsolete. With the almost infinite range of information available online, it hardly needs saying that many of the premises of different conceptions of media pluralism and diversity also need to be rethought. This chapter begins by surveying the different arguments about the effects of technological changes and then considers their conceptual implications for a meaningful notion of media pluralism.

It seems almost ironic that pluralism and diversity enjoy such broad popularity as media policy values at the very time when information and communication channels are proliferating at an unprecedented rate. In contrast to long-standing concerns over the homogenization of content and concentration of media power, many accounts of contemporary communicative abundance present an image of almost infinite choice and an unparalleled pluralization of voices that have access to the public sphere. John Ellis (2000) has defined three eras in the development of television: age of scarcity, age of availability, and the current age of plenty. Others have characterized the contemporary media environment with terms such as "communicative abundance" (Keane 1999), "supersaturation" (Gitlin 2002), and "cultural chaos" (McNair 2006).

It has been forecast over and over again that the Internet will inevitably break up concentrated media power and lay the foundation for "diversity, accessibility and affordability" (Compaine and Gomery 2000, 575). With more information available in public than ever before, concerns for media pluralism and diversity appear to have become not only increasingly contested but for some analytically obsolete or anachronistic. In what sense is it then meaningful to speak of pluralism when media systems in general are characterized more by abundance than scarcity?

The debate on media pluralism has largely been premised on the idea that the media act as powerful intermediaries or gatekeepers of public communication flows. It is this role that obviously makes it crucial to interrogate the openness of media systems to different voices, ideas, and interests in society. As Stefaan Verhulst (2007, 117) puts it, it is the fact of scarcity that imposes power; because of scarcity, those intermediaries that control the markets are in a privileged position to exercise power and shape public opinion.

However, with the shift to a demand- and search-driven media environment, it is thought that the new media have shifted the locus of control over communication toward individual users, as audiences now can increasingly filter and personalize information and choose how, when and where communication is received. For some, the expansion of choice and participatory potential has marked not only the end of scarcity, but also the end of powerful intermediaries and gatekeepers. As suggested by the proliferation of terms such as electronic, virtual, or digital democracy, the new modes of public communication enabled by the Internet seem to fulfill the promise of greater interchange and feedback between media institutions and citizens held out by many normative theories of the public sphere, without there being much need for regulation or public intervention.

Bruce Williams and Michael Delli Carpini (2004) argue that the new media environment disrupts the traditional "single axis system" of political influence and creates a fluid "multiaxity" of power. This has arguably also created new opportunities for nonmainstream political actors to influence the setting and framing of the political agenda.

On the other hand, there are skeptical voices that remind, as Mattelaart (2003, 23) does, that "each new generation revives the 'redemptive discourse' of liberating effects of new communication technology, only to be disappointed when old hierarchies of power prove to persist." To support this view, there is now considerable evidence that contrary to popular belief, the Internet has not fundamentally changed the concentrated structure typical of the mass media, but in fact brought about new forms of concentration, exclusion, and hierarchy (see, for example, Hindman 2009). And then finally, there are those who argue that today's problem is that there is too much diversity; that it is precisely the individualization and fragmentation of media use that is making publicly accountable media regulation and the principles of public service media more relevant than ever before (Sunstein 2007).

In short, there is little consensus on whether the technological and socio-cultural changes in the contemporary media environment have actually led to a meaningful plurality of voices. Instead, much of the debate on the implications of the Internet for media pluralism is characterized by a tension between a fascination with new technologies and their contribution to furthering democracy and, on the other hand, a critical view that highlights the importance of enduring power structures and hierarchies. This book has so far leaned towards the critical view that pluralism should be viewed broadly in terms of the distribution of communicative power and not in terms of increasing consumer choice only. The emphasis on the importance of surrounding cultural, political, and social factors also questions the capacity of technology itself to eradicate social hierarchies. Yet the changes in political, economic, ideological, and technological environments that are shaping media systems are in many ways real and can hardly be denounced as inconsequential.

FROM IDEOLOGICAL CONTROL TO CULTURAL CHAOS?

It has been commonplace in both academic and policy discourse to celebrate digital media as tools that will inevitably lead towards democratization and pluralization of the public sphere and to the emergence of different kinds of grassroots civil society activities.

Manuel Castells (2009, 55) has argued that the development of interactive, horizontal networks of communication has induced the rise of a new form of communication, which he calls "mass self-communication." While the communication system of industrial society was centered on the mass media, characterized by the distribution of a one-way message from one to many, the communication foundation of the network society is the global web of horizontal communication networks that include the multimodal exchange of interactive messages from many to many. For Castells, this opens up an unlimited diversity of autonomous communication flows and an unparalleled opportunity for insurgent political and social movements to intervene in the new communication space. To support these claims, Castells cites the exponential growth in the number of blogs, autonomous communication networks, new social movements, and alternative media that are largely organized in the Internet.

For media sociologist Brian McNair (2006, 10) these same changes have led to three interlinked developments: an exponential increase in journalistic and other forms of information available to citizens; the dissolution of spatial, cultural and social boundaries both globally and within nation-states; and the erosion of taste hierarchies used to police cultural consumption. As noted in Chapter 4, these have all been seen in media and cultural studies to represent a radical diversification and decentralization, even democratization of cultural production.

Both these visions also exemplify a broader argument about a fundamental shift in the dynamics of public communication and the public sphere from uniformity and control towards plurality and even anarchy. As a common denominator for most visions, lower costs of distribution and production appear to disrupt the traditional elite control of the media by amplifying the political voice of nonelites and allowing citizens to compete with journalists for the creation and dissemination of political information. As Richard Rogers (2004) puts it, the Internet has become a collision space for official and unofficial accounts of reality. Ranging from alternative health information to social movements' protests, the Internet is seen to unsettle the official and the familiar. Much in line with radical pluralist visions of democracy, the value of the Internet is thus seen to lie in the way it challenges mainstream news and official communication strategies by engendering a culture of dissent and argument (Rogers 2004, 163).

Besides technological advances, arguments saying that there is greater diversity in the contemporary media environment can also be couched in wider socio-cultural developments. According to Ellis (2000), the shift from the era of scarcity, when the media tended to build social consensus, to an "era of plenty" reflects not only changes in communication technologies, but also broader socio-cultural trends of individualization and pluralization. As the era of a mass market for standardized goods has given way to a market of differentiated products for more fragmented consumers, the logic of differentiation between social groups and individuals has also changed and the media market itself is increasingly engaged in the project of producing and giving significance to various differences. It can then be argued that an ever more differentiated and targeted communications market will produce more and more differentiation between people (ibid., 63–66).

For many, this is above all an emancipating development that broadens the opportunities available to citizens and breaks the paternalism and elitism associated with the old era of scarcity and unitary culture. As Catherine Lumby argues, "the past few decades have seen an overwhelming democratisation of our media—a diversification not only of voices, but of ways of speaking about personal, social and political life . . . the contemporary media sphere constitutes a highly diverse and inclusive forum in which a host of important social issues once deemed apolitical, trivial or personal are now being aired" (Lumby 1999, xiii).

Similarly, McNair (2006, 100) states: "There is a meaningful (rather than tokenistic) plurality of voices within contemporary cultural capitalism. . . . It is beyond dispute that the system can accommodate and give mainstream visibility to a more diverse, broader range of opinion." Contrary to critical media scholars, McNair adds that this has happened because of, not despite, the commodification of culture. In other words, dissent and counterculture are inherent to the very logic of contemporary cultural capitalism, not something that needs to be protected from it.

Consequently, it has become almost a truism that there has been a shift from few speakers and many listeners to a greater number of active participants and new communicative forms bringing a much wider spectrum of views to the public sphere. Even more importantly for the conception of media pluralism put forward here, the Internet is commonly thought to redistribute political influence and make the public sphere more inclusive to the political voice of ordinary citizens.

The narrative of diversification through technological and market developments has also been influential in communication policy, where the democratizing effects of the new media have often been used to justify less rigorous regulation of the old media.[1] Many writers have suggested that government regulation will no longer be necessary since the monolithic empires of mass media are dissolving anyway. As Nicholas Negroponte (1996, 57–58) argued in one of the early prophecies of the digital revolution: "The combined forces of technology and human nature will ultimately take a stronger hand in plurality than any laws Congress can invent."

The proliferation of channels, coupled with the capacity of audiences to actively interpret the media, is thus seen to make public regulation of the media increasingly unnecessary. The Internet, as an epitome of the "combined forces of technology and human nature," allows people to communicate across borders, to consume the growing amount of information and enter-

---

[1]This argument was central, for instance, when the US regulator FCC (2003, points 3–4) sought to relax its media ownership rules on the basis that people "have more media choices, more sources of news and information, and more varied entertainment programming available to them than ever before," so that "Americans can access virtually any information, anywhere, on any topic." Yet "broadcast ownership rules, like a distant echo from the past, continue to restrict who may hold radio and television licenses as if broadcasters were America's information gatekeepers."

tainment available, and to participate in multiple participatory platforms and applications. All these developments, which have seemingly emerged without any planning or regulatory intervention, also challenge the legitimacy of institutions such as public service media, subsidies, and other interventionist means to support media pluralism.

ENDURING ASYMMETRIES OF POWER

The relevance of these developments is hard to dismiss, as it seems evident that some communication technologies have the capacity to support a more pluralistic media landscape than others. Yet the assumption that the Internet and other new technologies have solved all concerns related to media pluralism is misguided in some very obvious ways. In contrast to the more enthusiastic visions, many activists and academics have recently pointed to growing concerns regarding new hierarchies of power and new forms of concentration in online media. There are many who claim that the new media environment only further privileges corporate interests, marginalizes alternative voices, and leads toward continued consolidation of media power.

In general, it can be argued that the disparities in the possibilities offered by new media largely reflect previously recognized socio-economic inequalities. Hence, the critics are right to argue that behind the veil of a multitude of resistances and critiques, we should also acknowledge the shape of certain "unmoved movers" (Suoranta and Vadén 2008, 1, 151). As Garnham (1999b) notes, patterns of power distribution change slowly, rarely, and with difficulty—so it is safe to assume that the new technologies alone are unlikely to be either as new or as dramatic in their impact, for good or ill, as the technologically focused approach assumes.

The assertion of an expanding range of available viewpoints does not go unchallenged either. As Todd Gitlin (2002, 7) argues, the media torrent itself seems somehow totalizing, propagating a uniform consumer culture with only limited room for genuine pluralism. There is no shortage of critical perspectives in either public debate or the academic domain that see the media as offering an ever more homogenized supply of market-driven entertainment and consumer culture. For these "more of the same" critics, the proliferation of media only encourages the tendency to follow the lowest common denominator and replicate standardized success recipes over and over, thereby homogenizing the supply even more. Despite the proliferation of various niche media, it can also be argued that the rise of the Internet and the demands of real-time news has only diminished the resources available to ambitious journalism and made mainstream news organizations increasingly reliant on established sources and routines, sometimes reducing journalism to the distribution of wire services and recycled news (see Baker 2007, 116; Fenton 2009, 14). Despite all the diversity, plenitude and complexity, the concerns over the concentration of power and the homogenization of content have thus not disappeared.

What most critical concerns share in common is the view that the diversity of options itself is not the only indicator of genuine pluralism, for it says nothing about the inherent hierarchies and relations of power within the media. In spite of claims about user-generated content, there is still a fundamental asymmetry between media producers and consumers. Questions about how media production is organized and about what shapes its output thus remain crucial issues for critical media research.

Aside from the continuing importance of existing institutional structures, the argument that new media technologies somehow autonomously, and without need for regulation, develop in a more democratic and pluralistic direction can be questioned as well. The fact that the capacity of governments to guide the direction of technological development is undermined hardly means that technological forces and human nature somehow automatically lead to harmony and inevitable democratization.

It is common to think of the Internet as something unruly, ungovernable, and characterized by openness and absence of control. Yet, in reality, the Internet raises a wide range of communication policy issues that are not only technical but also profoundly political. Regulatory mechanisms of various kinds are being put in place all the time, and as is the case with all communication technologies, Internet uses are shaped by different political, social and economic interests and managed by different powers (see Braman 2004; Zittrain 2008). Contrary to the rhetoric of autonomous technological progress, these mechanisms—many of which are informal and outside the scope of democratic accountability—continue to shape the media and their development. The control of information flows and use has thus become an even more effective form of power. This applies to many familiar topics such as media ownership, but also to other areas that are still poorly understood. For instance, design choices in network architecture, copyright rules, software codes, net neutrality, and other forms of information politics still largely determine the way that information is made available and who can speak to whom under what conditions.

Decisions about standards and protocols made within organizations such as the ITU, ICANN, and other Internet governance forums, and above all within and between corporations, can have a lasting impact on media pluralism, even if these organizations are not necessarily recognized as sites of media policy as such. Media regulation, in its various forms, is therefore no less important than before, but it must be based on a new set of premises and arguments that take into account the new situation of media abundance and the policy problems it raises.

Factors such as the ownership and control of media as well as unequal access to communication systems ensure that communicative abundance will not end questions about the unequal distribution of communicative power. The increase in the amount of information available has not brought about harmony, transparency, or unrestricted communication. Instead, it has created new controversies about the unequal distribution of and restricted access to means of communication. As John Keane (1999, 6) puts it, rather than being automatically solved, disagreements about "who gets, what, when, and how" are actually multiplying.

CONCENTRATION ONLINE

Instead of making overarching judgments about the value of technology itself, there is a need to consider more analytically the opportunities and obstacles presented by the new media technologies. First of all, even if the Internet provides an almost infinite diversity of voices in principle, this does not mean that all of this diversity is equally accessible to the majority of the public. Factors that come into play include not only technical obstacles, but also lack of skills or resources to find less prominent content and the structural power of new gatekeepers and content aggregators to influence what contents are most easily accessible to Internet users. As many observers have warned, certain logics and practices of information politics are taking the web away from its public spiritedness, leading to information exposure that is not in keeping with the principles of a pluralism of viewpoints or a collision of different accounts of reality (Dahlberg 2005a; Rogers 2004, 164; Zittrain 2008). Old hierarchies of media ownership and control continue to persist, but there are also new forms of domination and concentration that are only beginning to emerge. These create a need to critically reflect on the pluralism made possible by the new media, its limits, and the nature of the barriers that still persist.

The most basic obstacle, of course, is that not all have access to these new forms of media. As Castells (2009, 50) notes, a fundamental form of power that is common to all networks is exclusion from the network. A large part of the public is still not online, which bears implications for who will be left out of the conversation. But even if one leaves aside these questions of unequal access and the digital divide, which themselves are complex and multilayered enough, there are a number of other reasons to criticize the argument that the Internet will democratize the media by giving ordinary citizens the ability to compete in the marketplace of ideas against media corporations and political elites. One thing that is only starting to be recognized is that online media too have their own forms of concentration and hierarchies that in some ways go even deeper than those in traditional media. Space may be unlimited online, but other resources that are required to produce attractive content such as time, money, skills, and attention are not. The battles for the attention of audiences and the ownership of information have only intensified. American political scientist Matthew Hindman (2009) makes use of empirical research on Internet use to argue that the Internet has done little to broaden political discourse, but in fact it empowers a small set of elites—some new, but most familiar. While the Internet has increased some forms of political participation, elites still strongly shape the way that political material online is presented and accessed.

The competition among sources for the privilege to provide authoritative information thus continues to involve gatekeepers of various kinds. Furthermore, the nature of media commodities as a public good means that corporations are forced to devise strategies such as digital rights management to transform public into private goods and introduce new monopolies and new forms of scarcity throughout the media value chain. As Garnham (2000, 58) argues, concentration is an inherent tendency of media markets, because the economic survival of media companies depends upon the exploitation of scarcity. Since the business model of large content-producing corporations is based on the scarcity of content, which new technologies have the potential of removing, it is in the interest of media corporations to create mechanisms of artificial scarcity, such as copyright and patents, and to erect barriers to the abundance of digital content (see also Suoranta and Vadén 2008, 53).

Many commentators have taken it for granted that the Internet diffuses the attention of the public away from mainstream media outlets and towards more diversified sources. Some have viewed this positively, but others have been concerned that it may lead to the fragmentation of public discourse as people are exposed only to those ideas that fit their preexisting dispositions. Contrary to these assumptions, however, the empirical evidence suggests that the attention of the public still tends to converge on a limited number of sources that are not typically alternatives to mainstream media. Availability does not necessarily mean better accessibility and actual use, since much of Internet content comes from established suppliers of media content, and most of the most popular sites remain in the hands of the same players that dominate other media. As a consequence, Baker (2007, 112) concludes, "it does not appear that the Internet operates to substantially equalize influence among media entities; the number that dominate, that is, get the largest audience share, are even fewer than in the prior, exclusively offline world."

Even more troublingly, it has also been argued that the digital media reduce the likelihood of user exposure to unsought, but ultimately valuable media experiences (Goodman 2004, 1394). As Hindman (2009) shows, Internet traffic follows an extreme winners-take-all pattern. Relying on portals, link structures, and search engines, most people are directed to a few successful sites, while the rest remain invisible to the majority of users. Despite the wealth of independent websites, the online news audience is concentrated on very few outlets while blogs, for instance, receive only a miniscule portion of Internet traffic.

Using the methods commonly used to measure the concentration of resources (Gini-coefficient, the Herfindahl-Hirschman Index and the Noam Index), Hindman concludes that although the Internet greatly expands the amount of information sources that people can choose from, in practice the structure of the online medium creates a high degree of concentration of content among a small handful of sites.[2] For Hindman, online audience concentration thus equals or even exceeds that found in most traditional media; citizens seem to cluster around a top few information sources in any given category, while "most online content receives no links, attracts no eyeballs, and has minimal political relevance" (ibid., 18). At least according to this particular study, it is thus a myth to believe that the Internet levels the playing field and gives voice to the marginalized.

One concrete issue that is increasingly being recognized is the rising structural power of Internet search engines and their influence in determining what users worldwide can see and do online. The growth of available content makes the selection and mediation of relevant contents increasingly crucial, and to a large degree this function at the interface between public and individual communication is assumed by search engines and portals. In effect, they perform a function similar to that of traditional gatekeepers that effectively preselect the information available to users (Council of Europe 2012; Hargittai 2007; Hindman 2009; Machill et al. 2008). On the one hand, search engines are mediators that mirror the power of existing institutions and social structures. On the other hand, they are also new gatekeepers themselves, with autonomous influence in directing web traffic (Hindman 2009, 80). With the most visited pages ranked first, Hindman argues that the search engine's logic essentially reinforces the trend towards consolidation.

---

[2]Statistics cited by Hindman report that in the United States the top ten websites account for 29 percent of all web traffic, which is more than the audience share of the top ten newspapers, magazines, or radio stations in their respective media (Hindman 2009, 93). Similarly, Baker (2007, 112) shows that top blogs have almost eighty times the number of visits as the one-hundredth–ranked blog.

Popular sites become even more popular, while obscure sites recede even further into the ether. Factors such as search engines and the Internet's link structure are thus critical in determining what citizens see online, and they also explain the predominance of one or two sites in almost every category of online information (Hindman 2009, 14–15).

Another concept that is often used to criticize the expansion of corporate media power over the Internet is the notion of enclosure (see, for example, Castells 2009, 105–8; Dahlberg 2005a). Enclosure refers to restrictions on media content and the control of media uses, and it includes issues such as subscription services, absence of external links, lack of interoperability, software tie-ins, and other means of building walls around content by technical or economic means.[3] The notion of intellectual property also functions largely as a producer of scarcity, because it commodifies content by creating means and the ideological will to treat digital content as commodities (Suoranta and Vadén 2008, 67). Commercial actors, in particular, are increasingly seen to promote enclosure in ways that go against the ideal of open and unconstrained exchange of information that is typically associated with the Internet. This means, for instance, that companies behind the most popular online portals do their best to build walls around their sites, or construct virtual colonies by providing links only to other sites that the company controls (Dahlberg 2005a, 163, 168). More surprisingly, many "citizens' portals" set up by governments have also adopted similar means of controlling the format of contributions and disallowing external links (Rogers 2004, 11–12).

All in all, apart from the power of existing media conglomerates, new forms of concentration and control are emerging on the Internet. While many observers have claimed that the Internet's most important political impacts come from the elimination of old media gatekeepers, much of the recent research has shown that commercial websites and search engines, for example, play an increasingly important role in filtering information. These include both new types of structural concentrations such as bottlenecks controlled by providers, and new forms of exclusion that are due to media literacy. As Verhulst (2007, 121) argues, although new technologies have altered the role of the media, they have not marked the end of scarcity

---

[3]Electronic readers such as Amazon's Kindle and Apple's iPad provide an example of new forms of distribution that allow companies to control all the information that is made available through them. This possibility became news when Amazon remotely deleted some digital editions of two George Orwell novels from the devices of users who had bought them. Apple had a similar incident when it rejected a political cartoon application from its store because it ridiculed public figures, although it later reversed this decision because of bad publicity.

but are simply introducing new forms of scarcity. New intermediaries are looking to find new ways of controlling the flow of information, shaping the way people find information, and thus dominating the battle for attention.

All these issues remind us of the danger that the new media only reproduce the structure of traditional mass media, with time and attention becoming ever more subject to the power of money. As Verhulst (2007, 123) argues, "contrary to original assumptions, there is not an abundance (much less an infinity) of intermediaries today, but a segmented and fragmented market where the concentration of ownership and patterns of access appear very similar to the old market." Contrary to the claims that old media gatekeepers have been eliminated, gates and gatekeepers are still a critical part of the information landscape. Some of the ways in which online information is filtered are familiar and due to the enduring presence of old media organizations on the web, while other aspects of online filtering, such as search engines and portal sites, tags, blogs, rss feeds, meta-sites and tracking systems, are new and have received much less research from the perspective of media pluralism (see Rasmussen 2008, 76).

It is clear that the enormous variety of content available does not automatically encourage users to expand their media use. The argument that the Internet is a radically decentralized medium where large media outlets are unimportant, or that it necessarily increases the number of information sources that people actually see (exposure diversity) is not supported by the empirical evidence. More choice is available for those who have the knowledge and the time to search for more information beyond that selected and filtered by the editors of mainstream news sites, but not necessarily for the majority. While this may not be enough to dismiss the democratic and pluralistic potential of the Internet and the many opportunities it offers, it does highlight the need to reconsider many of the simplistic assumptions about what the Internet means for media pluralism.

As Castells (2007, 248) notes, the growing consolidation of old and new media conglomerates does not mean that the mainstream media are monopolizing the new, autonomous forms of content generation and distribution. What we are witnessing is the unfolding of a contradictory process that is leading to a new media reality whose effects will ultimately be decided through a series of political and business power struggles. The point here, therefore, is not to determine whether there is more or less genuine plurality now than there was before. Instead, the broader point to draw from this is that communicative abundance alone does not render questions about the distribution of communicative power and political voice obsolete, but only reconfigures them in a more complex form.

Another fear that has been invoked in debates on the impacts of new communicative abundance almost since the start of the Internet is the fragmentation of public discourse. Rather than too much concentration, some believe that the Internet provides too little. Even if technological advances did actually lead to a diversification of media uses, this has not been viewed only in a positive light, but it has also lead to fears of extreme individualism, fragmentation and loss of common public platforms. In particular, technological advances lead to questions about what the explosion of communication options means for the preconditions of democratic deliberation and the public sphere. Will the public sphere fracture into a number of self-radicalizing subpublics, or are there mechanisms that aggregate diverse voices in crosscutting debate and deliberation?

One of the criticisms against the Internet is that it undermines the quality of the public's information environment as well as the integrative role of the media in society (Dutton 2007; Keen 2007). As we no longer have widely shared and authoritative news media, some fear that the Internet may lead to a general decline in the scope and quality of public communication. Even though they have an almost unlimited array of content at their fingertips, Internet users can choose to access only a narrow spectrum of the subjects that interest them most. In the words of Cass Sunstein (2007), users can limit their own horizons by cocooning themselves in "echo chambers," in which their own personal prejudices are reinforced rather than challenged.

As noted above, there is empirical evidence that increasing availability does not necessarily lead individual citizens to more diversified media use. However, as commentators like Sunstein have emphasized, one of the most striking social consequences of new communication technologies is the growing power of consumers to filter what they see. Greater specialization allows people increasingly to avoid general interest media and to make choices that reflect their existing predispositions. This means it is possible for them to consciously avoid ideas that they don't like or agree with, or select material that confirms their existing beliefs and values. With people following only the sources that fit their existing predispositions, Sunstein (2007, 17) argues, there is the danger of a new herd mentality. Citizens can use the new power to filter information and insulate themselves in an information cocoon to systematically avoid dissenting voices, which increasingly leads to less common experiences with other citizens.

In other words, the more control people exercise over what they see and hear, the less prepared they are to be surprised (Verhulst 2007, 125–26). In this sense, the predicted decline of general interest media that provide a range of shared, common experiences and information for the public as a whole is often seen to have socially problematic consequences. As the media market is breaking down into smaller and smaller segments, people are arguably getting less and less exposed to competing views and unnoticed problems. Interestingly, this is in direct contradiction with the claim that the Internet somehow naturally tends to unsettle the familiar and create collisions between different versions of reality (see Rogers 2004).

While blogs and social media, for instance, have surely had some positive influence by giving exposure to previously ignored perspectives and by occasionally providing counterviews to the mainstream media, they are commonly read by like-minded people and feature little quality control. According to critics, this has the consequence that groups of like-minded people, after discussing the matter among themselves, are inclined to reach a more extreme version of their view. This is what Sunstein (2003) has called the "law of group polarization." In one empirical example of this tendency, a study by Adamic and Glance (2005) on American political blogs reported a divided blogosphere where liberals and conservatives linked primarily within their separate communities, with very few cross-links exchanged across ideological borders. Similarly, Markus Prior (2007) has argued that increasing media choice is one of the key factors in explaining the current partisan polarization in American politics.

Yet there is also evidence that suggests the opposite. Online political discussions need not necessarily become echo chambers of the like-minded. In an empirical analysis of the structural characteristics of political newsgroup discussion threads, researchers have found that debate, not agreement or reinforcement, is the dominant activity in political groups, and that replies to posts, and thus newsgroup interaction, are overwhelmingly across ideological or issue clusters, not within them (Kelly, Fisher, and Smith 2009). Another recent study, which tracked how people move around the web, found that most users do not stay within their communities (Gentzkow and Shapiro 2010). People still spend a lot of time on the sites of traditional media corporations with politically integrated audiences, and even when they leave these sites, they often go into areas where most people are not like themselves. According to this particular study, the Internet is actually more open to cross-ideological dialogue than old-fashioned forms of face-to-face association.

Studies that have assessed online discussions based on an operationalization of the Habermasian ideals of rational-critical discourse have also criticized online forums for being too oppositional rather than not oppositional enough, and thus for violating the values of reciprocity, reflexivity, and consensus (Dahlberg 2001; Graham 2009). In this sense, the tendency of many forums to collect dissonant voices around contested topics would seem to be more in line with the ideals of Mouffe's agonistic democracy and her views of healthy political contestation.

As discussed in part I of the book, the fears of fragmentation have been (pessimistically) acknowledged by both Habermas and Mouffe in their few comments about the implications of the Internet on the public sphere (Carpentier and Cammaerts 2006, 968; Habermas 2006, 422). From the perspective of democratic theory, fragmentation and polarization seem distressing to the advocates of both deliberative and agonistic conceptions of the public space. As Sunstein (2003, 91) states, it is important to ensure that like-minded people have access to enclave public spheres for deliberation, but it is also crucial that members of the relevant groups are not isolated from the diversity of different views in society. A functioning public sphere thus entails at least two conclusions about media and democracy: People should be exposed to materials and topics that they would not have chosen in advance, for unplanned, unanticipated encounters that involve new topics and points of view are essential for engagement between differing views and as guards against fragmentation and extremism. And to engage in public deliberation and to address social problems, many or most citizens should have a range of common experiences as a precursor for joint decision-making (Sunstein 2007, 5-6).

Based on the above-mentioned studies on web traffic, the justification of these fears remains contested. As noted above, the decline of intermediaries has been at least partly exaggerated, and in some cases the Internet has even led to the consolidation of attention. Communicative abundance does not necessarily mean anarchy, as there are still plenty of other mechanisms that bring a measure of coherence to political life. In this sense, fears of fragmentation assume a certain technological determinism and media-centrism that ignores all other sources of commonality and solidarity in society. Furthermore, there is often an unjustified assumption that the Internet will substitute for, rather than complement traditional media, when in reality it is probably better conceived as a functional complement to traditional mass media and face-to-face discussions (Dutton 2007; Rasmussen 2008, 80).

Furthermore, it is obviously problematic to make generalizations based on the nature of the Internet as a single medium. Individual motivations as well as the structural characteristics of different online forums vary. Different services rely on different modes of communication, facilitate very different uses and have different effects. While some modes of communication mirror the existing power of mass media intermediaries, others, such as blogs, empower one person to control agenda and content, and others still allow collaborative, group controls (see Kelly et al. 2009). The direction of future developments is also radically open, which means that the question of whether or not the Internet makes the public sphere more or less pluralistic is open-ended, both theoretically and empirically.

Given the traditional critique of mass culture and unitary conceptions of the public sphere, there is a certain irony in the nostalgia that romanticizes the shared experiences produced by mass media. It is widely held that the traditional mass media are the principal source of crosscutting political views available to all citizens. Yet, in the light of the critiques that the unitary model of the public sphere excludes less privileged groups within society, the "enclave deliberation" of multiple smaller public spheres can also be seen to promote the development of positions that would otherwise be silenced or marginalized in the wider public sphere. Also, as discussed previously, social groups are not coherent bounded entities, and as each citizen belongs to a number of different groups, it can be argued that due to this overlapping and changing identification, fears of online balkanization are sociologically perhaps somewhat misguided (see Young 2000, Benhabib 2002). As a final caveat, it also needs to be acknowledged that much of the empirical evidence cited above is from the United States, where patterns of regulation and media use differ quite notably from European and other national contexts.

Regardless, the debate clearly illustrates that the concerns we have about media pluralism are not only about having more or less choice. Instead, individual choices, perfectly reasonable in themselves, might produce various social difficulties. The question is, then, should media pluralism be conceptualized from the perspective of promoting a democratic public sphere or consumer sovereignty in the market? If one chooses the former, as Sunstein (2003, 95) argues, the public sphere requires "appropriate heterogeneity," which acknowledges that while all arguments can never be heard, the public sphere is above all a domain where multiple perspectives should collide. For Sunstein, the key precondition for this is the provision of full information, not only about facts but also about relevant values and political options. Similarly, Thomas Gibbons (2000, 308) argues that in addition to the availability of different media as an information resource, the full participation of individuals in the democratic process requires guidance about the context of information and ideas and their relationships, and above all engagement between different views, opinions, and policy choices.

REVALUING INTERMEDIARIES

Somewhat paradoxically, the fears of audience fragmentation have led to a new appreciation of general interest intermediaries, such as newspapers, magazines, and broadcasters, whose decline has been celebrated by some as enabling unprecedented pluralism,[4] In addition, the fears of audience fragmentation have also raised interest in the role of new intermediaries such as search engines, which increasingly determine how easily users find their way around the abundance of information. While such gatekeepers may in many cases represent bottlenecks that are seen to undermine pluralism and limit access, it is also recognized that they play a critical role in ensuring security or organizing the anarchy of information in the web.

Various proposals for new public interest intermediaries have also been put forward. Sunstein (2007, 193) has proposed the creation of specific, perhaps publicly subsidized "deliberative domains" that would ensure quality content and provide individuals with access to competing views. Subsequently, many other researchers of online deliberation have taken up the task of envisioning and developing new environments and situations where deliberative discussion can take place. In addition to online news media, which continue to centralize and manage debate on issues of shared political importance, these could include other co-operative systems, such as group software and learning systems based on the ideas of collaboration and deliberation (Peña Gangadharan 2009). In one concrete example, researchers have envisioned a specific search engine that, given a topic, will find threads of discussion where opposing opinions are expressed (Sack, Kelly, and Dale 2009). Similar technologies could conceivably be employed for finding opposing, political viewpoints in other online contexts.

In the European context, these functions are already strongly associated with public broadcasting systems, and increasingly they also seem to underlie arguments that try to justify the continued importance of public service media in the digital age.

Coherence and unity are of course traditionally among the basic rationales for public service broadcasting. According to Blumler (1992, 11), public service broadcasting should act as a "centripetal, socially integrative force," a national cultural cement by offering high-quality programming. In the current age of communicative abundance, such aims seem to be gaining traction in a revised form. Graham Murdock, for example, has called for a rethinking of

---

[4]In the context of the economic crisis and the commercial pressures of the digital revolution, some have even called for new public funding pools for traditional media to subsidize the continued provision of quality news (Currah 2009, 144–47).

the functions of public service media institutions by resituating their remit within what he calls a digital commons, "a linked space defined by its shared refusal of commercial enclosure and its commitment to free and universal access, reciprocity, and collaborative activity" (Murdock 2005, 227). The central position of public service media in the digital age seems largely to rest on the claim that public service media can facilitate between different ranges of material and thus counter the looming developments of marketization, fragmentation, and the enclosure of information (see Chapter 6).

In line with this, a recent study on the effects of different media systems on the level of public knowledge reported that a critical difference between public service and market models is the greater ability of the former to engage an "inadvertent" audience: people who might be generally disinclined to follow public affairs "cannot help encountering news while awaiting delivery of their favourite entertainment programmes" (Curran et al. 2009, 22). Therefore, the public service model also minimizes the knowledge gap between advantaged and disadvantaged groups and contributes to a more egalitarian pattern of citizenship.

The study in question refers to television, but the idea can easily be extended to online media. In keeping with normative theories that value the meeting of different social perspectives, there is a growing trend of argument that the importance of public service media online can be justified by reference to its function in building such links and forming a space where diverging interests can meet (see Coleman 2004; Craig 2000; Moe 2008).

NEW MEDIA AND THE REDISTRIBUTION OF COMMUNICATIVE POWER

As we have seen, current developments in media technology and media markets have been interpreted in widely different ways, and indeed it is hard to deny that some of those developments appear quite paradoxical. Whether these developments are seen as new forms of emancipation or new forms of domination largely depends on the perspective. As Lance Bennett (2003) notes, it is paradoxical that corporate media power and concentration seem stronger than ever and the resources available to promote neoliberal discourse through global communication networks are larger than ever. Yet it is also true that these same resources and networks are at the same time used by various social movements who aim to challenge the neoliberal discourse. Similarly, Williams and Delli Carpini (2004, 1209) sum up the ongoing debate by observing: "Optimistically we believe that the erosion of gatekeeping and the emergence of multiple axes of information provide new opportunities for citizens to challenge elite control of political issues. Pessimistically we are skeptical of the ability of ordinary citizens to make use of these opportunities and suspicious of the degree to which even multiple axes of power are still shaped by more fundamental structures of economic and political power."

It seems that the tendencies of pluralization, on the one hand, and centralization of control, on the other, are, more than anything, forces that simultaneously affect the media, regardless of their technological basis. The media create new differences, differentiate between subcultures, and bring forward new voices, but also homogenize tastes and generate social conformity. Yet these dynamics largely remain contested, and they certainly cannot be reduced to the effects of technology itself. Instead, they justify a continued concern for media pluralism, while also creating a need to rethink its meaning in the contemporary media environment.

It can be argued that the paradoxes associated with media pluralism speak of growing complexity that influences both the means of communication and the normative models against which we assess them. As Castells (2007, 259) puts it: "a new round of power making in the communication space is taking place." Assuming that the development of media systems is subject to various political and social struggles between different interests and values, the challenge is to show and clarify what these different alternative visions mean and to analyze their consequences for the communication of citizens and societies. There is no denying that some of the democratizing and diversifying effects of new media technologies are real, but so are many of their problems and biases.

From the point of view of radical pluralism and its emphasis on revealing structural hierarchies of power, the challenge is therefore to elaborate a conception of media pluralism that helps us to perceive and evaluate these developments.

One thing that seems evident from the above discussion is that instead of simply analyzing what is produced or what is available, we need to place greater emphasis on user competencies, questions of media use, digital literacy, and other aspects related to exposure diversity. In this sense, Nicholas Garnham (1999a) has interestingly discussed the application of Amartya Sen's capabilities approach to communication policy and argued that "we need to take into account both the range of communication options made available—and these must be real options, not mere choices between products and services with minimal real differences—and the ability of people actually to make use of those options" (Garnham 1999a, 121). Furthermore, Garnham argues that we need to think of the media as "enablers of a range of functionings rather than as providers of a stream of content to be consumed" (ibid., 121). Similarly, it has recently been argued that debates on media diversity should include "diversity of participation" as a new key aspect (Aslama 2009).

Media critics have long been concerned mostly with the availability of diverse content, but as Jan van Cuilenburg (1998, 45) claims, traditional concerns regarding the availability of diverse information and opinions are quickly turning into anachronistic aims with no practical meaning. Similarly, it is increasingly clear that a limitless number of options has little value in itself. As the logic of exclusivity is shifting from production to the filtering of information, it seems rather uncontroversial to argue that media policies should also focus more on information accessibility and exposure to different ideas (Hargittai 2007; Hindman 2009; Sunstein 2007; van Cuilenburg 1998). However, despite the calls from media policy scholars, these aspects have so far failed to gain very much traction in actual media policy discussions (Goodman 2004; Webster 2007).

According to theories of media and democracy, a heterogeneous citizenry must be exposed to the tastes and views of others. In other words, debates on media pluralism need to acknowledge other goals than satisfying consumers by providing a sufficiently broad (however defined) choice of media products and services. For instance, in some cases it can be considered more desirable that the public is exposed to content that is at least initially not demanded. To some extent at least, this would also entail access to shared contents and common experiences. This, of course, raises the question as to whether regulation should seek to influence or cultivate media use, and not just satisfy public tastes, and whether it can be coherently argued why certain ranges of cultural products should be made available if, at least at first, no audience demands them (Garnham 2000, 136; Goodman 2004).

My argument, however, is that the emphasis on users and individual competencies is not enough. If media pluralism is to serve as a critical concept, it must also acknowledge questions about the role of the media with regard to the distribution of power and influence in society. As argued above, communicative abundance has not diminished the fact that some actors and groups have more communicative power and political, economic, or cultural resources to get their voices heard than others. Technological changes have not changed the mundane fact that sources are in constant competition with one another for the privilege of providing authoritative information (Rogers 2004, 1). Despite the new opportunities offered by new technologies, public spheres everywhere will continue to be characterized by structural inequalities in the distribution of communicative power between individuals, social groups, corporations and states.

For a useful analysis and evaluation of such structural asymmetries, we need to have a broader conception of media pluralism that is concerned not only with consumer choice or specific issues such as media ownership, but more broadly with the democratic distribution of communicative power. In more concrete terms, such concerns relate to a number of issues, ranging from journalistic practices to net neutrality and other questions about the architecture of new media networks.

Policy issues relevant to pluralism in the new media environment inevitably also raise new questions about the appropriate extent of public intervention and its targets. Should governments subsidize the aims of achieving universal broadband access or otherwise intervene to ensure a more equitable development of the emerging infrastructure? Or should they regulate the new intermediaries and technical gatekeepers such as search engines and other recommendation and navigation systems to encourage user exposure to diverse content? And while the means of policy makers to steer these developments in any direct manner remain limited, questions about the conceptualization of pluralism also has clear implications for journalists and other actors who embrace pluralism and diversity as guiding principles.

In any case, the array of potential issues relevant to media pluralism thus only accentuates the critique that measures of plurality should not rest on the multiplication of genres or outlets, but on the actual success of a media system in representing and giving voice to different social actors.

This pursuit of media pluralism as a policy objective would thus be parallel to what Sophia Kaitatzi-Whitlock (2005, 168) has called "the equitable management of freedom of information." This understanding highlights the fact that the notion of media pluralism still refers above all to distributional questions: how much and what kinds of freedoms of information should be allocated to whom?

While the institutionalization and realization of the ideal of fair distribution of communicative power obviously remain contested, this gives the debates on media pluralism some normative grounding, which is not tied to specific media technologies. By taking the distribution of communicative power as a normative starting point, we can thus reclaim the concept of media pluralism from its technocratic and reductionist uses for the critical purpose of not only affirming consumer sovereignty, but identifying and evaluating new forms of exclusion and concentration as well as new forms of self-expression and participation that are emerging in the contemporary media environment.

CHAPTER 6

Uses of Pluralism in Contemporary Media Policy

This chapter presents two case studies of the different ways in which media pluralism has been conceptualized and used in contemporary European media policy. After briefly discussing the rise of media pluralism as one of the central principles of European media policy, I demonstrate the political rationalities associated with its different definitions by analyzing two cases in detail. The first case concerns the attempts to introduce a common European approach on media concentration and pluralism; the second deals with the arguments put forward in recent debates on the role and remit of public service media in the new digital landscape.

Both issues have recently culminated in the drafting of key policy documents. After almost two decades of discussions that never resulted in any meaningful action, the European Commission has finally published a new initiative on media concentration and pluralism that includes a study on indicators to assess media pluralism in EU member countries (EC 2007a). The debate on public service media, on the other hand, has recently focused on the communication from the European Commission on the application of state aid rules to public service broadcasting (also known as the Broadcasting Communication, see EC 2009). While both documents serve more as recommendations than binding regulations, the debates surrounding them provide a good example of the different interests and values in current European media policy debates. After a broader review of the context of these debates, I will proceed to analyze the argumentation of these particular documents and the accompanying public consultations to illustrate the implications of different political rationalities.

A central purpose of this chapter is to analyze which articulations of media pluralism have become hegemonic in European media policy and to identify the political rationalities on which they rely. As noted above, abstract principles such as media pluralism often function more as rhetorical devices used by self-interested agents than as analytical tools for policy makers. However, the different uses and abuses of guiding principles have consequences regardless of how reflectively or instrumentally they are used. In this sense, the intention here is not primarily to seek the foundations of the concept of media pluralism, but to identify the key arguments or ideas communicated in these policy debates and to examine how the concept has been used, defined, and operationalized in these contexts.

THE RISE OF PLURALISM AS A MEDIA POLICY PRINCIPLE

Although concerns over media pluralism are by no means new, I have argued that they have gained a more prominent place in the hierarchy of media policy goals, or at least in policy rhetoric in recent years. This has to do with both intellectual and more pragmatic institutional reasons. While current theories and philosophies of media and public communication offer some clues, their emergence as policy objectives can also be explained by reference to more concrete historical and political factors.

Pluralism and diversity have been among the key values of public communication in one form or another throughout the modern history of communication policy. However, they have played a different part and meant different things in different places and at different times, reflecting differences in both national media systems and between different areas of media policy.

Historically, media pluralism has been associated above all with the issue of media ownership concentration that has been debated since the beginning of commercial mass newspapers. The tension between media pluralism and concentration has also been prominent in many of the key media policy documents of the twentieth century. In the United States the Hutchins Commission's (1947) famous report on the freedom of the press, for instance, spoke of the "decreased proportion of the people who can express their opinion and ideas through the press" as one of the main threats to freedom of the press (Baker 2007, 2–3).

In Europe, governments have addressed the issue of media concentration at several points, especially during the latter half of the twentieth century, when most European countries saw a sharp decline in the number of daily newspapers (Cavallin 1998). The problem has been addressed in a variety of ways, but most countries have adopted at least some policies and legislation designed to protect and in some cases promote pluralism in media ownership through ownership restrictions or subsidy arrangements (Cavallin 1998; Doyle 2002; 2007; see also EC 2007a). At the pan-European level, the issues of media concentration and pluralism have also been acknowledged by the Council of Europe and the European Parliament at least since the 1970s.

In many European countries the protection of pluralism in public communication is also mentioned in the constitution. Constitutional courts in France, Italy, and Germany, for instance, have at various stages affirmed the interpretation that their constitution mandates the protection of media pluralism—not only negatively by placing limits on media ownership, but also by means of public broadcasting or other positive means (Baker 2007, 161).

Despite recurring arguments that the Internet and other new media are making these concerns obsolete, concerns over media concentration have not subsided even in the digital age. As I argue in the previous chapter, the Internet has not ended media concentration, and in some ways the globalization of media industries together with the technological changes in media distribution has even intensified these concerns (see Bagdikian 2004; Baker 2007; Herman and McChesney 1998). Similarly, the ongoing trend of media mergers and consolidation of media power in Europe, especially in countries such as Italy and Russia where media ownership is intertwined with political power, has continued to raise concerns about the concentration of media power to fewer, more powerful gatekeepers (see e.g. EP 2004).

While much of the debate on media pluralism has traditionally been associated with newspaper ownership, the issues raised by the electronic media are slightly different. As Denis McQuail (2007b, 45) notes, there was little trace of any meaningful idea of diversity or pluralism in the institutional arrangements for broadcasting that were made by nation-states in the early twentieth century. Early developments of electronic media were guided by centrally prescribed objectives that were characterized by unifying rather than diversifying ends. Broadcasting institutions were seen as unifying tools, as a means with which to cultivate a common identity in the population, and they were designed to maintain national identity by reaching the whole citizenry and bringing them together in a national public sphere (see Williams 1975, 28).

In contrast to the print media where pluralism has been a central value from the outset, definitions of public interest in broadcasting have only gradually come to involve principles that relate to the contemporary notion of media pluralism, such as localism, minority services, or political balance. In the electronic media, it was not until the 1960s and 1970s that the concepts of pluralism and diversity started to gain more prominence in media policy debates around Europe, at the same time when discussions centered on pluralism and diversity began to gain ground in different countries as well as on international forums such as UNESCO and the Council of Europe.

In Britain, for instance, pluralism began to gain currency in policy debates in response to the growth of ethnically more mixed, multicultural populations and mounting dissatisfaction with the existing, allegedly paternalistic media structures. The 1977 Annan Report on the future of broadcasting and other policy papers called for television and other media to allow a proliferation of voices and provide alternatives to the "straightjacket" of mainstream television (see Freedman 2003; O'Loughlin 2006). According to Freedman (2008, 75), these developments laid the basis for a pluralist approach that abandoned the objective of social consensus and sought to promote a multiplicity of independent voices, consumer choice, and competition.

In the Nordic countries, too, Henrik Kaare Nielsen (2003, 238) says the breakthrough of pluralism as an evaluative principle in debates on media and cultural policy came in the 1970s and 1980s. According to Nielsen, the idea that all forms of culture have their own quality criteria undermined the universal basis for defining cultural quality and led to a "pluralistic consensus" in media and cultural policy. The notions of quality, cultural value, or public interest thus became increasingly conceived in a relativist manner, avoiding the paternalism of the old paradigm of cultural policy. In media policy, this meant that the paternalism and elitism often associated with traditional public service values came under increasing criticism, spurring the need for new legitimating principles.

Interestingly though, Nielsen (2003, 238) notes that the emphasis on pluralism has not immediately created new opportunities for the orientation of public policy. Instead, it has created an open situation where the articulations and hegemonic definitions of pluralism and diversity were and still are contested. Reflecting this, Thomas Gibbons (2000, 307) even suggests that media pluralism has not been promoted primarily for the purpose of supporting a more democratic role for the media. Instead, "the idea was adopted as a transitional concept that conveniently assisted a shift from public service dominance to a market approach" (ibid., 307). This has had implications for the framing of the discussion about the democratic role of the media as a reasonable difference of opinion about two different ways of achieving the same goal. Implicit in such discourse is the idea that through the development of the new media and increased competition, the problems of market failure might be corrected and any special needs for public regulation annulled.

Similarly, Des Freedman (2005, 22) has argued that in contemporary policy arenas, where the objectives of diversity and pluralism are converging around the rhetoric of competition and choice, "appeals to both pluralism and diversity are increasingly becoming smokescreens behind which a significant restructuring and marketization of the media is taking place."

In this sense, current debates surrounding media pluralism in Europe can clearly be traced back to the 1980s when liberalization triggered not only increased competition in the media market, but also a certain paradigm shift in media policy. The rise of pluralism and diversity as policy objectives, therefore, is unarguably linked to the rise of commercial, market-oriented tendencies and an increased emphasis on free trade, competition, and deregulation; and it was in the wake of these developments that the concepts of pluralism and diversity began to gain more and more prominence in policy debates (Collins 1998, 62; Gibbons 2000, 307).

By the 1980s, pluralism and diversity in broadcasting also came to be understood more instrumentally as a matter of providing choice and serving various consumer tastes and interests. According to O'Loughlin (2006, 8), deregulation involved a reinterpretation of these objectives as well as a change in the instruments deployed to achieve them. Whereas pluralism, understood as fair access to different social groups, had in many European countries already been institutionalized by setting up either formal or informal mechanisms of control over broadcasting institutions to reflect different parts of the political spectrum or along linguistic and regional lines (McQuail 2007b, 46), the new market-oriented rationales increasingly emphasized the importance of independent producers, competition, and consumer choice.

However, the argument that the emphasis on pluralism only serves as a smokescreen for deregulation and marketization underestimates the extent to which critical thinking in media policy has also come to revolve around the notion of pluralism. At the same time when pluralism started to be articulated with competition and de-regulation, it also became one of the central values used to defend public service broadcasting and other nonprofit media. As many studies have shown, actual ideological and normative arguments for the legitimacy and justification of public broadcasting in general only started to gain prominence after the status of public service broadcasters was challenged in the 1980s (see Blumler 1992; Collins 1998; Hellman 1999, 58–60). Although European public broadcasting regimes in many ways conformed to some interpretations of diversity and pluralism even before their monopoly was challenged, as a legitimating principle used to defend certain broadcasting institutions and structures pluralism is a more recent addition.

The struggles over the conceptualization of pluralism thus reflect wider controversies in European media policy, between economic and industry aims on the one hand and socio-cultural public interest values, on the other. In this context, the fact that pluralism and diversity can easily be applied to defending both public service obligations and free competition goes a long way towards explaining their popularity in contemporary media policy debates.

It seems that the growing policy use of media pluralism is directly linked to its increasing ambiguity. No longer just a matter of ownership or any particular issue, media pluralism can be used to refer to almost anything. In this sense, pluralism can be seen more as a contested philosophical principle, or a political ethos, than a specific policy goal. As McQuail (2007b) notes, most of the commonly listed key policy principles, such as competition, localism, universal service, or maintaining cultural and linguistic identities, can in fact be seen as aspects of pluralism. In one way or another, pluralism and diversity seem to lie behind most policy arguments as overarching policy principles, even more so than the notion of media quality, for instance, does today. This inclusiveness, however, also exposes the weakness and potential emptiness of the concepts. As McQuail (2007b, 47) argues, the ambiguity of pluralism and diversity means that policies designed to promote them can be "exposed as lacking any cutting edge, if not actually bankrupt." Arguably this conceptual vacuity has become even clearer when established policy models and arguments have been challenged by new technological developments and the complexity of the contemporary media landscape.

MEDIA PLURALISM ON THE EUROPEAN AGENDA

On the European level, the roots of the current debate on media pluralism can be traced back to the 1970s when both the Council of Europe and the European Parliament first put the issue on their agenda. These institutions have also articulated the policy discourse around some basic questions that still occupy policy makers, including the role of public service broadcasting and the concentration of media ownership (see Cavallin 1998; Michalis 2007, 36; Nesti 2007, 3).

Going even further back, the commitment to pluralism and freedom in the media can be traced back to the European Convention for the Protection of Human Rights and Fundamental Freedoms, which was adopted in 1950. The article in the convention on the freedom of expression is often interpreted to also include citizens' right to receive diverse information. The European Court of Human Rights (ECHR), for instance, has stated in numerous judgments that without a plurality of voices and opinions in the media, the media cannot fulfill their role in democracy. The Council of Europe and the ECHR have therefore advocated a positive interpretation where states are under a "duty to protect" and, when necessary, to take positive action to ensure diversity of opinion in the media (see Council of Europe 2002).

In particular, this positive interpretation has been furthered by the Council of Europe, which has traditionally given much attention to the issue of media pluralism. As a forum for political discussion, analyses and research, the council has limited political power, but especially since the creation of a monitoring framework for media pluralism and concentration in 1989 it has produced a series of reports, overviews, and recommendations that discuss the various aspects of media pluralism and diversity.[1] Overall, the Council of Europe has addressed a wider and politically more sensitive set of media issues—including pluralism, media freedom, independence, and public service broadcasting—than the EU, which has mainly focused on the creation of common European audiovisual markets. In this sense, the work done by the Council of Europe also is important because in stressing political and cultural aspects, it has been thought to represent a counterweight to the more economic and market-oriented debates around EU audiovisual policy (see Michalis 2007, 174).

This role has been frequently acknowledged by other, more powerful European institutions such as the European Parliament and the European Commission. In addition to the Council of Europe, there are a number of other monitoring agencies and civil society organizations that have influenced the policy debate on media pluralism through reports, statistics, and monitoring. Alongside various professional and industry organizations, these civil society organizations have played a role in providing definitions and framing for broader policy debates. These informal policy debates have also provided a concrete forum where concepts and ideas can travel between academic and policy spheres, and it is perhaps partly due to these efforts that pluralism has emerged on the European policy agenda in recent years.

Recently the political salience of the issue has been reinforced by a number of international organizations. The World Summit on the Information Society declared its commitment to the principles of "the independence, pluralism and diversity of media, which are essential to the Information Society" (WSIS 2003). Similarly, the UNESCO Convention on the Protection and Promotion of the Diversity of Cultural Expressions (adopted in

---

[1]The Committee of Experts on Media Concentrations and Pluralism (MM-CM) gathered information throughout the 1990s. Since then, the Advisory Panel on Media Diversity (AP-MD) has followed up this work by monitoring transnational concentrations (see Council of Europe 2000; 2002; 2004b; 2007a). Most recently, the Group of Specialists on Media Diversity (MC-S-MD) was instructed to "elaborate a detailed proposal for a methodology for the monitoring of media concentration and, if possible, for measuring the impact of media concentration on media pluralism and content diversity" (Council of Europe 2009).

2005 and put into force in 2007) acknowledges the importance of media pluralism and the need for positive intervention (including public service broadcasting) to create conditions conducive to pluralism. In principle, the latter constitutes a new legally binding instrument at the international level, although it too falls short of defining exactly what it means by pluralism in the context of media policy.

Although all the different declarations and contexts in which pluralism and diversity have been raised have slightly different conceptions of these concepts, they all serve to reinforce the political salience of the concepts as general guiding principles in contemporary media policy discourse. As Freedman (2005) notes, media, and communication policies that have been drawn up to confront the new challenges of technological convergence and globalization are practically littered with positive references to pluralism and diversity. This seems to hold true equally at the international, European, and national level.

The EU, in particular, has confirmed its commitment to the defense and promotion of media pluralism in various declarations and documents. Most notably, the status of media pluralism is now enshrined in article 11 of the Charter for Fundamental Rights of the EU and in its article on the right to information and freedom of expression, which states, "freedom and pluralism of the media shall be respected." Another key document that is often raised in debates on media pluralism and particularly on public service broadcasting is the infamous Protocol of the Treaty of Amsterdam (1997), and its acknowledgment that "the system of public broadcasting in the Member States is directly related to the democratic, social and cultural needs of each society and to the need to preserve media pluralism."

The most recent step that affirms the place of media pluralism on the political agenda in the EU is the publication of the Commission Staff Working Paper on Media Pluralism in 2007. Growing out of controversial debates that have been going on since the early 1990s, the document acknowledges that "the European Union is committed to protecting media pluralism as an essential pillar of the right to information and freedom of expression," and then goes on to propose the next steps necessary to engage in further dialogue on the issue. The paper and the ensuing study also explicitly acknowledge that media pluralism is a broader issue than media ownership, stating, "media pluralism is a concept that embraces a number of aspects, such as diversity of ownership, variety in the sources of information and in the range of contents available in the different Member States" (EC 2007a). Even though it has not yet led to any concrete results, as one of the most ambitious attempts to explicitly define "objective indicators" for assessing media pluralism, the initiative and the eventual reactions of various stakeholders to it provide a particularly interesting opportunity to analyze the definitional power and the current terms of debate on media pluralism.

ON THE NATURE AND TENSIONS OF EUROPEAN MEDIA POLICY

Most commentators tend to regard European media policy as market-oriented and focused on economic integration and liberalization. Rather than concentrating on positive integration or market correcting measures, EU policy has been seen as biased towards "negative integration," which means that media policy debates have largely been framed in terms of market liberalization and the exercise of extensive competition powers (see Harcourt 2005, 2). Recently, the rise of information society and competitiveness discourse in European media policy has been seen to further reinforce economic and industrial policy arguments at the expense of the politically controversial questions surrounding culture (Michalis 2007, 164–65).

One of the main drivers of the shift from public service–oriented regulation to a model of free market doctrine and media commercialization in Europe has been the growth of supranational regulation. EU policy is commonly seen to erode national capacities to promote public service values and cultural or democratic aims in media policy (see Venturelli 1998, Kaitatzi-Whitlock 2005). As Kaitatzi-Whitlock (2005, 7) bluntly argues, the power of commercial media interests together with the economistically trapped framework of the EU itself "has led from the 1980s onwards to the systematic liberalisation of the European media and their concomitant disastrous weakening as essential organs of public spaces for political communication."

In part, this asymmetry is due to the EU's limited mandate in areas other than economic policy. At EU level media issues are mostly governed by economic policy, whereas issues regarded as cultural policy have remained the sole responsibility of individual member states (Harcourt 2005, 37). While the European Parliament in particular has actively emphasized public interest goals such as media pluralism, the implementation of EU policies has continued to concentrate mainly on market liberalization. This is because both the Commission and the European Court of Justice have considerable powers to intervene with regard to competition rules, whereas any positive interventions have to be negotiated with member states and between different EU institutions (Humphreys 2007, 92–93). Consequently, the priority tends to be on economic considerations pursued on the basis of strong legal governance instruments, while noneconomic and public service objectives are pursued on the basis of voluntary governance tools and within politically weaker European organizations. Accordingly, concerns over issues such as media pluralism typically get more support from weaker European institutions such as the Council of Europe, the European Parliament and Commission departments of lower standing that form a so-called "coalition of the weak" (Michalis 2007, 14).

It follows then that much of the debate on media pluralism tends to reinforce the established tension between economic and cultural or democratic concerns in European media policy (see, for example, Collins 1998; Harcourt 2005; Kaitatzi-Whitlock 2005; Michalis 2007; Nieminen 2010). Accordingly, it has become commonplace to consider some institutions such as the European Parliament to represent a more interventionist position, while the Commission, particularly its departments for competition and internal markets, and the European Court of Justice are taken to represent a more market-oriented approach.

However, there are notable differences of emphasis even within the Commission, and the negative assessment of the capacity or the will of the European Commission to take into account democratic, social and cultural aims is not indisputable. David Ward (2001, 89), for instance, has offered a much more favorable assessment of European media policy rationales by arguing that "the Commission has developed an extremely sophisticated understanding of the role of broadcasting in terms of its importance in the democratic life of societies."

Cultural concerns have not been completely absent from the Commission's approach, but it is certainly fair to say that consumer choice and free competition have become more and more pervasive in the language of most European Commission media policy documents. One example is the articulation of pluralism with freedom of choice for consumers and the general framework of market competition and consumer sovereignty (see Pauwels 1999). Partly this reflects the neoliberal trends that are shaping policy making all over the world, but in the European case this approach is arguably even further strengthened by the structural bias of EU policy towards its basic aims of liberalization and the removal of obstacles to the internal market.

However, as influential as it has been, it would be misleading to argue that the neoliberal articulation of pluralism with free markets and consumer choice is unquestioned in European debates. Pluralism is also a key public interest value, and proponents of public service broadcasting in particular have adopted it at the core of their self-legitimating rhetoric. As will become clear in the following analysis of various stakeholders' contributions to recent policy processes, the Council of Europe, the European Parliament, organizations such as the European Federation of Journalists (EFJ) and the

European Broadcasting Union (EBU), as well as many academic scholars have emphasized the democratic and cultural aspects of media policy and thus supported a more interventionist, public service–oriented paradigm in European media policy.

The positive resonance of pluralism has been put to use not only in formal declarations, but also in a more mundane way in arguments for various other political objectives. Besides public service broadcasting, many other interventionist policy measures have been justified by reference to pluralism and diversity. "Cultural diversity," in particular, has served as a justification for a variety of measures, from state aid to the film and audiovisual industries to support mechanisms or quotas for European works and independent producers.[2]

However, it can be argued that the motives here have as much to do with industrial policy as with cultural concerns. Cultural diversity has been defined and employed not as an end in itself but as a resource for economic development, and particularly as a justification for the efforts to protect the interests of European media industry against US dominance. In this sense, discourse around pluralism and diversity has been convenient for policy makers, because it can be molded for so many purposes, including the aim of increasing the competitiveness of European media and communication industries (see Klimkiewicz 2008).

As Maria Michalis (2007, 162) has argued, another reason for the rhetorical endorsement of pluralism in the EU is that it is seen as a less controversial and more realistic goal than building cultural unity or European identity, which still dominated the debate on European audiovisual policy in the 1980s. While in the 1980s the EU pursued "a collective European cultural identity" and European unity by means of satellite broadcasting, the more modest aims of today's policies are captured in the ambiguous "unity in diversity" slogan (see also Collins 1998).

The use of pluralism and diversity in media policy is thus highly opportunistic, and the way that pluralism and diversity are defined is tied in large part to self-serving motives. However, this is not to deny the existence of genuine ideological differences. The discourses of the free market approach and the public service ethos, in particular, rely on very different political rationalities when interpreting diversity and pluralism as media policy goals. The former is based on competition and freedom of choice, and the latter

---

[2]The MEDIA program, for instance, has conveniently combined the aims of protecting cultural diversity and strengthening the European audiovisual industry; see http://ec.europa.eu/information_society/media/index_en.htm.

on a broader and more ambivalent attempt to serve the whole society with various political views and cultural values. To elaborate this tension, I will turn now to analyze two empirical cases that are especially illustrative of the contested nature of media pluralism as a policy objective.

CASE STUDY I: DEBATES ON MEDIA CONCENTRATION AND PLURALISM

Until recently, media pluralism has been debated in Europe most prominently in the context of media ownership concentration. Fears of excessive concentration and the risks it poses to pluralism have led to increasing demands for more harmonized European rules and for measures to curb the increasingly transnational concentration of media ownership. According to these demands, the deregulation of media markets together with technological advances has encouraged companies to expand both vertically and horizontally, leading to larger and fewer dominant media groups with a web of common interests. Based on these developments in the European media landscape, many have argued that national measures are not sufficient and that there is a more compelling case than ever for EU-level intervention (see Doyle 2007, 140). As Sophia Kaitatzi-Whitlock (2005, 166) states, once the media begin to operate transnationally, the issue of media pluralism becomes a European as well as a national problem, and should therefore become an object of EU policy.

As noted above, ownership concentration has featured on the EU political agenda since the beginning of common European audiovisual policy. The European Parliament first drew attention to media pluralism and the dangers of concentration in drafting the original Television without Frontiers directive in the 1980s (see EC 1984). However, this directive was eventually conceived as primarily an industrial policy tool, and apart from provisions that aim to promote European content and the role of independent producers it does not contain any means specifically aimed at safeguarding media pluralism.

The current Audiovisual Media Services Directive[3] adopted in 2007 acknowledges that "pluralism of information should be a fundamental principle of the European Union," but despite demands for a harmonized European approach on media pluralism as a specific policy issue, the EU still has limited formal powers and policies in the field beyond competition law

---

[3]The Television without Frontiers (TWF) directive was first adopted in 1989, revised in 1997, and subsequently extended and renamed the Audiovisual Media Services Directive (AVMSD) in 2007.

and other internal market instruments.[4] Most European countries meanwhile have retained at least some mechanisms to restrict the concentration of media ownership and protect pluralism beyond simple competition rules. Furthermore, a recent survey by the Council of Europe (2009) indicates that almost all European countries have no legal definitions of either media pluralism or media diversity. Despite pressures to relax existing national restrictions on media ownership, however, support remains in principle for the notion that media pluralism requires special protection beyond the aims of general competition and antitrust policy.

As the AVMS directive (2007, point 3) acknowledges:

> Audiovisual media services are as much cultural services as they are economic services. Their growing importance for societies, democracy— in particular by ensuring freedom of information, diversity of opinion and media pluralism—education and culture justifies the application of specific rules to these services.

So far, the need for special rules beyond competition policy has been highlighted above all by the European Parliament, which has repeatedly expressed concerns over media pluralism on the level of both ownership and media content. The subject has been raised in a number of reports and resolutions, opinions, and parliamentary debates. For instance, the Parliament has called for a specific anticoncentration directive and urged that the above commitment to protect media pluralism must be added to the fundamental principles of the AVMS directive. In its highly controversial report, the Parliament particularly mentioned the situation in Italy as an argument for minimum standards (EP 2004), but more recently it has also drawn attention to problems with the concentration of media ownership in a number of other member states (see EP 2006; 2008a; 2011). European-wide limits on concentration and ownership have also received backing from many professional and civil society organizations.

Despite the commitments in official documents, however, there is ongoing controversy over whether the EU has competence to pursue policies aimed at protecting pluralism or whether the whole issue should be left to the member states and organizations such as the Council of Europe. More interestingly for the present purposes though, there is also controversy over how warranted these concerns are, especially since there are more channels

---

[4]Even though media policy concerns are not totally absent from the European Commission's competition practice, it has been noted that the competition rules themselves tend to leave less and less scope for noneconomic considerations (Ariño 2004).

than ever and since the barriers for private citizens to publish any type of content seem to be falling away.

Opponents of new regulations generally argue that pluralism is best assured through channel proliferation and that unrestricted media ownership is imperative to allow the European "national champion" companies to compete successfully against competitors in the global market (EC 2005, 5; see also Kaitatzi-Whitlock 2005, 169). Thus, the industrial imperatives of the information society and the convergence of different media sectors have so far effectively hindered attempts to tackle media concentration. As Peter Humphreys (1996, 304) noted of the situation in the 1990s: "There is every sign that oligopolistic developments in the mainstream European industry are the price to be paid for the sector's growth and for the development of new technologies."

More recently, new technologies and economic developments have threatened to undermine the business models of most media industry sectors that have been in the center of attention in debates on ownership concentration. This has further strengthened the view that concentration is a necessity for preserving traditional media organizations and their contribution to the media system. As a result, the window of opportunity for meaningful policies to curb ownership concentration can be seen as being closed even more resolutely (Napoli 2011).

The outcome of the European Parliament's efforts so far remains uncertain. On the one hand, the inaction of the EU in the area of media pluralism and concentration has been described by some commentators as one of the biggest failures of the European Parliament and the most spectacular case of nondecision making (Kaitatzi-Whitlock 2005; Sarikakis 2004, 132). This is because the efforts to create common standards for media pluralism have so far produced no tangible results and no legally binding action has been taken on the European level. There are many policy studies that describe how the attempts to build on a political and cultural definition of pluralism and diversity have repeatedly failed due to the opposition of the media industry, the reluctance of the Commission, and their ability to redefine the terms of the debate (see Doyle 1997; Harcourt 2005; Kaitatzi-Whitlock 1996; 2005; Michalis 2007; Sarikakis 2004). As a consequence, attempts to seriously tackle media concentration at the European level seem to have little chance of success.

On the other hand, it is largely due to the efforts of the European Parliament that the concept of media pluralism has entered the terminology of European media policy. Even though media pluralism, as other socially and culturally sensitive media policy issues, remains mainly under the competence of individual member states, the debate on the European level has not abated and the question of media pluralism now seems irreversibly entrenched in the policy agenda. The most evident sign of this is the European Commission's initiative which outlined a new "three-step approach for advancing the debate on media pluralism," acknowledging that the "European Union is committed to protecting media pluralism as an essential pillar of the right to information and freedom of expression enshrined in Article 11 of the Charter of Fundamental Rights" (EC 2007a, 4).

CONTESTING A NONPOLICY

Despite frequent references to media pluralism as the fundamental principle of EU media policy, the efforts to place media pluralism on the agenda of audiovisual regulation have so far had limited success because of at least two reasons. On the one hand, there is the question of competence—does the EU have the legal right to pursue media pluralism by means other than competition policy. On the other hand, there have always been divergent views about the fundamental aims of European media policy, and there is often intense rivalry between different interests, member states, and different institutions and actors within the EU, all of which have different conceptions of what media pluralism means.

These entrenched conflicts, of course, are nothing new in European media policy. The European Commission first responded to the repeated demands of the European Parliament in 1992 by issuing a Green Paper on Pluralism and Media Concentration in the Internal Market with the purpose of assessing the need for Community action on the question of concentration in the media (EC 1992). The document acknowledged the issue of media concentration and the need to maintain pluralism in the media sector, and outlined three possible policy options: no action, action to improve transparency measures, and positive intervention (a new directive). After lengthy consultations and lobbying from major media groups (see EC 1994a), the issue was revisited in 1996 in the form of a draft of a possible EU directive on Concentration and Pluralism in the Internal Market, and again in 1997 with a new draft called Media Ownership in the Internal Market. According to Doyle (1997), the change of name indicated an attempt to deflect the focus away from the issue of cultural and political pluralism, where the competence of the EU would be in question, to the aim of removing obstacles to the internal market.

The proposed initiatives, neither of which led to a directive, were based on determining the upper limits of ownership and audience shares for media companies. Unsurprisingly, however, it proved difficult to establish any harmonized rules that would take into consideration such factors as differences between market sizes, media cultures, and the variety of measures used in different member states to assess a company's influence on the market (Council of Europe 2009; Doyle 1997; 2007; EC 2005, 6; Papathanassopoulos 2002, 105–16). As noted above, however, the biggest reason for the failure was that the media industry ferociously lobbied against any new rules that would restrict their operations and create a competitive disadvantage.

Aside from conflicting economic interests, it is not difficult to discern an ideological divide between the political demands of the European Parliament and many civil society actors, on the one hand, and the media industry and its associations, on the other hand. Reflecting one of the more extreme positions, a statement by the European Newspaper Publishers' Association (ENPA 2005, 4), for instance, noted that the suggestion that the state should practice active measures to support content that would otherwise be unable to survive on the media market is fundamentally undemocratic and would be "a dangerous move supporting a state-controlled media."

The failures of the follow-up consultation process are well documented in European media policy research. In general, the interest organizations consulted formed two directly oppositional groups roughly expressing commercial and noncommercial interests, respectively. As Giorgia Nesti (2007, 16) has documented, media owners, industry organizations and other actors who for political and economic reasons took advantage of the status quo tended to oppose any further European regulation because it represented an impediment to investment and to the aspirations of European media corporations to gain foothold in the global information markets. The second group, which included the European Parliament, the Economic and Social Committee, along with consumer federations, journalists' professional organizations, and civil society actors, called for immediate action, many of them proposing more comprehensive measures than the Commission had recommended.

The debate has also sparked controversies within the Commission. The departments (DGs) responsible for competition, industrial policy and internal markets have generally been opposed to any further restrictions on media ownership on economic grounds, while the departments for culture and audiovisual policy have been in favor of ownership regulation and emphasized the cultural and political dimensions of media pluralism (Michalis 2007, 165; Papathanassopoulos 2002, 112). The main concern for the Commission, however, has been that overly restrictive ownership rules in Europe, in its view, would hinder the ability of European corporations to compete internationally, especially as ownership rules are gradually being relaxed in the US and in third countries (see EC 2005, 5).

As it has turned out, no new rules on media ownership have been adopted, and although the European debate is ongoing, questions concerning media pluralism have been mostly relegated to national policies, which continue to feature diverging approaches (see Council of Europe 2002; EC 2007a; Doyle 2007; Meier 2007; Valcke 2009). However, as Kaitatzi-Whitlock (2005, 181) has argued, inaction has not meant maintaining the status quo but de facto deregulation, since it has only given more time for powerful operators to create irreversible concentrations in the media sector. This is partly because national measures are ineffective in dealing with the increasingly transnational scale of media markets, but also because whenever member states attempt to unilaterally establish proactive national policies for media pluralism, they risk intervention from the Commission or the European Court of Justice on grounds of breaching European competition rules. In other words, the argument that the EU should not intervene in the regulation of media pluralism because it belongs to the competence of member states is highly contradictory. The decision not to intervene is therefore no less political in this case, which illustrates the argument made in Chapter 4 that it is often misleading to frame policy debates as disputes over the extent of regulation instead of different forms of regulation with different aims.

Furthermore, there is a clear conflict between economic interests, on the one hand, and democratic, social, and cultural aims, on the other hand. In addition to traditional political bargaining, however, the debate is increasingly about how to define the problem.

The contrasting definitions of the problem can easily be illustrated by examining the comments of various stakeholders to these debates. According to the comments by Campaign for Press and Broadcasting Freedom (CPBF 2005) to the European Commission issue paper on media pluralism, "the threats to diversity and pluralism in our media have never been greater, and there will also be a damaging impact both culturally and on the range and quality of the work that journalists produce." Civil society organizations are also highly critical of existing national measures. The CPBF (2005, 2) argued that "most European governments have enacted legislation to speed up the process of concentration," while the European Federation of Journalists (EFJ 2005a, 1) warned that the media industries' demand to lift "too restrictive rules" in the name of global competitiveness is "dangerous for media pluralism and a threat to the European model of mixed broadcasting systems."

Commercial actors and industry associations, on the other hand, tend to argue that the liberalization of the internal European media market creates a win-win situation, where media industries can attract greater audiences while consumers benefit from a wider choice of outlets. Based on the position papers analyzed, this argument is essentially threefold: media pluralism is a matter for individual member states and there is no added value in further EU measures, new digital media will increase competition anyway, and even if there is consolidation, it may also bring benefits.

The European Newspaper Publishers' Association (ENPA 2005, 2) argued that: "Restrictive action would risk greatly reducing the ability of the traditional media to effectively compete with emerging competitors in the telecoms and other electronic 'communications' operators that are beginning to see opportunities on the markets." Furthermore, "traditional media providers will face huge competition from new forms of digital news providers on the Internet and therefore concentration is unlikely to have a significant effect on pluralism." And even if there were increased concentration, it may also bring many benefits, including "better training for journalists, better investment in materials, and *increased* media pluralism" (ibid.).

Similarly, the Association of Commercial Television in Europe (2009b) has argued that fears for media pluralism "ignore the impact of the explosive growth in consumer choice in media since the 1980s (a growth which has come in successive stages including the market entry of private television groups, the move to digital television and the growth of the internet)."

The position of the main industrial lobby, which has also carried over into the European Commission's documents, has thus been that the proliferation of outlets and technological advances automatically lead to freedom of information and pluralism. By invoking concepts such as competitiveness and consumer choice, the commercial interests have been able to ignore the efforts of the European Parliament and other progressive actors by reframing the issue of media pluralism in terms of the internal market and competition policy. Therefore, the real confrontation between the conflicting interests and values has never been allowed to be decided politically.

One of the reasons for this is that policy approaches to ownership and pluralism have been essentially means rather than ends based. In the absence of clear normative arguments about the nature of the media systems envisioned by the different parties, media concentration has been reduced to a narrow internal market issue.

While the issue of media concentration has traditionally been closely interwoven with normative debates on political and cultural pluralism, the arguments about the relationship between ownership and pluralism are rarely explicated. The European Parliament and the Council of Europe have consistently regarded the concentration of media ownership as first and foremost a cultural and political problem and as a threat to pluralism and democracy. As such, it has been strongly linked to public service values, journalistic independence and citizens' right to information. Media pluralism has thus served as a conceptual shell that has often elided with media ownership and anticoncentration measures, but also carried a number of other values and connotations.

This has allowed industry representatives to suggest that the arguments of those advocating further regulation are less than well defined and that they confuse the issues of media pluralism, media concentration and media professionalism (see ENPA 2005, 2). Furthermore, a discursive configuration has evolved where civil society organizations argue that media pluralism should be considered on a democratic and cultural basis, "beyond the framework of ratings, profits and commercial objectives" (CPBF 2005, 2). Commercial interests, in turn, maintain that the arguments of proponents of regulation are abstract and emotional, while their own views are based on a more realistic basis of hard economic data.

In general, the Commission and the media industry have tended to emphasize a definition of media pluralism that is couched in economic discourse of competitiveness and consumer choice. By employing the argument that cultural and political aspects of media pluralism belong to the competence of member states, they have been able to shift the debate away from cultural and political concerns towards internal markets and competitiveness, which in effect has buried the problem of media pluralism as a cultural and democratic media policy issue in its own right.

As a consequence, media pluralism has become conceptualized as the optimum number of distribution operators, conflating quantitative plurality with pluralism (see Kaitatzi-Whitlock 2005, 178). Contrary to the position of the European Parliament, the Commission has disregarded the role of public service broadcasting and other nonprofit media and treated them like any other market competitors. This has fostered a broader shift in European media policy from cultural and democratic arguments to economic and technological concerns. It can also be argued that the vague policy discourse about what media pluralism should be, together with questions about competence, has allowed the Commission as well as the interest groups to act opportunistically and shift the policy discourse back and forth between the legal-economic discourse of competition policy and the cultural and social rhetoric used in political declarations.

Yet concerns over media pluralism and concentration have not subsided, perhaps because the ambiguity of the concept has allowed it to return to policy discussion in various guises, and in reference to various policy concerns. However the political configuration has essentially remained the same. The European Parliament has kept the issue firmly on the agenda by publishing a series of documents in which it has proposed various forms of public interest regulation, including an anticoncentration directive, the creation of the European media ombudsman (EP 2008a), and more support for nonprofit community media (EP 2008b). In addition, the importance of media pluralism has been further highlighted by professional and consumer organizations, which claim that the issue requires not only a national but also a European response. Reflecting these pressures, the European Commission convened in 2011 a new High Level Group on Media Freedom and Pluralism to provide advice and recommendations. A number of national and international civil society organizations together with four European parliamentary groups have also established a new alliance called the European Initiative for Media Pluralism to further promote the political will needed to develop the capacity of the EU to protect media pluralism. At the same time, the European media industry has raised equally strong arguments against any intervention. Instead of new legislation, the industry has demanded regulatory solutions that refrain from excessive regulation and support the competitiveness of the European media industry on a global scale.

A FRESH START? MONITORING AND SOFT GOVERNANCE

Acknowledging the insurmountable political obstacles to a harmonized European policy, the European Commission has shifted its emphasis away from the stalled attempts to introduce new binding legislation. As a result of the Liverpool audiovisual conference in 2005 it was agreed instead that the Commission would take steps to upgrade the monitoring and measuring of media pluralism in Europe (EC 2005; 2007a). Rather than proposing new legislation, the Commission has thus responded to the repeated claims and demands of the European Parliament and non-governmental organizations by promoting a new "three-step approach," which emphasizes the creation of new monitoring and measuring tools aimed at advancing debate and enhancing "the auditability of media pluralism" (EC 2007a). Of the options proposed in the 1992 Green Paper on Media Pluralism, taking "no action" seems to have finally given way to "action to improve transparency measures."

The Commission working paper, which introduced the new approach, states:

> The identification of concrete indicators marks a new approach and will
> enable citizens and all interested parties to assess more objectively media
> pluralism in the Member States. A successful study will help to introduce
> a greater measure of clarity into a debate on a very complex
> and multifaceted issue. (EC 2007a, 17)

Below I will analyze in more detail the implications of this approach based on the initial Commission Staff Working Paper on Media Pluralism (EC 2007a), the eventual study that unveiled the Media Pluralism Monitor (ICRI et al. 2009), its explanatory appendices and finally the stakeholder comments to the study.

The new approach as a whole indicates that the Commission has clearly opted to support the creation of various monitoring and transparency mechanisms, instead of formal legislation dealing explicitly with media pluralism. This is in line with a more general tendency in European media governance towards coregulation and softer policy measures, such as best practices and recommendations for the member states (see Michalis 2007, Harcourt 2008). Soft governance, meaning nonbinding agreements made between participating actors established outside the Community method, is thus seen above all as a way of bypassing political stagnation in the European Union (Harcourt 2008).

As noted above, the debate on media pluralism involves an inherent tension. On the one hand, there is the recognition that pluralism must be protected in the name of public interest and democracy, while on the other hand there is the desire to serve certain economic and industrial goals, particularly the need to build national and European champions able to compete with US companies. These conflicting interests are clearly accommodated in this new initiative.

The first stage in elaborating the new approach included a working paper (EC 2007a), which recognizes that "it is of decisive importance for democracy in the individual Member States and the European Union as a whole to preserve and further expand media pluralism." The paper documents the current status of the ongoing efforts by member states to promote pluralism, covering both electronic and print media. The second step was to commission an independent study to determine "objective indicators for the assessment of media pluralism in the EU Member States." Finally, in the third step, the Commission intended to submit a communication on the subject, followed by a broad public consultation. So far, however, the plan has not yielded any concrete results, and despite expectations, the new Commission had not by 2011 announced any new initiatives to systematically apply the indicators to all EU member states (see Komorek 2009; Valcke 2011).

In the original initiative the Commission sustained a familiar argument against the submission of an EU initiative on pluralism at present, but it emphasized the need to closely monitor the situation with the help of empirical indicators developed in the study (ICRI et al. 2009; see also Valcke 2011, Valcke et al. 2010). The areas that these indicators were to cover are: policies and legal instruments that support pluralism in different member states, the range of media available to citizens in different countries, and the supply side indicators on the economics of the media.

The eventual study that was published in 2009 discusses the definition and measurement of media pluralism on a general level and gives an overview of the technological and economic trends in the media sector, and their likely impact on media pluralism. Finally, it introduced a prototype for the European Media Pluralism Monitor (MPM).

The introduction of the study clearly recognizes the political sensitivities surrounding the subject, noting how prior attempts to harmonize a common European approach have failed and how the enlargement of the EU has further diminished the feasibility of a uniform approach to media pluralism (ICRI et al. 2009, 2).

The study also explicitly recognizes the multifaceted and normative character of media pluralism as a policy objective. Yet it is repeatedly emphasized in the study that it offers a diagnostic, not a prescriptive tool and that it does not prescribe specific remedies or policy responses (ibid., 6). Furthermore, it stresses that the formulation of an EU-wide harmonized definition of media pluralism for policy purposes was not within the remit of this study, as "this would entail normative discussions that this study was not supposed to embark on" (ibid., 5).

Instead, it provides data that can "subsequently be used to stimulate public debate and underpin robust policy making." Despite its political cautiousness, however, the study can still be taken as a welcome step towards clarifying the issues and opening a new debate on policy goals. As a whole, the study discusses the nature of media pluralism and its different aspects from a variety of perspectives by engaging with the academic literature as well as policy documents. Based on this, it also claims to take into account the "more dynamic and contextual aspects of diversity and pluralism that have been called for in academic literature" (ibid., 8).

Significantly, both the Commission working paper and the eventual study now explicitly define media pluralism as an issue that goes beyond media ownership. They make reference to its many aspects, ranging from merger control rules to content requirements in broadcasting licensing systems, the establishment of editorial freedoms, the independence and status of public service broadcasters, the professional situation of journalists and the relationship between media and political actors. In all, media pluralism is seen to encompass all measures that ensure citizens' access to a variety of information sources and voices, allowing them to form opinions without the undue influence of one dominant opinion-forming power. Moreover, the Commission acknowledges that media pluralism must take into account both pluralism of ownership (external pluralism) and pluralism of content (internal pluralism).

Making numerous references to the reports and resolutions of the Council of Europe and the European Parliament, the approach is also seemingly influenced by the culturally and socially oriented approach of the Council of Europe and the European Parliament. As a concession to the more interventionist approach advocated by the European Parliament and civil society actors, the working paper notes that "intense competition between newspapers or television channels may not itself guarantee pluralistic content" (EC 2007a, 11). The Commission also explicitly notes the importance of public service broadcasting and its contribution to media pluralism (ibid., 12–13).

Going far beyond the scope of ownership restrictions, the traditional focus of research and policy documents dealing with media pluralism, the study takes the debate significantly forward, at least compared to earlier EU policy documents from the 1990s, where media pluralism was framed almost exclusively in terms of market competition and competition policy.

Drawing on various Council of Europe documents, the indicator study adopts a broad working definition of media pluralism as "the scope for a wide range of social, political and cultural values, opinions, information and interests to find expression through the media" (ICRI et al. 2009, 5). More specifically, it understands media pluralism to mean the diversity of media supply, use and distribution in relation to ownership and control, media types and genres, political viewpoints, cultural expressions, and local and regional interests. Making reference to various definitions in policy documents and the academic literature, the study also claims to incorporate the numerous dimensions of media pluralism, such as internal and external pluralism, cultural and political pluralism, open and representative pluralism, structural and content pluralism, polarized and moderate pluralism, organized and spontaneous pluralism, reactive, interactive and proactive pluralism, and descriptive and evaluative pluralism (ibid., 5).

Furthermore, in line with the developments discussed in Chapter 5, the authors recognize that not only the supply aspects but also distribution mechanisms and potential access to media are relevant aspects of media pluralism that need to be assessed. Finally, reflecting its overall spirit of inclusiveness, it is also emphasizes that media of all types—public service, commercial, and community media—play an important role in creating pluralism (ibid., vii).

The concept of media pluralism itself is also problematized by the Commission. In particular, the tender for the study on pluralism indicators demands that the study takes into account the implications of recent technological changes for the pluralism and diversity debate. It is noted in the working paper of the Commission that "concern over media pluralism and diversity comes at a time when there are more TV channels than ever before and entry barriers for publishing any type of content on the Internet—even for private citizens—have fallen away" and that "to some commentators, this would imply dilution of media power across more fragmented markets than in the past" (EC 2007a, 2). Moreover, it is noted that "concern expressed regarding media pluralism and diversity may inter alia also be concern regarding structural changes that are taking place as a result of new technology, and the impact these may be having on media output" (ibid.). As an example of such structural changes, the paper mentions the alleged "dumbing down" of the media.

The study itself, however, makes clear that the changes in the media environment have important benefits but also create new types of potential harm to pluralism: "Consequently policy makers must broaden their consideration of pluralism, the roles of public service and commercial media, and the array of measures available to protect and promote pluralism" (ICRI et al. 2009, 9).

In contrast to previous policy documents, the study also recognizes the different normative approaches (market, political) to media pluralism and their different rationalities. However, even the acknowledgment of the complexities and problems of incorporating pluralism into empirical research does not seem to prevent the aim to create "objective indicators" for assessing media pluralism. Instead, it is claimed that the new Media Pluralism Monitor is compatible with both approaches, as it includes both economic and socio-demographic indicators and thus offers "the most neutral measurement tool conceivable in policy terms" (ibid., 6, 20).

While acknowledging the complexity of the concept and the contradictions between its different definitions, the study thus ultimately holds that the conflicting values and political rationalities can be reconciled with the help of concrete and objective indicators for assessing media pluralism: "Nevertheless, it is feasible to search for general and substantive criteria to measure media pluralism, and to develop tools for empirical assessments of diversity in the media sector, without jeopardizing the multi-faceted and normative character of media pluralism. In this spirit, this study aspires to reconcile the different normative approaches to media pluralism, and to media policy in general, that exist in Europe, with the enhancement of the auditability of media pluralism" (ICRI et al. 2009, 5). The solution adopted in the study to the problem of conflicting normative frameworks is simply to increase the number of indicators, some of which are purely economic and quantitative, and others more qualitative and "political" in character. By incorporating both, the study claims to be compatible with both these approaches, making "the concept of media pluralism concrete, measurable and comparative" (ibid., 22). Despite repeatedly suggesting that media pluralism is not only a technical but also a normative and political issue, the study also argues that the monitoring tool itself is not political in any way.

It can be questioned, however, whether it is possible to avoid normative conflicts simply through the inclusion of indicators of both kinds. By including different types of indicators, the MPM acknowledges that different normative approaches may imply different indicators. However, it does not recognize that different normative approaches may also lead to conflicting interpretations of the same indicator.

This becomes clear when we look at the proposed indicators that aim to measure the existence of regulatory safeguards. As noted above, there is continuing controversy over the desirability of specific ownership restrictions, for instance, which according to many critics may also have unforeseen negative consequences for pluralism, or at least some aspect of it.

The problems of interpretation are even more evident in some of the more qualitative indicators. Among the risks to pluralism mentioned by the study are: "lack of resources to support public service media" and "insufficient engagement of public service media in new media" (ICRI et al. 2009, 41, 140). In their feedback to the published study, however, the commercial media companies and their representatives were quick to point out that in their view the biggest threats to media pluralism were posed not by lack of resources to support public service media but on the contrary by "overcompensated public broadcasters" and "market foreclosure by a dominant publicly funded broadcaster" (see ACT 2009b).

It is difficult to see how it is possible, without normative and political debate, to determine the proper representation of public service institutions in the new media. In this sense, the monitoring approach hardly avoids the normative problems and conflicts of interest discussed above. Instead, the choice of definitions, border values and criteria inevitably give rise to normative discussions.

In this sense, the approach of the MPM can be criticized for assuming a somewhat naïve belief in technocratic rationality and empirical measures of pluralism as a way of surpassing different normative definitions of the concept. That said, there are many reasons to offer a much more positive assessment of the new approach, including its transparency, broader concept of pluralism, and its basic aim to stimulate further debate.

Because of entrenched industry opposition and diverging normative approaches and regulatory cultures in Europe, it is unlikely that the MPM will bring an immediate change to current EU media policy making. As the report on indicators emphasizes, however, it is not intended as a prescriptive tool, but rather brings together a host of previously disparate concerns in order to offer a multifaceted approach to media pluralism. The use of the proposed indicators is thus left to the discretion of the policy makers, who remain "free to opt for a more market-driven approach of diversity, emphasising choice and deregulation, or for one tending more towards public regulation and which relies on cultural-political norms of cultural diversity, civic equality, and universalism" (ICRI et al. 2009, 6).

The industrial imperatives of the global competiveness and information society have by no means weakened in the EU, and given the past experiences, it seems unrealistic that policy makers on the EU level will be able to reach consensus on any far-reaching policy measures. This became clear already in the public consultation that followed the publication of the MPM, where industry representatives expressed concerns that the monitor would be used to justify more regulation at national or EU level or to check on media contents, which they readily interpreted as interfering with the freedom of expression (see ICRI et al. 2009, 134).

Given the industry opposition, it has been generally assessed that the so-called three-step plan itself will not bring major changes to the current market-oriented approach of the EU on media pluralism. As Ewa Komorek (2009, 53) sums up, "one cannot shed the feeling that 'the three-step plan' is a road to nowhere . . . that it is simply meant to quiet the demands of the European Parliament and the likes of the European Federation of Journalists (EFJ) who continue to call on the Commission to take action on the issue of media pluralism."

However, the results of the study and the aim to establish concrete criteria for media pluralism are of obvious importance for the future framing and the agenda of the debate on media pluralism. To some extent, the study and the debate it has inspired have already taken the debate forward and beyond earlier policy documents where media pluralism was defined only in terms of internal markets and competition policy. Yet, given the complex nature of the concept it is easy to anticipate problems that the demand for concrete indicators will entail. As is indicated by the assessment of the contribution of public service broadcasting to pluralism, for instance, objective indicators will hardly solve the normative conflicts flowing from the different conceptions of media pluralism. However, even if the indicators do not succeed in solving these normative conflicts, there is reason to consider the new approach at least a modestly positive step in the broader European media policy debate on media pluralism.

CLASH OF POLITICAL RATIONALITIES

Based on the numerous references in policy documents, there is a strong consensus on the importance of media pluralism for democracy. However, the debate on pluralism and media concentration since the 1990s clearly illustrates that there are two contrasting conceptions of media pluralism in European policy debates.

First, there is the conception that regards media pluralism as a broader social and political value, grounded in the concepts of democracy and the public sphere. As such, media pluralism provides an umbrella for various policy issues, such as those concerning the range of ideas, viewpoints, and forms of cultural expression in media content, the abuse of political power by media owners, and journalistic freedom and independence. It appears then that the core value associated with media pluralism in this conception is the protection of different, independent voices in the media that offer different opinions and perspectives as well as a range of cultural representations. More often than not, it is this kind of rationale that motivates anticoncentration measures as well as the remit of public service broadcasting and other interventionist means of promoting media pluralism.

Overall, it seems that media pluralism is employed as an umbrella value that is used to mobilize support for various good causes. The problem is that the analytical value of the concept remains dubious, undermining the strength of many of the arguments in actual policy consultations. In practice, the more abstract conception of media pluralism has thus also suffered from the conflation of means and ends in media policy.

Secondly, media pluralism is increasingly seen in economic and technocratic terms, as free competition and the satisfaction of consumer preferences. Although it is acknowledged that media pluralism is related to a number of cultural and political concerns, these are generally either marginalized or elided with the quantitative and consumer-led conception of pluralism. As Freedman (2005) argues, policy makers increasingly associate pluralism and diversity with the expansion of consumer choice in the marketplace, with the result that their meanings have, to a certain extent, converged around the dynamics of competition. The conception of pluralism that is expressed in contemporary neoliberal policy initiatives is therefore rather partial. It is based on the conviction that market forces are best able to support the provision of different views and that regulatory intervention, while necessary to correct "market failure," is to be minimized and avoided where possible.

The two logics can be paralleled with the distinction between commodified and noncommodified logics discussed by Edwin Baker (2007) in the context of American debates on media concentration. The *noncommodified* rationale for defending media pluralism derives essentially from democratic theory and the egalitarian commitment to the democratic distribution of communicative power in the public sphere. Pluralism is seen as a "wide and fair dispersal of power and ubiquitous opportunities to present preferences, views, visions" (Baker 2007, 7). Importantly, this principle is an end in itself, not a means predicted to lead causally to some other desirable result. Thus its appeal is mainly normative and it cannot be justified only by empirical evidence.

According to Baker (2007, 74), economic analyses and empirical diversity indexes, no matter how sophisticated, tend to share an ultimate concern with fair competition and the provision of commodities to consumers. This lends further strength to a rationality where pluralism is advanced primarily in terms of catering to different tastes and preferences, rather than giving expression to different perspectives and cultures (see also Curran 2002, 212). In other words, such conceptions rest on a private-choice view of public space, replacing the framework of the public sphere with the framework of the market (see also Venturelli 1998).

In the recent European debate, the European Parliament and the Council of Europe have clearly represented a more socially and politically oriented rationality. Although different parties in the European Parliament have expressed different views about media pluralism (see Sarikakis 2004, 120–21), there has been a relatively strong view that associates pluralism with broader public interest goals and the fundamental values of freedom of expression, democracy and the rights of the citizens. Although the exact goals often remain poorly articulated, one of the key features of this discourse has been a general opposition to the "internationalisation of the American model," understood as excessive commercialization and corporate expansion (see Sarikakis 2004, 121).

In line with this, some scholars continue to insist that despite all the differences, there could indeed be something like a "European consensus" in embracing a rather positive approach to press freedom and pluralism: "As opposed to the US-American market liberal approach ('freedom from . . .') there seems to be wider support in Europe for a model that actively supports and regulates press freedom and media pluralism ('freedom to . . .') in order to ensure the representation of checks and balances, of critique and controversy, and of minority opinions and interests in a changing media world" (Czepek, Hellwig and Novak 2009, 11). In contrast, while acknowledging the importance of pluralism in principle, the European

Commission and the commercial interests that influence its work have clearly adopted the *commodified* rationality. Although at times it has acknowledged the broader social and political context of the debate, the Commission still tends to emphasize economic factors and employ a discourse where the free flow of media content is seen to provide maximum choice for consumers in the market. In this discourse, commercial viability, more choice and diversity typically go hand in hand, creating a win-win situation for consumers and media producers alike. As Beata Klimkiewicz (2008) puts it, competitiveness provides a key perspective through which European media policy in general, and media pluralism as a particular policy objective, are "filtered through."

In some ways, the Media Pluralism Monitor can be seen as having challenged this perspective by providing a basis for a much more in-depth discussion of the different aspects of media pluralism. Whether it will succeed in influencing the terms of the policy debate more permanently, however, remains to be seen.

It is of course nothing new in politics to have more than one interpretation of an ambiguous normative term. What is particularly problematic about the contemporary debate on media pluralism is that the two rationalities are rarely brought into direct confrontation with each other as genuinely contrasting positions or alternatives. Instead, the commodified and market-oriented rationality seems to end up perpetuating its ideology through the back door. Cultural and democratic values are routinely acknowledged in speeches and declarations, but the actual policy measures and indicators used in policy formation still rely almost exclusively on considerations that can be translated into quantifiable economic data. Thus, battles concerning the definition of media pluralism as a policy issue, its assessment and measurement, and its relationship to institutional arrangements such as public service broadcasting or market competition are not weighed on political arenas. Rather, they are subjected to expert discourse and empirical indicators, which further reinforce the commodification and de-politicization of media policy.

CASE STUDY 2: DEBATES ON PUBLIC SERVICE MEDIA

Another issue that has brought different conceptions of media pluralism to the surface in European media policy revolves around the status and role of public service broadcasting. The question of whether and to what extent public broadcasting, or perhaps more appositely public service media,[5]

---

[5]*Public service media* is a term that has been adopted recently by many scholars to emphasize the point that the public service remit should no longer be limited to traditional broadcasting (Bardoel & Lowe 2007; Council of Europe 2007b).

should be sustained and publicly supported in the digital media landscape has been at the heart of European media policy debates for several decades now. Like the attempts to regulate media pluralism discussed above, the contestation over public service media can be interpreted as a series of definitional struggles over the criteria used to assess broadcasting institutions in particular and the role of media in society in general.

Similarly to the debates on media concentration, the debate on public service media clearly reflects the conflicting interests of the European media industry, public service institutions, and the policy traditions in different EU member states. However, despite the rhetoric about the challenges facing public service media or indeed the crisis in public service media, and at times intense debate about their funding and organization, there has been less political debate about the fundamental objectives of public service institutions or the values that justify their operation. Even though the importance of public service media as an institution is widely acknowledged, there also remains a sense of inevitable decline—in terms of audience shares, funding, as well as general influence—in debates about its role and remit in the digital media landscape.

Analogously with media pluralism indicators, my argument in this chapter is that instead of attacking directly the values and principles of public service ethos, European media policy runs the risk of defining and often curbing the legitimate scope of public service media "through the back door," by means of the highly inaccessible, technocratic, and undemocratic apparatus of European competition policy and state aid rules. To counter these trends, I suggest that there is a need to rethink and reassert the guiding principles of public service media and their contribution to a pluralistic public sphere from a theoretical, normative, and political perspective.

Although public service media have taken very different institutional forms in different parts of Europe, they are commonly accepted as one of the foundations of the "European model" in media policy. From the 1980s onwards, however, public broadcasters have come under increasing commercial, political, and ideological pressure (see, for example, Collins 1998; Syvertsen 2003). These pressures are usually thought to come from a combination of ideological factors, such as the rise of neoliberalism and the decline in the legitimacy of public services together with more concrete technological and economic factors, including technological convergence and digitalization. In short, many of the central ideas on which public service broadcasting were based in Europe, ranging from the old spectrum scarcity and market failure arguments to the value-laden notion of program quality, have lost much of their persuasive force.

As noted above, the dominant attitude within the European Union to public enterprise is also generally considered to be hostile. The view that the abolition of spectrum scarcity delegitimates political intervention in the broadcasting market has been strongly embraced especially in the early phases of common European audiovisual policy (Collins 1998, 51–53). This hostility derives from a mismatch between fundamental EU assumptions that competitive markets are normal and normative, and the legacy of public sector enterprise, including public service broadcasting as well as public libraries and others arrangements that do not fit that paradigm. Perhaps the most outspoken example of this is the 1994 Bangemann report,[6] which infamously urged the EU to "put its faith in market mechanisms as the motive power to carry us into the Information Age," while arguing that the "the prime task of government is to safeguard competitive forces" and eradicate competitive disadvantages such as "public money, financial assistance, subsidies, dirigisme, or protectionism" (EC 1994b).

Since the 1980s the challenges to the public service ethos have led to a reexamination of the rationales of media policy and public service media in particular, and it is in that context that much of the current debate on media pluralism is still weighed. One of the consequences of this is that public service broadcasters have been forced to rethink their legitimating principles and to articulate and assert them even more forcefully (see Collins 1998, 53).

Unsurprisingly, public service broadcasting is increasingly defended in the name of pluralism and diversity. As key principles of the public service remit, they are characteristically also enshrined in the mandates of European public service broadcasters, referring variably to different aspects of political, social, cultural and linguistic pluralism and diversity (Blumler 1992, 9–11; Collins 1998, 62–63; Humphreys 1996, 158). On the European level, the role of public service media in protecting media pluralism is also acknowledged in the Protocol on the system of public broadcasting of the Treaty of Amsterdam (1997) and in numerous resolutions of the Council of Europe and the European Parliament (see Council of Europe 1994b; 1996; 2003; 2004a; 2007b; EP 1996; 2004; 2008a, 2010).

Judging by political declarations only, there is indeed strong political and ideological support for public service media. Public broadcasting is identified in the recommendations, declarations, and reports of the

---

[6] A report prepared for the European Council on the development of information society by a high-level group chaired by Martin Bangemann, then European Commissioner for Industrial affairs and information and telecommunications technologies.

European Parliament, the Council of Europe, and many other institutions as a necessary core of democratic media systems and described as being closely associated with pluralism, informed citizenship, social cohesion, and almost everything good expected of the media. As noted above, the European Commission's recent documents on media pluralism also invariably recognize the importance and special role played by public service media in safeguarding pluralism and diversity (see EC 2005; EC 2007a).

As Collins (1998, 62–63) notes, the inclusion of pluralism and diversity among the legitimating principles of public service broadcasting may reflect the apprehension that this is the most vulnerable value in the current situation, but on the other hand it may also reflect the fact that as a normative value it is seen as much less problematic than quality or national identity, for instance. Historically, a key feature of European broadcasting regulation has been the imposition of certain standards of quality of information and culture that deserve protection through regulation and support (see McQuail 2007a, 12; Syvertsen 2003, 163). In today's more postmodern intellectual climate, however, these value judgments are increasingly associated with traditional taste and cultural hierarchies that are no longer viable. A recent study of the legitimation strategies employed by Swedish and Norwegian public service broadcasters notes that these broadcasters have consciously taken distance from the paternalistic attitude that characterized the original idea of PSB, and substituted it with an emphasis on their "diversified offerings" (Larsen 2010). Therefore, it appears that the popularity of pluralism and diversity as legitimating principles also has to do with more opportunistic and self-serving reasons. In other words, they have become politically correct substitutes for the notion of quality.

The inclusiveness of the concepts, of course, means that commercial media can equally claim to provide diversity and pluralism. While advocates of public service broadcasting argue that market mechanisms lead to a concentration of ownership and homogenization of content and thus diminish media pluralism, commercial media can equally criticize public broadcasting for elitism and paternalism, while defending their own operation as based on popular sovereignty and freedom of choice.

As reflected in the position papers analyzed below, the commercial media have consistently argued that the pursuit of pluralism through government intervention is illegitimate and often counterproductive to the aim of increasing free competition and consumer choice. Based on this, the neoliberal forces in European media policy have repeatedly argued that the remit of public service institutions should be limited to services that commercial companies do not provide.

The inevitable inference from all this is that the relationship between public service media and the notion of media pluralism is much more complicated and controversial than suggested by the political declarations. The contemporary contestation of the public service remit and its legitimate scope clearly revolves around different interpretations of pluralism. While the rhetoric employed by commercial media defines pluralism in terms of competition and choice, the public service ethos is based on more abstract, and admittedly indefinite, values of informed citizenship, universal access and the public sphere. More often than ideological arguments though, the critics of public broadcasting invoke the pragmatic reasoning of economics or technology, arguing that while the public service cause itself may well be laudable, its time has definitely passed. As Sarikakis (2004, 114) notes, this had led to an interesting mismatch where arguments in support of public broadcasting are almost always political, whereas arguments against it are more firmly grounded in economic or technological considerations. However, as I argue in the previous chapter, the technocratic discourse itself is by no means value free, but it comes embedded with a certain normalized political rationality, including a certain conception of media pluralism.

PUBLIC SERVICE MEDIA AND COMPETITION POLICY

The role of public service media is debated and treated in different ways in different European countries, but my focus here is on some recent debates on the pan-European level. The reason for this is that although developments have taken a different course in different member states, the significance of European regulation is clearly expanding, and in many ways the current European discussion about the proper scope of public service broadcasting in the digital age is also illustrative of the different political rationalities in media policy.

As noted before, one of the problems for European media policy is that because of EU institutions' lack of direct competence in media and cultural policy, media issues have been relegated under competition policy, which means that any problems specific to the media sector tend to be easily marginalized. If this was evident in the debate on media pluralism, it also affects the debate on public service media. In the competition policy framework, the position of public service media in particular is dubious from the very outset. Even if public service media continue to receive political support, they will always be framed as an exception to normal market conditions.

As the Commission Green paper on services of general interest states: "The purpose of existing Community law instruments is to ensure a certain economic balance between market operators: these instruments, therefore affect the media sector as an area of economic activity and not—or at least only very indirectly—as a means of delivering information to the citizen" (EC 2003, 22). This has not precluded the Commission from acknowledging elsewhere the importance of public service media or even committing to its protection in a number of other instances. The working papers of the Commission on media pluralism, for instance, clearly note that "public service broadcasting has an important role to play in ensuring media pluralism" (EC 2005, 3) and that "both public service broadcasters and commercial broadcasters contribute to media pluralism and this dualism itself further strengthens pluralism" (EC 2007a, 12).

Similarly, the Commission's communication on the principles and guidelines for the community's audiovisual policy from 1999 notes that: "Public service television plays an important role in the Member States of the European Community: this is true with regard to cultural and linguistic diversity, educational programming, in objectively informing public opinion, in generating pluralism and in supplying, on a free-to-air basis, quality programming" (EC 1999, 12).

However, despite routinely acknowledging the public interest objectives associated with public broadcasting, it is evident that in practice the EU has approached public service media primarily from the perspective of competition policy. As a consequence, even though there is broad support for public broadcasting from member states and other European institutions, there has been a constant tension between European competition rules and the commitment to preserve public broadcasting on the grounds of "the democratic, social and cultural needs of society," as the protocol on public broadcasting in the Treaty of Amsterdam states. According to a number of scholars of European media policy, this is because the European policy regime itself is biased towards a commodified understanding of the media, in which political and nonmeasurable public service values tend to appear less logical and natural than in the national context where they were originally conceived (Venturelli 1998, Syvertsen 2003, Kaitatzi-Whitlock 2006).

This bias also explains why commercial media lobbyists have so heavily relied on the European institutions to argue for curbing the role of public service media in the new digital age. Since the early 1990s, private media companies have filed over thirty complaints to the Commission about public broadcasting services and their "unfair competitive advantages." Based on these complaints, commercial broadcasters have attempted to limit competition from public service broadcasters by challenging both their funding and their comprehensive remit. As a consequence, the decisions of the European Commission together with the case law of the European Court of Justice (ECJ) have become central arenas in the battle over the future remit of European public service media.

The argument developed by private broadcasting companies, and sympathized by some European regulators, has essentially been that public service broadcasting should be defined in terms of programs and not in terms of an overall remit or institutional values. Instead of their traditional comprehensive remit, public broadcasters should thereby concentrate on services not supplied by private broadcasters. Public service broadcasting should be defined as unprofitable programming, which would essentially limit its scope and exclude program types that are seen to compete directly with commercial providers, such as imported fiction, sports, and entertainment (see Coppens 2005, 80–81; Michalis 2007, 172; Sarikakis 2004, 112). While controversial, the assumption that public service media should be defined by their dissimilarity to existing commercial offers has formed an implicit frame of reference for much of the debate reviewed below.

The complaints from private media about unfair competition have resulted in two documents that constitute some of the key reference points of current European media policy. The first is the Protocol on the system of public broadcasting in the member states attached to the Treaty of Amsterdam (1997). The second key document is the European Commission's Communication on the application of state aid rules to public service broadcasting, which was originally issued in 2001 and revised with much controversy in 2009.

The Amsterdam Protocol has been very influential since it explicitly acknowledges, on the level of the EC Treaty, that public service broadcasting "is directly related to the democratic, social and cultural needs of each society and to the need to preserve media pluralism." Furthermore, the protocol states that:

> The provisions of the Treaty establishing the European Community
> shall be without prejudice to the competence of the Member States to
> provide for the funding of public service broadcasting insofar as such
> funding is granted to broadcasting organisations for the fulfilment of the
> public service remit as conferred, defined and organised by each Member
> State, and insofar as such funding does not affect trading conditions and
> competition in the Community to an extent which would be contrary
> to the common interest, while the realisation of the remit of that public
> service shall be taken into account. (Treaty of Amsterdam 1997, 87)

On the basis of the text it seems clear that EU policy cannot be blatantly opposed to public broadcasters. Rather, the EU has respected a certain free zone for public service broadcasting outside competition regulations, defining it in EU terminology as a "service of general interest" to be concretely defined by each member state. Furthermore, the protocol explicitly recognizes the importance of public service media and their value for pluralism in particular. Therefore, it has been interpreted as a commitment to protect the strong European-style concept of public service, rather than the American-style marginalized concept that private broadcasters were seen to advocate (Humphreys 2007, 102). In the short term at least, the protocol was thus considered a victory for public service companies and their supporters, particularly the European Parliament, which has traditionally emphasized the social and political role of the media.

The protocol was especially significant because at the time of the treaty in the 1990s there was strong pressure from commercial media companies as well as the liberalizing forces within the EU Commission to further deregulate the media industry. In line with this spirit, the Commission and private broadcasters had insisted in the build-up to the Amsterdam Protocol on guidelines that would narrow the scope of public broadcasting and limit it to specific program types (Michalis 2007, 172). The neoliberal spirit was thus seen to threaten the future status of public service broadcasting.

Sarikakis (2004, 113) notes that if the guidelines proposed by the Commission in the mid-1990s had been accepted, public broadcasters would have faced dramatic consequences and above all further marginalization. The controversy led the European Parliament to initiate a series of discussions and consultations with academics, professionals, and public broadcasting representatives. These discussions and the so-called Tongue report (EP 1996) later proved to have an unexpected impact on the future of media policy. According to Sarikakis (2004, 107), not only did the alliance formed by the defenders of public service broadcasting succeed in blocking the attempts to marginalize public broadcasting, but they also reintroduced and strengthened the discourse of public interest and citizenship in European media policy. The report and the ensuing policy reactions, including the Amsterdam Protocol, strengthened policy discourses that demonstrated the relevance and continuing support of public service media in the new era and thus provided an influential counter-discourse to the commodified approach of European competition policy.

Civil society lobbying, public broadcasting companies, and organizations such as the European Broadcasting Union and the European Parliament have thus built up a rather broad alliance of political forces in defense of the public broadcasting model (Syvertsen 2003, 165). As a result, the most controversial proposals to curb the remit of public broadcasting have officially been abandoned, although many of the same arguments still feature in public broadcasting debates.

However, the Amsterdam Protocol is a compromise that cuts both ways. This is because the protocol also says that public funding for broadcasting services "may not affect trading conditions and competition in the Community to an extent which would be contrary to the common interest." Therefore, it leaves the Commission the power to review the scope of public service broadcasting in the interest of the "common interest" and in particular, in the light of competition policy.

As a result, controversies around the funding of public service broadcasting, its remit, and competition have continued. Recently, these controversies have culminated in the revision of the Commission's Communication on the application of state aid rules to public service broadcasting (EC 2009). In particular, the communication and related consultation process have given commercial media companies yet another opportunity to resist the development of public service media in the name of "fair competition" and "a level playing field."[7]

Despite all the lobbying, the new communication acknowledges—once more—the importance of public broadcasting and its specificity compared to a general interest service in areas such as transport and energy. Furthermore, the guidelines described in the Commission's communication do not attempt to restrict the scope of the public service broadcasting remit to programs not supplied by commercial providers, but acknowledge public broadcasters' broad remit, which includes "varied programming." Accordingly, "it is in the common interest to maintain a plurality of balanced public and private media offer also in the current dynamic media environment" (EC 2009, 7). The communication does not, however, give public broadcasting companies a free pass. Instead, the Commission demands that the public service remit must be clearly defined to exclude activities that do not meet the "the democratic, social and cultural needs of each society" (ibid., 14).

Both the Amsterdam Protocol and the Broadcasting Communication have become examples of how different institutions and actors, including academic scholars, can arrive at different conclusions from the same texts. According to David Ward (2001), the Commission has developed an extremely sophisticated understanding of the role of broadcasting in terms of its importance to the democratic life of societies. On the grounds of the

---

[7]These arguments can be found in the responses of media industry associations to the Commission's consultation on the new Broadcasting communication. See below for a closer analysis of the arguments.

Commission's earlier decisions on complaints about state aid to PSB, Ward concluded that the Commission has largely acknowledged the status of public service broadcasting as an exception to competition rules and recognized its value for internal pluralism (Ward 2001, 88).

For many others, the implication is that EU policy discourse is so impregnated with neoliberal ideology that public service broadcasting must be legitimated as an exception to the normal principles of competition, deregulation, and market forces. Therefore, the whole apparatus is another step in the general direction towards marginalizing public service broadcasting and naturalizing consumer sovereignty and direct market competition as normative cornerstones of media governance (see Jakubowicz 2004a; Kaitatzi-Whitlock 2005; Venturelli 1998).

The current guidelines on the funding of public service media seem to strike a somewhat uneasy balance between private companies' demands that the provision of new media services by public service broadcasters must be restricted, and on the other hand the public broadcasters' argument that their remit must be defined in a dynamic way so that they can adapt to the changing environment and new technologies. What is particularly clear from these debates is that the discussion on the European level is not primarily about developing or strengthening the role of public service media, but about ways of restricting their operation in such a way as not to distort free competition. The whole debate on the definition of public service remit has thus arguably strengthened a discourse where pluralism is conceived in terms of free competition and the satisfaction of consumer preferences.

THE POWER OF DEFINITIONS

One of the most significant outcomes of the increased scrutiny on public service broadcasting has been the seemingly mundane demand that its scope and nature be defined more precisely. There have been a number of attempts to arrive at a definition of the common elements of public service broadcasting in Council of Europe documents as well as in the academic literature (see, for example, Council of Europe 1994b, 2007b). However, due to the different interpretations of the guiding principles of public service broadcasting and different national traditions in Europe, it has proved difficult to define what public service broadcasting actually means in any simple and unambiguous terms (see Harrison and Woods 2001; Humphreys 2007; McQuail 1992, 49–64; Syvertsen 1999; Syvertsen 2003). Although there seems to be a general consensus about the core values, such as pluralism, quality, universality, and independence, it is often unclear how these abstract goals should be realized in practice.

Apart from the fact that public broadcasting has traditionally meant different things in different countries, the problems of definition today also reflect the conflict of interests between commercial media, who advocate a strict definition that would limit the expansion of public service media into new services, and public broadcasters, who worry that such a definition would curtail their role in the wake of the decline of traditional broadcasting. The different conceptions of pluralism also illustrate the two different underlying rationalities. In the competition discourse, pluralism is almost exclusively taken to mean consumer choice between certain program types or genres. This raises an immediate concern with respect to the limiting of the public service remit to producing content that is not profitable or not supplied by commercial content providers. Commercial interests have therefore consistently argued that public service broadcasting should be limited to noncommercial areas only and largely to old linear broadcasting. As the representatives of the commercial television industry argued in their statements to the European Commission's Broadcasting Communication, public broadcasters should be given "as tight a definition as possible" and "the starting point should be assessing which services will certainly not be offered by the market and these should be the cornerstone of the public service remit" (FACT 2009, 2).

For the advocates of public service media, however, this would effectively mean relegating public service broadcasting into a minority service, or "a museum of 20th-century broadcasting, rather than serving the public of the 21st century" (EBU 2004, 5). Compared to the discourse of consumer choice, defenders of public service values in European media policy tend to have a more ambitious conception of pluralism, which includes the aim of promoting social cohesion, universal access, and other values that cannot be reduced to satisfying individual preferences. As opposed to being a minority service and filling the gap left by commercial services, public broadcasters are committed to serve society as a whole according to their comprehensive ethos. As one EBU document puts it, this means putting individual pieces of information in a meaningful context, explaining the world in all its variety and diversity, and providing a guard against the danger of "a two-tier information society" (EBU 2004, 2–3).

As these arguments indicate, the public service remit is considered intangible, normative and embedded in the values of democracy and the public sphere. As Tomas Coppens (2005, 81) sarcastically puts it, "pluralism, citizenship, creativity or national culture are difficult ideas (or ideals) to calculate with a price tag. What is the retail price for a healthy public sphere these days? Is there citizenship inflation or a pluralistic deficit?"

The problem is that although they are widely acknowledged and supported, these values are much more difficult to quantify for purposes of independent assessment and monitoring and therefore they are a priori ill-suited for the present policy regime. Furthermore, the idea of a comprehensive remit that is based on normative and intangible values is at odds with the commercial competitors' demands for a predictable and stable environment. Therefore, even though the majority of policy makers remain somewhat sympathetic to public service broadcasting in principle, the terms of the debate are not without consequences.

In the light of the attempts to restrict the scope of public service broadcasting, the mere definition of public service has thus become politically charged. As Jakubowicz (2004b, 20) argues, the campaign against public service operators "usually begins with a demand for a clear definition," for the real objective of such formulations is to halt the evolution of public service broadcasting on the basis that any new developments not covered in the definition could be challenged and subsequently reversed. Therefore, it can be argued that definitions serve the purpose of straightjackets which actually prevents public broadcasters from adapting their strategies and moving into the new media (Freedman 2008, 156).

This became evident in the Commission's public consultation on the new Broadcasting Communication where commercial interests have systematically called for as tight a definition as possible, including detailed criteria and market impact assessments for the approval of new media services delivered by public service broadcasters.

Since there is no general consensus on the definition of public service broadcasting, most complaints about the funding of public broadcasters have so far been dealt with on a case-by-case basis. According to Donders and Pauwels (2008, 296–98), this has created a situation where the Commission, by means of the "state aid regime," has considerable competence to shape not only the scope of the public service sector, but also the substance of the remit of public broadcasting. A broader implication of this is that the debate over the proper remit and scope of public service media in the contemporary European media landscape is not conducted through public political decisions. Instead, there are fears that the Commission will define the public service remit through the back door, by means of the decisions taken on individual complaints.

Furthermore, because state aid cases are considered on the basis of narrow competition rules, the Commission has very limited flexibility to take account of noneconomic factors in assessing public service broadcasting (Michalis 2007, 241). According to the Commission guidelines, it is up to the

Commission to decide whether or not state aid to public broadcasters is compatible with the EC Treaty on the basis of three criteria: definition, entrustment and monitoring, and proportionality. In short, definition means that the remit and mandate of public broadcasting should be clearly defined. Entrustment and monitoring necessitates independent assessment to establish whether broadcasters are living up to define their mandate. Finally, proportionality means that PSB should not be overcompensated for the services it is entrusted to perform.

The highly technocratic nature of decision making in this area is obvious and not without consequences. For instance, if the positive externality that public service media are entrusted to provide is pluralistic content, the decision-making procedure requires that there must also be a monitoring apparatus in place to assess the broadcasters' performance and their impact on the overall media market. In this sense, then, the nature of EU policy in this area again seems to necessitate the type of reforms that further depoliticize policy making and strengthen the commodified and technocratic approach to the role of media in society.

NEW MEDIA AND NEW ARGUMENTS

So far the decisions taken on actual cases have been rather mixed. Generally it has been accepted that, in accordance with the Amsterdam Protocol, the funding of public service broadcasting as such does not infringe European competition law and that it is up to the member states to define the exact remit of these services.[8] The revision of the Broadcasting Communication in 2009, however, has revived many of the controversies over the proper remit of public service media in the digital age and raised concerns that the Commission might be becoming more hostile towards public broadcasters.

Below I will demonstrate these controversies by analyzing in more detail the arguments put forward in the Broadcasting Communication itself and the various consultation documents that reflect the contrasting positions of public service broadcasters and the private media industry.[9]

Questions about the public service remit have recently centered around the involvement of public service broadcasters on new media platforms.

---

[8]The Commission's decisions on state aid for public service broadcasting since 2000 can be found online at http://ec.europa.eu/competition/state_aid/register/. For a review of the cases so far, see also Ward (2008).

[9]The consultation documents, drafts and reactions to the Broadcasting Communication are all available at: http://ec.europa.eu/competition/state_aid/reform/archive.html#broadcasting. Unless indicated otherwise, the views expressed here rely on a review of these documents.

With the changes that are sweeping the media landscape, public service broadcasters have increasingly embraced the Internet and the new opportunities it opens for service delivery. The branching out of public broadcasters onto new distribution platforms, niche channels and websites has prompted a new wave of complaints from their commercial rivals to the European Commission. In recent years these complaints have also spread beyond the broadcasting sector, with newspaper publishers and other private content providers expressing fears that state aid may be used excessively to fund the online activities of public service broadcasters. The entry of public service broadcasters into the new markets has thereby only aggravated the conflict between the public service sector and commercial interests.

The Commission's current rules on state aid to public service broadcasting make it clear that the public service remit may also include online and other new services. The 2009 Broadcasting Communication states that "public service broadcasters should be able to use the opportunities offered by digitisation and the diversification of distribution platforms on a technology neutral basis, to the benefit of society" (EC 2009, point 81). Yet public broadcasters may use state aid to provide such services only when it is "provided that they are addressing the same democratic, social, and cultural needs of the society in question, and do not entail disproportionate effects on the market, which are not necessary for the fulfilment of the public service remit" (ibid.).

According to some commentators, however, the Commission has recently taken a more unfavorable stand towards public service media. In particular, the Commission's Competition and Information Society directorates, which traditionally have strong links with industry, have shown an increasingly hostile attitude towards the aspirations of public service broadcasters to expand their remit to new media platforms (see Donders and Pauwels 2008; Humphreys 2007; Moe 2009).

This sentiment can also be read in the comments of the stakeholders to the Commission's communication. While commercial interests generally welcome the new communication and consider it an improvement over the existing guidelines, representatives of public service broadcasters as well as most nongovernmental organizations take a much more critical stand on the need for new rules.

A common position paper signed by most of the member states also criticized the Commission draft communication for laying down too detailed criteria of evaluation that would restrict the flexibility of both member states and public service broadcasters to adapt to the changing needs of citizens. Most member states, public broadcasters, and civil society organizations would only need to make small changes to adapt the communication to the digital age.

Furthermore, public service broadcasters are strongly opposed to the detailed ex ante evaluations of new services and market analysis obligations proposed in the draft communication (see EBU 2009; Nordic PSB 2009). A number of comments noted that it would be inappropriate to assume that the new services of public service companies need more far-reaching regulation than traditional television and radio. The EBU (2009, 2), for instance, has argued more generally that the Commission should avoid perpetuating the distinction between "old media" and "new media" in European media policy.

The main argument for opposing excessively detailed regulation of the new services is that such rules would not be suited to the requirements of a quickly changing communications environment and restrict the role of public service media in the development of new services. Some comments also criticize the Commission's approach and its underlying assumptions more generally. The Open Society Institute, for instance, questioned the Commission's approach and general tone. The Commission communication as a whole, it said, is based on the false assumption that public service broadcasters present a serious danger to the health of Europe's audiovisual sector and that there is an urgent need to strengthen protections against their expansion into new media. The same comment is also critical of the assumption that public service broadcasting should be defined in contrast to "existing commercial offers," for such arguments are usually associated with commercial actors' vested interest in keeping public service broadcasters away from the mass audience (OSI 2009).

In particular, there has been controversy over the notion that any new media activities in which public broadcasters engage should be closely associated with their traditional remit, which for some is tantamount to curbing the expansion of public service activities into digital platforms (see Donders and Pauwels 2008, 305). It is felt that the Commission is in this way trying to discourage the innovation of new services or the expansion of the public service remit beyond its traditional domain. However, as public broadcasters argue, such stagnation in the changing media environment would not mean upholding the status quo, but on the contrary further marginalize the scope of public service communication.

Moreover, the attempts to curb the expansion of public service media are in stark contrast with the general vision of the future shared by both public broadcasters and most media policy scholars, who now tend to see public service media as a broader principle or a model of media governance that is not limited to traditional broadcasting or its specific institutions.

As discussed in Chapter 5, public service media are seen in this vision as playing an important role as an innovator of new services and in providing cohesion and guidance in the new media environment (Born 2006; Enli 2008; Harrison and Wessels 2005; Murdock 2005; Syvertsen 2003).

In contrast to the calls to limit the public service remit to certain genres or platforms, organizations such as the EBU, the Council of Europe, and the European Parliament have made a strong case for a broader technology and platform neutral definition of public service media. A recent Council of Europe recommendation on the remit of public service media (2007b) states that "the public service remit is all the more important in the information society and that it can be discharged by public service organisations via diverse platforms and an offer of various services, resulting in the emergence of public service media." In its resolution on the risks of violation of freedom of expression and information, the European Parliament (2004) similarly emphasizes that the concept of public service broadcasting needs to evolve beyond traditional broadcasting, for "the development of new media services is becoming increasingly important in order to fulfill their remit to provide pluralistic content," and that it "is important that public service broadcasting content reaches audiences through as many distribution networks and systems as possible."

Moreover, in its resolution on concentration and pluralism, the European Parliament (2008a) has further demanded that the regulations governing state aid should be implemented in a way that takes these needs into account. The EBU also urges member states to make comprehensive use of this competence "rather than allowing the State aid experts of the Commission to second-guess what exactly is covered, or, worse still, in their view is not covered by a given national definition of the public broadcasting remit" (EBU 2004).

All these documents furthermore forcefully emphasize the importance of assuring adequate funds for public service organizations so that they can fulfill these services. Accordingly, in the consultation process for the review of the Broadcasting Communication, advocates of public service broadcasting argued for a more flexible framework and against detailed criteria for an ex ante evaluation of new media activities. The rationale here is that in the digital age, public service broadcasters should be allowed to reach the public by all possible means, including innovative and experimental use of new media.

According to Hallvard Moe (2009), the EU's emerging approach to public broadcasters' online services seems to signal a break with such visions of a comprehensive remit in at least three ways. Firstly, public broadcasters are ascribed only a supplementary role on the Internet, meaning that they should only complement market actors. Secondly, instead of assessing whole program schedules or broadcast channels, the Commission gauges the delivery of specific new services in isolation. In so doing, the Commission also seeks to separate services tailored to individual demand from those catering to social needs. Thirdly, there is a tendency to see online activities merely as supportive of existing broadcast programs.

As Moe (2009) argues, such an approach, although not blatantly hostile to the idea of public service media beyond broadcasting, is insufficient to grasp the potential value of new platforms. The tendency to assess services in isolation, as individual products for consumers, clearly implies a rationality in which media services and contents are assigned only an economic value and treated as commodities like any others. The implication of these tendencies is that media pluralism becomes conceptualized even more narrowly from the point of view of consumer choice. Altogether this again reflects the broader commodity-oriented approach in media policy, where goals such as coherence, comprehensiveness, and quality are marginalized because they do not fit into the cost-benefit calculus used by the "state aid experts."

The conflict between the contrasting logics of public service media and free competition thus seems to linger and become increasingly complex. With the continuing ambiguity as to what constitutes public service in the changing media landscape, it is likely that the controversies and complaints will not abate but extend to new areas besides funding, including issues such as copyright, program rights, and must-carry requirements.

EXCEPTIONALIZATION OF PUBLIC SERVICE MEDIA

The actual policy outputs on the European level are of course compromises between various demands, and it is difficult to assess their long-term consequences. As noted, public service broadcasters have managed to gather enough support so that their immediate existence is not really in danger. More generally though, a closer analysis of the policy argumentation will help to assess the general intellectual and ideological trends in media policy. In this sense, it seems clear that although not devoid of cultural policy considerations in rhetoric, the dominant approach in EU media policy is fundamentally based on the logic of competition law and the normative framework of consumer choice. Furthermore, there are signs that the perspective guided by competition law, which seeks to level the market across national borders, has increasingly rubbed off on national policy actors' arguments. Today, national authorities increasingly draw on a competition law rationale when addressing the status of public service broadcasting in the national context (see Moe 2009). Even though political actors continue to support the principles of public service broadcasting, the terms of the current European policy debate increasingly indicate its status as a historical anomaly or an exception to "normal" market rules. This consequently restricts the scope of public service media as a comprehensive ethos or a model of governance.

Even though the Commission's communication on state aid rules, for instance, appears to be somewhat sympathetic to the presence of public service media on all platforms, it clearly defines the agenda in terms of fair competition and exceptions granted to existing institutions, and not in terms of actually considering how the principles of public service media could be extended or reimagined.

As Donders and Pauwels (2008, 298) put it, the debate is framed in such a way that "public broadcasting organizations in the broadcasting market are thus a priori inhibitors of market functioning, rather than market and innovation facilitators." Both from an ideological and regulatory point of view, the continuous questioning of public broadcasting also attests to the fact that public support is no longer taken for granted as an essential tool of media policy. Premised on the aim of creating a level playing field for media companies, the whole apparatus of applying state aid rules to public broadcasters clearly expresses the idea that public service broadcasters are primarily seen as market competitors of commercial companies (ibid.). All this is compatible with the broader shift where all media, including public service broadcasting, are increasingly seen as serving consumer needs, instead of the earlier rationales that saw public service broadcasting as a universal public utility or as a tool for active citizenship and the public sphere (see Syvertsen 2004). This further supports the idea that European media policy has evolved beyond its public service phase to a new paradigm, devoted primarily to economic goals (cf. van Cuilenburg and McQuail 2003).

The European Union's state aid regime is only one example of a broader trend where the activities of public broadcasters have become subject to more scrutiny overall. Due to the increasing scrutiny from the private broadcasting lobby and the EU, several European countries have developed new accountability frameworks whereby public broadcasters must meet specific targets in the shape of performance indicators or broadcasting audits (Bardoel et al. 2005; Coppens 2005).

Unsurprisingly, such mechanisms have been particularly advocated by commercial interests. As the Association of Commercial Television in Europe puts it in one of its position papers, "the role of state aid in the media [ought] to be considered with appropriate economic rigour rather than on the abstract or emotional criteria often advanced by some stakeholders" (ACT 2009a, 1). In line with this, the new Broadcasting Communication includes demands for more new control mechanisms and performance metrics to make sure that public broadcasters comply with the competition rules. One way to assess the relevance, market impact, and cost/value of any new public service is provided by so-called *public value tests* that have been introduced in different versions in various member states of the EU (see Donders and Pauwels 2010; Moe 2010).

As a result, the idea of empirical performance analysis is now firmly embedded in public service broadcasting policy. Although the idea that public service media need to account for their actions to some independent regulatory body is hardly unreasonable in itself, it is evident that the analysis of the public broadcaster's performance involves huge methodological problems, both in principle and in practice.

Performance analysis, in whatever form, can be valuable if it furthers public discussion on the values that public broadcasters are expected to serve. However as Coppens (2005) notes, there will always be the danger that the very wording of the criteria and the way in which they are applied become excessively important, thereby shifting the focus of media policy further away from public political discussion to technocratic expert assessment. According to Freedman (2008, 157), public value tests, for instance, will generate enormous amounts of data "that are far better suited to an understanding of broadcasting as a straightforward economic, rather than a complex social and cultural practice."

Although public value tests have already been implemented in many countries, with varying scope and measures, their actual political consequences remain open to debate and further empirical scrutiny. For the purposes of this book, however, it is noteworthy that they indicate a commitment to a certain type of political reasoning, regardless of how they will eventually be used.

In general, it seems that soft governance and the increasing reliance on self-regulation and coregulation by industry and internal committee governance have not furthered public political discussion. While soft governance methods can make strides in forwarding policy consensus, they also create problems in terms of transparency, accountability, legitimacy, and democratic input (see Harcourt 2008; Michalis 2007; Moe 2009). As such, the model of soft governance has some clear parallels with technocratic and depoliticized governance that takes place in isolation from public debate. In the case of evaluation criteria, these fears are reinforced by the fact that the media industry itself can exert significant influence on the criteria and their application.

The approach that conceives of public broadcasting as an island of social responsibility with obligations and that maintains that further deregulation is needed in the commercial sector for success in global competition, can also be seen as a clear paradigm shift in European media policy. In many European countries, the main commercial channels are subject to various forms of public interest regulation. Traditionally, the dual system operated in many European countries provided a structural incentive for commercial broadcasters to compete qualitatively with public broadcasters. Public service broadcasting was seen to constitute the core of the media system, and it was expected to have a role in upholding quality standards for the commercial media, too. Furthermore, many media policy scholars have argued that this public service element in commercial television should be further strengthened through more effective regulation.

It seems that the idea of public service institutions as the core of media systems has increasingly been abandoned and that they are explicitly seen as an exception to the dominant form of market-based media governance. This makes it increasingly difficult to examine or assess the performance of public service media with anything other than market criteria.

The extent to which this rationality has prevailed over a more cultural and social agenda in various contexts is debatable. However, it seems clear that the recent debates on public service broadcasting strengthen a political rationality where competitive markets are increasingly seen as unquestioned and normalized. Even if public broadcasters are granted a continued exception to serve "the democratic, social and cultural needs of each society" in the current regulatory climate, the regime as a whole only seems to naturalize free market competition as the main form of media governance.

Another consequence of this framing of the debate is that almost all attempts to justify public service media tend to be defensive and aimed at protecting existing institutions. Even policies that are presented as victories for public service broadcasting, such as the Amsterdam Protocol, only serve to maintain the status quo. Arguments for a more ambitious media policy reform that would seek to expand the principles of public service media, on the other hand, are practically off the agenda.

RETHINKING PUBLIC SERVICE MEDIA AND PLURALISM

The changing environment and increasing scrutiny on public service media have created a need to rethink the guiding principles of public service media and the type of institutions best suited to put these principles into practice. However, the argument here is that this rethinking should not take place on the basis of quantitative economic indicators only or by state aid experts.

Instead, it should be based on a public and transparent political debate over the values and principles we expect from public communication. As Karol Jakubowicz (2007) argues, a discussion about public service media is inevitably about different social principles and value systems, even though it is often veiled in the pragmatic rhetoric of inevitable technological and economic adaptation.

In this sense, the attempts to rethink the notion of public service media in the digital age have arguably been limited by their lack of grounding in broader social and political debates (see Born 2006). To contribute to such debate, this section will leave aside immediate policy concerns and discuss the guiding principles of public service media from the perspective of democratic theory and the discussion in the first part of this book.

As noted above, public service broadcasters in Europe have generated enough support and lobbying power to assure their continued existence. Unlike in the United States, most European countries share at least a provisional consensus that guarantees public service media a sustained role in the evolving media environment. The problem with the argumentation of the public service organizations and their defenders, however, is that instead of genuine reflection on the future of public service values, it is mostly aimed at preserving existing institutions. Consequently, their use of principles such as pluralism, diversity, and quality too tends to be as self-serving as it is for commercial media companies. Therefore, public broadcasters too can be criticized for failing to articulate adequate intellectual arguments for their continued relevance.

In this sense, many observers have argued that the reactive treatment of existing public service institutions as the epitome of quality, pluralism, balance, and universal accessibility is myopic and too defensive (Curran 2002; Keane 1991). Instead, academic commentators of public broadcasting policy tend to agree that there is a need for a shift of focus from the specific institutions of public service broadcasting to a broader notion of public service media or public service communication (see Born 2006; Bardoel and Lowe 2007; Lowe 2008).

Even in academic debates, however, there are different ways of understanding the notion of public service media. The concrete reason for replacing the notion of public service broadcasting with public service media is of course provided by technological change. Many scholars have argued, for instance, that traditional public service objectives are constrained by particular institutional arrangements that do not necessarily enable audiences and users to shape and produce their own public service communication. Instead, new forms of public service communication should allow for new forms of audience participation (Aslama 2009; Harrison and Wessels 2005, 835–36; Lowe 2008).

In many ways, existing public service organizations can already claim that they are moving in this direction with their multiplatform strategies. In addition to this, however, there is a broader notion of public service media which is not limited to old public service organizations. This is evident in the argument of Graham Murdock (2005), for instance: "We have to stop thinking of public broadcasting as a stand-alone organisation and see it as the principal node in an emerging network of public and civil initiatives that taken together, provide the basis for new shared cultural space, a digital commons, that can help forge new communal connections and stand against the continual pressure for enclosure coming from commercial interests on the one hand and the new moral essentialism on the other" (Murdock 2005, 213–14). In line with this, the conception of public service media used here refers not only to a characterization or description of certain existing institutions, but to a particular model of media governance. Rather than tying the fate of public service media to those existing institutions, the notion of public service media could provide an alternative logic to the hegemony of the free market model in media policy and also serve the broader attempts to create communication structures that are accountable neither to the market nor the state but to the public at large (Syvertsen 2003, 156–58).

A broader approach would also avoid the opposition of public and commercial television, which continues to dominate European policy debates. As noted above, public service media are increasingly conceived in the present regime as an island of social responsibility with obligations, while commercial actors should be further deregulated in order to succeed in the global competition. If understood more broadly as a logic of media governance, however, public service regulation could be seen as something that can be applied to different institutions to a varying degree (see Nieminen 2010).

But what are the guiding principles on which the new public service media should be based? Rather than the ritualistic invocation of pluralism or quality, there is a need to fundamentally rethink how public service media can contribute to a pluralistic public sphere.

Even though pluralism and diversity are increasingly invoked as the key values in the name of which public service broadcasting is defended, the relationship of public broadcasting and pluralism is somewhat contradictory. As noted above, it is hard to deny that historically, public service broadcasting has often had a rather conservative and socially exclusive character. As centralized, bureaucratic organizations that were characterized by unifying rather than diversifying ends, they have been conceived as means to cement national cultural values and to cultivate a common identity (Blumler 1992, 11; Williams 1975, 28).

Accordingly, the concern for unity and cohesion is still present in many contemporary discussions on the role of public service media in providing national identity, social cohesion, and political integration. In European media policy debates, public service media and their mass audience programming are seen to generate a shared sense of community, social cohesion, and belonging (EBU 2004; Harrison and Woods 2001, 483). As noted in Chapter 5, these functions are often regarded as even more vital at a time of audience fragmentation.

Overall, public service broadcasters are faced with the partly conflicting demands of contributing to both pluralism and coherence. As Richard Collins (1998, 58) has argued, the role of public broadcasting as "an emancipator of its audience" is potentially at odds with its role of "providing a national cultural cement." The cultural mandate of public broadcasting has traditionally included the idea that broadcasters should lead rather than follow public and popular taste. With the rise of the new logic of consumer sovereignty and freedom of choice, broadcasters have found themselves skewered on the contradiction of satisfying the public as audience and fulfilling their educational and cultural mandate (Collins 1998, 59).

Because of these tensions, defending the institution of public service broadcasting in the name of pluralism requires some qualifications, or at least more elaboration than the straightforward arguments based on consumer choice employed by commercial media. It is perhaps more justified to consider public service broadcasting as an institutional compromise that reflects the necessity to reconcile the needs for unity and pluralism, which both can be justified with reference to democratic theory. Public service broadcasting can be understood as a media policy tool usable for differently conceived functions based on different social and cultural aims.

Of course, there is no point in trying to look for equivalence between the institutional practices of public service media and some theoretical model of democracy. Rather, critical normative theories can be seen as resources with which to reflect upon those institutions, their deficiencies, shortcomings, and promises. The problem raised by the above discussion, however, is that such reflection is quickly losing its arenas if the assessment of public service media is confined to technocratic and managerial public value tests—rather than being weighed in a thorough political discussion.

Since the 1980s the theoretical defense of public service broadcasting has drawn heavily on the Habermasian public sphere thesis. Within this paradigm, public service broadcasting has been put forward as the institutional space which is in the best position to realize the principles of communicative action in the public sphere: it has been seen to foster rational debate, enlighten the population, and provide a common, universalistic space for public deliberation. As Nicholas Garnham (1992, 371) prominently argued, more than any other media, public service broadcasters have been seen to provide forums "of matching scale that occupy the same social space as that over which economic or political decisions will impact." In this discourse, public service broadcasting is seen not only as a bulwark against commercialization, but also as a counterforce to audience fragmentation, a means of public communication within a unitary public sphere.

In the current situation, the attempts to legitimate public service broadcasting with reference to the Habermasian public sphere have been questioned on several levels. First, they can be criticized for portraying public service broadcasting too simplistically and uncritically as the institutional guarantor and embodiment of the public sphere. Secondly, the contributions in question have mostly built on a reading of Habermas's early public sphere theory, which has often been criticized for its biases towards a certain conception of rationality and consensus. Therefore, many scholars have sought to contest the mobilization of the public sphere thesis by problematizing the affinity assumed between a unitary model of a public sphere and public service broadcasting and by invoking a more pluralistic conception of multiple public spheres (see Curran 2002; Jacka 2003; Keane 1991). Reflecting the general pluralist ethos, Keane argued that instead of monolithic organizations, fulfilling public service require the "development of a plurality of nonstate and nonmarket media that function as permanent thorns in the side of state power, and serve as the primary means of communication for citizens living within a diverse and horizontally organized civil society" (Keane 1991, 150).

More recently, other scholars have argued that in a political and cultural environment that has promoted difference and diversity, arguments for public service media also need to consider more fully the issues of pluralism. According to Georgina Born (2006), writers have either advocated the public service model in which television is seen in terms of a unified public sphere, or they have welcomed the likely demise of public broadcasting, linking it to the rise of digital and narrowcast media which allow for the articulation of new identities and politics and the growth of plural public spheres. New normative thinking about democratic functions of public service media, Born continues, should therefore be sought not from old idealizations of the unitary public sphere, but from the political philosophy of radical and plural democracy.

So far, writers who have based their arguments on post-Habermasian democratic theory have mostly seen public service broadcasting as an outdated notion that bears no relevance in postmodern semiotic democracy (see Jacka 2003). The argument here, however, is that the radical pluralism of theorists such as Chantal Mouffe can also be used to defend and justify a continued role for public service media.

From the perspective of radical pluralism, public service media can also be seen as a space for exhibiting and experiencing differences and disagreements—as something akin to the agonistic and open contestation of views advocated by theorists of radical and plural democracy. No longer an agent for standardizing national unity or imposing consensus, it has been implied that public service media could then be reinvented as a medium for creating new relations between varied publics, conflicting ideas, perspectives, and multiple identities (see Craig 2000; Ellis 2000; Lowe 2008).

Such arguments clearly reflect the pluralist tendencies in contemporary democratic theory. In line with the radical pluralist approach, it is possible to think of public service broadcasting as a meeting point for conflicting ideas and perspectives, or as Murdock (2005) puts it, as a node in the network of various public and civil initiatives. This would involve, as Sunstein (2007, 192) has noted, the "creative use of links to draw people's attention to multiple views." However, such a conception remains fundamentally ill-suited to the policy framework where public service broadcasting is conceptualized as the lone institutional exception to market-based media. In contrast to the technocratic paradigm that dominates European policy debates, these visions thus require a more qualitative and holistic conception of media pluralism, which is not something that can be discovered through quantitative studies.

As many academic scholars have argued, public service media cannot be complicit with the debate that reduces pluralism to consumer choice. Instead, they need to defend a more principled justification of a noncommodified communication system. As James Curran (2002, 204) argues, this is only possible if public service theorists step outside the framework of market thinking: "In the nature of things, the market is an aggregation of individual decisions, and does not have a conception of the needs of society. What a revised rationale for public service broadcasting should attempt to do is to identify these wider needs, and explain why they are best fulfilled through public service arrangements."

In the current rationality of competition policy, public service broadcasting too has increasingly been redefined as service delivery to the consumer rather than serving the needs of society. And if public broadcasters defend pluralism only in terms of catering to different tastes and preferences rather than the broader democratic rationale of giving expression to various perspectives and cultures, then they have already conceded the terms of the debate to the rationality of the marketplace. In this sense, arguments based on "market failure," for instance, provide only short-term legitimation for public service media, for it can always be argued that the reason for market failures is only that markets are underdeveloped.

The argument that legitimates public service media in terms of correcting market failures is thus too lame in that it yields to the general discourse of consumer choice and market competition. The problem remains, however, that the space for developing alternative political arguments about the future role of public service media seems to be withering away as media policy moves in a more technocratic direction and towards a system that assesses public service broadcasting as a single institutional exception to the otherwise unquestioned virtues of "fair" competition and unrestrained market forces.

The contention here, by contrast, is that the ideal of media pluralism and the institutional models it implies have to be evaluated in the light of (different) conceptions of pluralistic democracy and the public sphere, and not simply by reference to the criteria of effective competition and consumer choice in media markets. With the emergence of empirical indicators and audits in European media policy it seems inevitable that "the politics of criteria" will only gain further importance as definitions and measurements become even more crucial points of political contestation.

CHAPTER 7

Empirical Indicators and the Politics of Criteria

This chapter analyzes in more detail the implications of the increasing tendency to treat media pluralism and diversity as tangible, empirically measurable concepts. As noted above, the demand for objective empirical data has recently been growing in the field of media policy. Reflecting the application of various empirical indicators and performance metrics in policy making, there is also a growing body of academic research that addresses media pluralism and diversity as measurable concepts.

The justification of policies by reference to empirical, objective data can be viewed as an attempt to bring closure to the political contestation in the name of scientific objectivity or expert knowledge. However, for the purposes of this book, the metrics and indicators can be seen as another arena where the meaning of the concept of media pluralism is contested. This is because the selection of data, definitions, and criteria always involves choices of what aspects of pluralism are deemed more important than others. So rather than viewing empirical indicators as more neutral tools, I argue that it is more useful to view diversity indexes and metrics as "governmental technologies" through which certain definitions and political rationalities become institutionalized and normalized.

My argument is not directed against the use of empirical data in media policy as such, for it is easy to see how they can serve as a knowledge base for public policy and debate. Instead, my aim is to show that the use of empirical data is also political. It does not offer a means to evade the need to tackle the normative questions raised in this book, and it certainly does not relieve policy makers from making normative judgments.

In contrast to terms such as media quality, freedom, or social responsibility, there is something about the notions of pluralism and diversity themselves that seems to make them appear more compatible with the needs of technocratic expert assessment in media policy. In policy debates, this has become evident in the development of the infamous Diversity Index by the US policy makers as well as in the attempts of the European Commission to develop the indicators of the Media Pluralism Monitor. As the study that outlined the Media Pluralism Monitor states, empirical indicators are seen to give "a stronger evidentiary basis to define priorities and actions for improving media pluralism" and "ensure a uniform basis for dealing with pluralism issues and provide a more objective basis for the often heated political and economic arguments" (ICRI et al. 2009, 3).

This marks a notable difference from the concept of quality. Pluralism and diversity imply value-freedom and objectivity that is better suited for the purposes of objective policy analysis, and they give the policy discourse a certain veneer of scientific neutrality. However, the tendency to conceive of pluralism as an empirically measurable value also implies a shift from normative and political questions to more narrowly defined technocratic and market-driven definitions of media and culture, a move which itself is not without normative and political implications. At worst, the reliance on empirical data can veil political conflicts and obscure the normative aspects of evaluating media performance and setting policy objectives. In this sense, this chapter seeks to repoliticize the empirical indicators of media pluralism.

FROM POLITICAL RATIONALITIES TO GOVERNMENTAL TECHNOLOGIES

Throughout this book I have emphasized that all policy paradigms need some kind of theoretical basis that is made up of concepts as well as a way of defining and measuring those concepts. So far I have dealt with some of the problems and normative contradictions involved in media pluralism as a theoretical and political concept. However, policy making cannot be viewed simply as a process of implementing particular political or normative doctrines. As neo-Foucauldian perspectives on governmentality in particular have emphasized, the incorporation of these concepts and theories into governmental practice always necessitates connection with various administrative techniques and forms of calculation which modify, if not transform, the theories and their objectives (Dean 1999; Rose and Miller 1992). The political rationalities that I analyze in the previous chapter cannot thus be divorced from the mechanisms or technologies through which they are put into effect and through which they become institutionalized and normalized in the practices and calculations of policy making.

If political rationalities refer to the discursive fields within which politics and its aims and limits are justified, then governmental technologies refer to the complex of mundane programs, calculations, techniques, apparatuses, documents, and procedures through which these rationalities are institutionalized and solidified into part of political common sense (see Rose and Miller 1992, 175–76). While political rationalities can be conceived as paradigms or cognitive schemas through which political problems are conceptualized, then governmental technologies are the means by which they are institutionalized and put into practice.

Based on the recent research into the role of ideas and concepts in public policy, it can be argued that the success of political ideas and paradigms often relies not on grand ideological clashes, but on their ability to become institutionalized and embedded in the norms, standard practices and calculations of policy making (see Hay 2004; regarding media policy, see also Napoli 2007). Reports, discussion papers and other policy documents themselves can thus be conceived as governmental technologies. However, in addition to political declarations and regulations, it is especially apposite to analyze how different statistical measures of media pluralism and diversity have been generated and mobilized by both policy actors and researchers and to examine their consequences for the broader debate on media pluralism.

Notwithstanding the importance of rendering the performance of the media in indexes, metrics, and numbers, it is widely acknowledged that empirical measures cannot give a complete picture of the complex issues involved. Yet such statistical exercises can become self-fulfilling prophecies. In a policy-making environment driven by the demand for empirical data, the aspects that are measurable easily become the focus of policy debate, which further distances media policy from broader political and democratic values.

THE DEMAND FOR EMPIRICAL EVIDENCE IN POLICY MAKING

The growing efforts in the media policy field to bring a stronger empirical-objective orientation to the principles of diversity and pluralism are by no means exceptional. The tendency to rely on empirical measurement and metrics is in many ways typical of contemporary politics and can be viewed as part of a broader turn towards evidence-driven policy making, in which policy making across all fields has become more data and research-driven and the mindsets of policy makers have become more and more weighed in favor of arguments based on empirical data in contrast to value judgments.

As Napoli and Seaton (2007) argue, regulatory decision making inevitably involves the blending and balancing of empirical findings with normative judgments. As noted above though, the role of value judgments is currently being marginalized by a greater reliance on empirical research, as part of a greater "rationalization" of policy decision making.

This reflects a broader tendency to rely on what policy makers see as more reliable quantitative methods. According to Des Freedman's (2008, 97–98) interviews with American and British policy makers, there is an increasing sentiment that "decision-making about the media, like any other area of public policy, should be guided by scientific, rather than abstract principles and by objective, not politicized sources of information." The reliance on empirical evidence is thus commonly seen as a safeguard against vested interests, as a tool for more objective decision making.

On the other hand, the use of empirical data can also be associated with the institutionalization of the new neoliberal policy paradigm and a shift from normative to technocratic political rationalities (Hay 2004). Following from this, Hay argues, political rhetoric is increasingly couched in terms of the non-negotiable character of external, either economic or empirical-objective imperatives, which are difficult to reconcile with the various normative views on public interest.

As part of this trend in media policy, efforts ranging from public value tests to various empirical indicators of media pluralism and diversity seek to empirically assess the performance of the media.[1] The roots and most visible signs of this development can be seen in the United States, where economic analysis has traditionally had a greater role in media policy than in Europe (Hitchens 2006, Freedman 2008).

While the use of empirical tools has been especially contested in recent debates on media diversity and concentration in the United States, the broader trend remains unchanged. In European media policy the logic of empirical assessment only seems to be strengthening, as is clear from the development of ever more specific objectives and performance criteria. In all, the need for empirical diversity measurement and assessment largely derives from demands for a stronger base for the legitimation of public policy intervention. The simple reliance on the policy rhetoric of public interest and its component values such as pluralism is considered insufficient for

---

[1] Aside from the measurement of media pluralism, the proliferation of various empirical indexes can also be seen in many other areas, such as democracy and human rights, freedom of expression, media development, and media sustainability (see ICRI et al. 2009, 14; Napoli 2007, xviii)

policy makers who seek empirical data with which to justify their actions. It seems that the idea of performance assessment based on "reliable and objective evidence" is now firmly embedded in European media policy too, as it has been in American debates for some time.

Aside from the initiative of the European Commission, the demand for empirical evidence has also been raised by the Council of Europe (2009, 11), which has recently recommended that all "member states should set up, if this has not been done yet, specialized bodies for, and establish systems of, monitoring media landscape with special emphasis on media pluralism and diversity." The survey conducted by the Council of Europe (2009) indicates that existing measures can take many forms, from qualitative reports to different types of quantitative information.

While it is difficult for anyone to dispute the benefits of improved monitoring, the demand for empirical data makes it crucial to consider the political implications of different types of measures and to determine the most useful ways of using these monitoring tools.

EXCURSION: LESSONS FROM THE UNITED STATES

Although the focus of this book has been on European debates, it is worth making a brief excursion into recent communication policy debates over media pluralism and diversity in the United States. For some time now, US policy makers have shown a tendency to approach media diversity as a tangible and empirically measurable concept rather than merely a normative justification for policy initiatives (see Baker 2007; Howley 2005; Napoli 1999; 2007). However, with the recent politicization of the debate on media ownership, the definitions of the concept of diversity and its measurement have also begun to attract unprecedented debate. Now that the European debates on media pluralism are moving in the direction of developing new empirical indicators, it is useful to reflect briefly on these experiences.

Media ownership and diversity emerged as issues of public debate in 2003 when the Federal Communications Commission (FCC) announced its plans to overhaul (relax) existing restrictions on media ownership and introduced its ill-fated Diversity Index[2] to assess the level of diversity in various markets (FCC 2003). The index was essentially based on a methodology

---

[2]The FCC's Diversity Index (DI) was designed to reflect the degree of concentration in local markets by measuring the availability of outlets of various types. It assigns a weight to each class of outlet (radio, newspaper, television, and so on) based on their relative value to consumers. The Diversity Index was modeled on the Herfindahl-Hirschmann Index (HHI), which is used in antitrust analysis to measure the degree of concentration in an economic market.

for measuring the effects of market concentration on viewpoint diversity in any given media markets. As we have seen with many European proponents of liberalization, the argument put forward by the FCC and the major media corporations that supported the Commission was that because of the growth of competition and the new technologies, ownership concentration presented little threat to media diversity.

Reflecting a firm conviction in the liberating effects of markets and new technologies and following the deregulatory agenda set in the Telecommunications Act of 1996, the FCC argued that today's media marketplace is characterized above all by abundance:

> Americans today have more media choices, more sources of news and information, and more varied entertainment programming available to them than ever before . . . and, via the Internet, Americans can access virtually any information, anywhere, on any topic. (FCC 2003, point 3)
>   Nonetheless, . . . our broadcast ownership rules, like a distant echo from the past, continue to restrict who may hold radio and television licenses as if broadcasters were America's information gatekeepers. Our current rules inadequately account for the competitive presence of cable, ignore the diversity-enhancing value of the Internet, and lack any sound basis for a national audience reach cap. (Ibid., point 4)

In short, these arguments repeat a version of the familiar refrain of policy makers all over the world, including the current debates within the European Union: the existing rules no longer reflect the current media environment; technological advances have provided access to more media and information; scarcity is no longer a constraint; industries must be allowed to expand and exploit the opportunities offered by new media; and regulation should be removed where the marketplace can provide services (see Hitchens 2006, 3). The new rules proposed by the FCC would have increased the number of television and radio stations that one entity can own in a local market, relaxed the ban on owning a television station and a newspaper in the same market, and raised the cap on the proportion of television households a single corporation can reach nationally from 35 percent to 45 percent.

However, the decision ignited a surprising storm of criticism, sparking arguably more public debate than media policy questions ever had before. According to McChesney (2007, 159): "What was crucial in 2003 was that the light switch went on for millions of Americans. They did not have to accept all the problems with the media as an 'unalterable' given. The media system was not natural; it resulted from policies." An unusual coalition of public interest organizations and private citizens from across the political spectrum banded together to oppose the FCC's decision and tried to get it overturned. Subsequently this criticism also led to the FCC decision being challenged and eventually frozen in Congress and the federal courts.

In hindsight, the assessment of the magnitude of the political awakening and its long-term implications may be slightly overstated. The debate on media ownership and diversity has since continued, with the FCC reviewing further regulatory revisions, many of them still intensely contested. However, among other things the developments have generated a continuing debate on the proper ways to empirically measure diversity and on how to conceptualize diversity and pluralism in the media (Baker 2007; Howley 2005; Napoli 2007; Napoli 2011). The legal challenge to the rules that was brought by a number of public interest groups revolved largely around whether the FCC's diversity index provided a reasoned basis for assessing media ownership rules. Following these debates, the failure of the original diversity index is now broadly recognized and the approach taken by the FCC has been discredited. While some scholars have taken the route of redesigning and developing better indexes, others have more categorically rejected the idea that diversity can be empirically measured (Baker 2007, Howley 2005). Baker (2007, 77), for instance, argues that the empirical measurement of diversity "represents a misguided but increasingly common empiricist belief that quantifiable facts can give answers to normative questions—and can do so without any coherent explanation for how the quantified facts even relate to the normative questions."

Essentially, the diversity index was developed in response to the courts' demand for reliable objective evidence on media performance with regard to the policy goals of diversity and pluralism. This was preceded by developments in the early 1990s when judicial courts in the United States expressed increasing irritation at what they saw as unreflective, ritualistic invocation of diversity in defense of various forms of structural regulation on media ownership (Horwitz 2007; Wildman 2007). The courts began to insist on new "nonconjectural" empirical evidence of concentration and diversity and of the efficacy of regulatory remedies. This bears clear similarities with current European debates on media ownership regulation.

As Horwitz (2007) argues, the empirical emphasis also highlights the change in what diversity is understood to mean and the rationales behind media regulation in general. The new rationales cast doubt on the long-standing logic of the assumed relationship between diversity of ownership and diversity of viewpoints and replace it with diversity metrics based on purely quantitative measures. The obvious problem with this is that all the aspects of media pluralism and diversity that cannot be empirically measured are suddenly marginalized.

Furthermore, many critics note that the empirical diversity index itself was antiscientific and designed with a specific purpose in mind. With only a few exceptions, the studies used in the process of developing the index employed either economic or management perspectives and ignored alternative, social, or cultural perspectives. It was later also revealed that the FCC refused to distribute reports that did not support its goals and that it broadly ignored the protests of concerned citizens (Freedman 2008, 99). Besides the problems involved in reducing the complexities of media diversity to a single empirical index, the diversity index was never presented for public review, nor was it peer reviewed or even piloted. Instead, it has been argued that the index was used above all as a means of pleading for certain interest groups and industry interests. Therefore, the decision to relax the ownership rules that was prepared closely with industry representatives was a classic example of the closed nature of communication policy-making—and the problems of objective policy making based on empirical data. While the drafting of the European Media Pluralism Monitor has been more transparent in many ways, it is worth keeping these problems in mind.

Interestingly, the FCC itself has since given up its attempts to measure diversity by means of a single index. According to a more recent communication, in the future the FCC will "not employ any single metric, such as the Diversity Index, because . . . there are too many qualitative and quantitative variables in evaluating different markets and combinations to reduce the task at hand to a precise mathematical formula" (FCC 2008, 43).

The reason for bringing up the debate on the Diversity Index here is that it embodies the two main problems in the debate on media pluralism. First, it highlights the tension between seeing pluralism and diversity as a commodity value (equating it with consumer choice) and a noncommodified and intangible socio-political and democratic value. Secondly, it exposes the various problems in seeing diversity as a linear value that can easily be measured or quantified.

According to Lesley Hitchens (2006, 137–38), this type of empirical economic analysis has had an especially strong influence in US media policy and ownership policy. Even more so than in Europe, US communication policy documents are replete with economic data and competition analysis, presented as evidence of the degree of diversity to be found in a given market. However, as the experiences of the American diversity index indicate, it is not always clear whether this makes the outcome less or more arbitrary.

In fact, it can be argued that the nature of communication policy decision making and the reliance on empirical data tends to systematically skew policy making towards market-driven objectives and prejudice against intangible cultural and social objectives. This is because the industry arguments and the commodified aspects of media pluralism in general, are often easier to articulate and measure in economic terms—not to mention the fact that industry has overwhelming resources to gather and influence such data.

A more positive outcome of these developments was that they sparked widespread public debate on the value and meaning of media diversity. Given the ambiguity of pluralism and diversity as media policy objectives, the value-freedom implicit in attempts to render them empirically measurable have only highlighted their contestability. This also lends weight to my argument that despite the veneer of scientific neutrality, no discourses on media pluralism are neutral either socially or scientifically. Instead, they inevitably involve a number of presuppositions about the nature of the media, the public sphere, and its functions in society.

Europe has not seen any similar turning point in the debates on media pluralism. Media pluralism has not become an issue of public concern or advocacy campaigns to the same extent as in the United States. Yet the developments in the United States are bound to have consequences in Europe as well. The European Commission's recent approach and the study it commissioned on empirical indicators of media pluralism point not only to a renewed interest in pluralism as a policy issue, but also to an acute need to debate alternative definitions of media pluralism and the consequences of its different conceptualizations and empirical operationalization. If the empirical measurement of diversity and pluralism has been controversial in the American context, where media policy is traditionally much more market-oriented than in Europe, there are bound to be problems in Europe, too, where the tradition of public service broadcasting and other seemingly nonmeasurable media policy arrangements have much stronger historical roots.

THE TROUBLE WITH METRICS: PERFORMANCE ASSESSMENT AND POLICY MAKING

According to Philip Napoli (2005, 6), scholars and advocates concerned with the role of the media in a democratic public sphere must choose between the lesser of two evils: "One is to cede the increasingly influential empirical space that policymakers increasingly are asking to have filled to those who may have different policy priorities. The other is to risk undermining the policies and principles at the core of the role of the media in a democratic public sphere by treating these principles and policies as requiring empirical support via methods that may in fact be somewhat ineffective in doing so." While Napoli readily declares that the latter choice is more productive,

I argue in this chapter that it is also necessary to retain more radical criticism of the technocratic trends in media policy.

The trend towards greater quantitative rigor in public policy making has itself been the subject of much debate, discussion, and critique. The tendency to introduce empirical indicators and metrics in media policy can be seen as part of a wider phenomenon through which the "room for real political change has been displaced by a technology of expertise" (Edkins 1999, xii). Arguably, decision making in the EU provides an especially clear example of this phenomenon where the role of citizens is simply to be persuaded by the arguments of experts, while the only role of politicians is to engage more fully in that task of persuasion. Similarly, equally vital to European politics is the recurrent emphasis on the claim to a type of economic knowledge that is technically correct, universal, and apolitical.

According to Nielsen (2003), the roots of these ideas lie in the diminishing possibilities of political decisions to shape policy, and on the other hand, the increasing needs to control social complexity. This has created a need for new administrative instruments of control, "disciplining mechanisms that formally, but potentially also in practice, ensure central government's continued control over the tasks it has delegated to decentralised levels" (ibid., 240).

It can be argued that the emphasis on empirical and objective data echoes the current neoliberal policy discourse and its vision of a society driven by individualistic cost-benefit thinking. Critically speaking, the role of expertise is often acknowledged as a central legitimating feature of neoliberalism. As Pierre Bourdieu and Loïc Wanquant (2001, 5) argued, neoliberal "NewSpeak" relies on experts employed in ministries, corporations and think tanks to come up with highly technical documents and justifications for neoliberal policy decisions that are actually made on ideological rather than spuriously technical grounds. Their mission is thus to give a scientific veneer to the political projects of state and business elites.

It is not difficult to identify several problems in the administrative discourse of evaluation. First, it seems evident that it involves inherent oversimplifications that result from the translation of political issues or concepts as complex as media pluralism into objective empirical measures. It is unsurprising therefore that the measurement paradigm has received some criticism from those advocating a more qualitative concept, in which pluralism is conceived more as "a way of thinking, something discoverable through qualitative studies" (O'Loughlin 2006, 4).

There is an obvious danger that the adoption of a more intensive empirical orientation towards normative policy principles such as pluralism could ultimately rob these principles of some of their power and influence in the policy-making arena. As Napoli (2005, 6) notes, "in adopting a more intensely empirical stance toward these principles, there is the risk that the empirical support of their value, or of the policies traditionally employed on their behalf, could prove lacking when examined with the limited toolkit of the social sciences. Such results could then undermine the rhetorical strength of these principles in the policymaking and policy advocacy processes."

Secondly, however, empirical data can be questioned on the same grounds with which they are originally justified. Concerns remain about whether it represents a legitimate effort to bring greater objectivity and analysis to policy making, or whether research and empirical analysis itself has been utilized more in support of predetermined policy outcomes. As Napoli and Seaton (2007) acknowledge, rather than necessarily bringing greater objectivity, a greater reliance on research also involves the possibility of biased analyses being injected into the policy process by stakeholders with vested interests in specific policy outcomes (see also Baker 2007; Braman 2008).

As noted above, it can be argued that the nature of communication policy decision making and the reliance on empirical data tends to systematically skew policy making towards market-driven objectives and prejudice against intangible, social, and political objectives. This is because the industry arguments tend to be easier to articulate in terms of economic empirical measurement, while significant actors in the policy process, such as academic researchers and public interest organizations, lack the resources of industry to gain access and influence the data that will be used in policy making (Napoli & Seaton 2007). The privileging of quantitative data and large-scale statistical evidence in particular tends to disempower less well-resourced groups, who cannot afford such data (Freedman 2008, 101). Furthermore, the hostility to "abstract ideas" involved in this tendency has also meant that many of the critical academics are excluded from policy circles (ibid.).

In the case of media policy making regarding media ownership and diversity issues in the United States, Napoli and Seaton (2007) found that the policy arguments of stakeholders who have research to support their arguments (usually industry) typically receive much more serious consideration by policy makers than those with less resources to utilize research, such as public interest organizations.

As Napoli (2008) has observed, it also seems ironic that while the demand for rigorous, defensible empirical analyses has increased in virtually all quarters, the quality, scope, and accessibility of the data necessary to engage in such analyses have not improved respectively. Although it would seem axiomatic that public policy should be based on publicly available data, policy makers at least in the United States tend to rely increasingly on commercial data sources, with much of the data gathering outsourced to commercial firms (Napoli 2008, 806; Braman 2008). The obvious concerns that arise from this are that the terms of access and provisions associated with commercial databases often are too restrictive for an open and transparent policy-making process, and that the data often are gathered with the needs of commercial clients in mind, rather than the needs of policy makers and policy researchers (Braman 2008; Napoli and Seaton 2007; Napoli 2008).

As the case of the diversity index illustrates, if the original criteria for data selection are inaccessible to the public, their objectivity and reliability inevitably falls under suspicion. This is arguably true of administrative policy research more generally. Based on an analysis of evaluation practices in cultural policy, Nielsen has concluded that the evaluation criteria in such studies often remain poorly illuminated and the assessment appears as a goal in itself, as control for control's sake, as "secular rituals that modern, fundamentally incalculable and intractable society invents in order to maintain confidence in its own rationality" (Nielsen 2003, 240).

Overall, there is little reason to assume that the evidence-based approach is impartial or free from bias or political influence. Instead, it simply means that the tensions between different policy objectives, or different political rationalities, are presented as genuinely contrasting choices as they are increasingly veiled in the discourses of expert assessment and empirical criteria.

Furthermore, a broader conception of media pluralism as fair distribution of communicative power in the public sphere is easily marginalized in this kind of policy environment, as it does not readily suit the needs of empirical assessment. This applies to other goals as well. Because the bulk of empirical data used in media policy is currently produced in industrial audience research measuring a market demand, policy legitimation is skewed towards measures that conceptualize public interest as "what the public is interested in," that is, what people are prepared to consume (Raboy, Proulx and Dahlgren 2003, 324). This in turn further strengthens the discourse of consumer sovereignty in media policy.

Similarly, as the above discussion shows, while the market definition of pluralism as consumer choice is rather easily quantified and measured, the more qualitative and multifaceted public service ideals clearly are not. On the contrary, the remit of public service broadcasting, for instance, is especially intangible and normative, embedded in the ideas of public sphere, citizenship, pluralism, creativity, and national culture, all values that are notoriously difficult to define in an unambiguous way, let alone measure empirically (see Coppens 2005). Therefore, the distinction between the market approach of media pluralism, which emphasizes choice and deregulation, and the broader approach, which relies on cultural-political norms of openness and equality, clearly has political consequences.

More fundamental problems arise from the trends where policy making is dominated by a narrow legal-economic framework, rather than a concern for the democratic public sphere or other explicitly normative and usually radically immeasurable goals. To critical theorists concerned with the depoliticization of policy making, the emphasis on instrumental reason and expert knowledge has always been problematic. As Jürgen Habermas (1996b, 45) has put it, rationality in the choice of means often accompanies irrationality in orientation to values, goals, and needs, essentially depriving democratic decision-making of its object. With this in mind, all attempts to define or measure media pluralism involve political and normative choices and contestation over the meaningful norms and criteria of setting policy goals that cannot be reduced to mere facts and figures. Consequently, attempts to impose common criteria or a conceptual framework for analyzing media can be seen as attempts to reach political closure, or attempts to stabilize the political contestation and establish certain criteria and concepts as hegemonic.

Following Nielsen's (2003) critique of evaluation practices in cultural policy, it is easy to concur that a formal and technocratic control discourse that makes no reference to the general normative debate on the functions of the public sphere and the media can have comprehensive consequences for media policy as well. These would potentially include weak public debate on the normative issues related to the media as well as arbitrariness and unintentional consequences in setting policy objectives. Empirical indicators do not remove the need to discuss the underlying rationales of media policies, such as supporting a pluralistic public sphere, and their relation to other objectives such as economic growth or political integration. The use of "objective criteria" in policy decision-making easily misses the fact that these are often contradictory goals whose relative priorities should be politically settled. In any case, in order to make appropriate assessments and develop meaningful metrics, it is necessary at the very least to decide on the value space within which the assessment and measurements are to take place.

WHAT TO MEASURE? ON THE BIASES OF EMPIRICAL INDICATORS

Leaving the more principled critique of technocratic decision-making aside, it is also possible to analyze the efforts to measure pluralism and diversity in a more immanent manner, by examining what it is that the various indexes actually claim to measure. As Edwin Baker (2007, 19–23) notes, the relevance of empirical evidence and the type of evidence needed for any media policy inquiry depends entirely on the issue at hand. However, as some issues are obviously less amenable to measurement by empirical indicators than others, there is the risk that the availability of particular objective data arbitrarily determines what issues are debated. It is necessary therefore to analyze what kind of empirical data would be relevant for debates on media pluralism and what kind of explanations of evidence can and cannot be drawn from that data.

In order to illustrate the kind of political choices that are involved in any empirical tools, I will focus my critique on a few specific problems of some commonly used empirical approaches. Finally, I return to discuss the European Commission's Media Pluralism Monitor and evaluate its claim to be the most comprehensive tool currently available for measuring media pluralism. The main argument here is that the description of media pluralism by reference to any empirical index instead of viewing it in the context of political contestation has political consequences more insidious than the debate on methods of measurement implies.

A variety of approaches are used in different countries to measure media pluralism and diversity, with the indicators used ranging from elaborate frameworks of qualitative and quantitative assessment to rough calculations of market structures or program type diversity (see Council of Europe 2009; Hellman, 2001; McDonald and Dimmick 2003, Coppens 2005, Valcke 2009; van Cuilenburg and van der Wurff 2007). The fact that the study commissioned by the European Commission settled on no less than 166 indicators for assessing media pluralism is a good illustration of this variety.

Traditionally, efforts to measure media pluralism have focused most heavily on the market structure, that is, on measuring the number of sources available. This emphasis is probably explained by a number of factors (see, for example, Harcourt and Picard 2009; Napoli 1999; Napoli 2011). The first is the assumption that plurality of sources represents a fundamental policy objective, regardless of any potential relationships between source diversity and content or exposure diversity. Even if there are no unambiguous methods for establishing the link between source and content diversity, it can be argued that the concentration of media power itself raises obvious concerns. As Jens Cavallin (1998) argues, in terms of democracy and pluralism, as well as freedom of expression and opinion, it is crucial that different social actors are given equal opportunity to exercise influence—power itself is thus at the center of political life. Therefore, the examination should focus on the structures underlying the distribution of power rather than on allegations of abuses of such power.

The second reason for focusing on market structure is that policy makers have embraced the commonly held (though contested) assumption that source diversity serves as an appropriate proxy for content diversity. The third factor involves the hesitancy among policy makers to provoke the concerns that can arise from governmental assessments of media content, as well as their hesitancy to engage with the substantial methodological challenges associated with objectively and reliably measuring content in ways that are sufficiently acceptable to all stakeholders (see Napoli and Gillis 2008). Finally, to the extent that diversity of exposure has resided at the margins of contemporary media policy discourse, it also has resided at the periphery of contemporary media policy research. In contrast to questions about content diversity, let alone exposure diversity, information on the structural aspects of the media system has also been relatively easily available in research on market shares, concentration of ownership, and the sheer number of outlets.

Given the difficulties involved in measuring content or exposure diversity, it may thus be reasonable to suggest that it is better to rely on structural statistics describing media markets and concentration. As noted in the previous chapter, the initiatives put forward in European media policy, for instance, have typically been based on upper limits of ownership and audience shares. However, it has proved difficult to establish any harmonized rules that take into consideration differences between countries, market sizes and the variety of measures used in different member states to assess a company's influence on the market (Doyle 1997; 2007; EC 2005, 6; Harcourt and Picard 2009; Papathanassopoulos 2002, 105–16). To combat these problems, a number of new instruments and methods have recently been introduced in many countries for the assessment and judgment of market power, concentration and media pluralism in communications markers (see Harcourt and Picard 2009; Just 2009; Valcke 2009).

Despite these new methodologies, there remains the more fundamental problem (discussed in Chapter 4) that the relationship between media concentration and pluralism is highly complicated and often appears even contradictory. Preserving a range of separate and autonomous media outlets seems in many ways an obvious and central aspect of protecting media pluralism, yet the relationship between ownership and content diversity is far from linear, and the range of variables that impact pluralism is nearly endless. Despite the fact that in most discussions about media ownership and media pluralism the terms are often elided, the two concepts are not necessarily even related in any linear way; and if the relationship between structural pluralism and content pluralism is not known or is not linear, then the conventional policy approach to inferentially assess pluralism from market concentration and competition does not seem to make much sense (see van Cuilenburg and van Wurff 2007; Ward 2006).

Although it is unarguably important to have access to data on developments in the media market and patterns of ownership, it seems evident that it is impossible on this basis alone to draw any meaningful conclusions about the state of media pluralism. Various attempts have been made to operationalize media pluralism on the level of media content with a view to establishing the link between ownership and content. However, when pluralism is understood in terms of media contents alone, the empirical approach becomes even more problematic both methodologically and politically.

Regardless of the obvious difficulties, there is now an established field of academic research on content diversity, especially concerning television programming. Many European countries have government and regulatory commissioned studies on the diversity of television programming (see Aslama et al. 2004; Aslama et al. 2007; Hellman 2001; van der Wurff 2004). In principle, such research can take any aspect of diversity as a meaningful variable, but in most cases, studies on television programming have focused on the diversity of program types.

According to van der Wurff (2005, 250), program-type diversity is considered a "good, comprehensive and illustrative" indicator of diversity because of two reasons: It is deemed a relevant criterion when making viewing choices; and regulators and governments have deemed it an important policy indicator and monitor about the performance of license holders, and of whether (public) service broadcasters offer enough specific program types.

In reality though, one may well suspect that pragmatic reasons, such as the ease of operationalization and classification, also have as much to do with it. In any case, the interpretation of diversity in terms of program types or genres has become a common focus for both scholarly and policy debates on media diversity (see also McDonald and Dimmick 2003, van Cuilenburg and van der Wurff 2007). Using a standard genre system, these studies usually calculate the range and diversity of program genres on television, identify the balance between different program genres and establish their frequency (Ward 2006, 6).

In Finland, for example, the Ministry of Transport and Communications publishes an annual report that measures the diversity of television programming by calculating the proportion of different program types (such as foreign fiction, factual programming, sports, and so on) and analyzes their relative distribution on the basis of a relative entropy index (see Lehtinen and Aslama 2009). The results of the study indicate that Finnish television continues to offer "a very diverse supply" (ibid., 14).

While this may be convenient methodologically, there are some obvious concerns and questions. For one, such an approach is fully dependent on how genres or program types are classified (what counts as entertainment, current affairs, documentary, and so on). Usually these studies rely on industry-generated categorizations, that is, existing definitions produced by the very same institutions whose performance they are claiming to assess. It can also be questioned whether program type diversity actually has anything to do with the fundamental aims of promoting a variety of opinions and debate that typically lies behind the principle of media pluralism.

These measurements tend to presume consumers whose differentiated preferences are best satisfied by offering a variety of different types of programming. Format variety may have its merits in terms of enhanced consumer choice, but it is a different matter altogether whether that has anything to do with the normative goal of a pluralistic public sphere. In such discourse, media are conceptualized as a consumer good like any other, with no reflection on different social values, openness to new ideas, or other aspects associated with political and cultural pluralism. The general premises of democratic media policy, however, are not conceived simply with respect to creating satisfied customers. At least this by no means exhausts the meaning of declarations on the value of freedom, pluralism and other routinely and consensually praised objectives of public media policies. Such measurements of media pluralism that are based on narrow criteria such as program type diversity can thus be viewed as a governmental technology that, perhaps unintentionally, ends up supporting a political rationality that conceptualizes pluralism in a very narrow and biased way.

In Chapter 6 I suggest that there are some particular problems with empirical research into program type diversity and the institution of public service broadcasting. Although public broadcasters have been in no hurry to discredit those frameworks of performance assessment where they fare well, there are some principled problems that are incompatible with the ethos of public service media. Defining public service media in terms of program type or genres, an assumption that is implicit in much of the debate, is in many ways inconsistent with their broad-ranging cultural and social aspirations that are not based on any quantitative or measurable criteria (Harrison and Woods 2001, 495). Also implicit in much of diversity research is the idea of a division of labor between channels, which easily leads to the conclusion that the public service remit should be limited to serving underprivileged audiences with commercially nonprofitable content.

In addition to program types, it is of course technically possible to use a variety of other measures. There have been individual studies on number of different aspects of pluralism, including subjects and actors that have access to newspaper articles or newscasts. However, each of these is bound to be dependent on the categorizations they use, which typically limits their ability to adopt any broader conception of media pluralism understood as distribution of power. As is amply clear from the measurement of the range of different program types, each choice of criteria will also inevitably have political consequences. As noted above, market-driven media may well provide a diversity of formats or program types while at the same time narrowing the ideological range of voices available. Thus, empirical measurement not only marginalizes any qualitative or holistic ideals of media pluralism, but also always entails choices about the aspects of pluralism that are most valued.

EVALUATING THE MEDIA PLURALISM MONITOR

Given these critiques, the Media Pluralism Monitor (MPM) introduced by the European Commission is an interesting step forward. In comparison with most other measurement tools in current use, it is much more ambitious and represents one of the most sophisticated and comprehensive attempts to bring together various empirical indicators. As noted in Chapter 6, in order to account for the multifaceted character of media pluralism, the MPM indicators relate to various domains, including media ownership, media types and genres, and political, cultural, and geographic pluralism. Furthermore, they claim to cover the various stages of the media value chain, including supply, distribution and use (ICRI et al. 2009, 11–13).

The broad-ranging nature of the MPM also implies that the individual indicators are not intended to be assessed in isolation, but need to be interpreted in the light of related indicators in order to produce "a complete and correct analysis" of the situation (ibid., 21). At least in theory, this is a clear improvement from previous attempts to assess pluralism based on any single criterion, such as ownership or program types.

In its introduction, the study even explicitly acknowledges some of the criticism directed at the empirical measurement of media pluralism, such as the Diversity Index in the United States. In response, the Media Pluralism Monitor seeks to combine quantitative and qualitative indicators in order to account for the various aspects of media pluralism. It also claims to take a holistic approach by measuring not only ownership and concentration, but also other restrictive forces.

Departing from most previous approaches, the design of the study is intended to identify potential risks to media pluralism. This means that the formulation of indicators always start from the question, "what situation could possibly represent risks or threats to media pluralism" (ibid., 21). It can be debated whether this choice has normative implications in itself. The radical pluralist perspectives outlined in the first part of this book, for instance, emphasize that pluralism should be seen as a critical orientation or a radical transformative ideal, rather than as a static state of affairs. In this sense, a risk-based approach can be criticized for producing a somewhat static conception of pluralism. On the other hand, one expert involved in testing the MPM noted that the focus on risks, rather than new opportunities, might lead to a one-sidedly negative assessment of media pluralism (ibid., 131). Yet the approach also has some clear benefits, for it remains open to threats arising from a variety of factors, including both government and market pressures.

In accordance with the broad notion of pluralism, the study includes three types of indicators. The first set of indicators measures the presence of policies and regulatory instruments (including co- and self-regulation) that support pluralism. The second set measures the range of media actually available to citizens in the light of socio-demographic factors, such as geographic location, social class, age, and gender. Finally, a third set of indicators assesses the supply and economic performance of the media, including the number of media companies, competition levels, and concentration ratios. In addition, the MPM includes a supplementary domain that contains indicators for the "essential basic preconditions" of media pluralism, such as regulatory safeguards for freedom of expression, independent regulatory authorities, and policies for promoting media literacy (ibid., 29–30).

Overall, the study seems to take into account most of the aspects and dimensions of pluralism discussed in the academic literature, including this book. In this sense, the range of indicators represents a definite improvement over previous studies where pluralism is reduced to single arbitrary indicators. However, despite its claims that it promotes a comprehensive approach that recognizes the complexity of the issue, questions still remain regarding the practicability of the apparatus.

The obvious critique, acknowledged by the authors of the study themselves, is whether the larger number of different areas and indicators jeopardizes the feasibility of the tool (ICRI et al. 2009, 21, 136). While it cannot be criticized for reducing pluralism to any single indicator, the MPM involves other obvious problems regarding its interpretation and prioritization of different indicators. Given its complexity, the full application of the MPM may thus prove to be very difficult, which may then undermine the holistic purpose of the tool.

The response of the study to this criticism is that the added value of the MPM "lies precisely in the fact that it brings together a host of previously disparate concerns to offer a multi-faceted approach to media pluralism and this is only feasible through a balanced combination of a wide range of indicators" (ibid., 21).

Unsurprisingly, there are some inherent problems in the approach adopted in the study, and especially in the attempt to avert normative judgments by combining both economic and socio-cultural indicators. Despite the rhetoric of objectivity, it is evident that most of the indicators included in the MPM require subjective assessment. The claim that the MPM offers the most neutral measurement tool conceivable in policy terms is thus open to criticism. Given the project's proclaimed aim of providing the "highest possible level of neutrality in this sensitive debate" (ibid., 141), it can be questioned whether the attempt to remain neutral and avoid any divisive issues leads to conservative implications in the sense that potentially sensitive indicators are dropped or undermined, because they would involve normative discussions that the study is not prepared to undertake.

While the study repeatedly emphasizes its objectivity and neutrality, and underplays the normative and political implications of the monitor, it is clear that the monitoring tool is not free from normative choices any more than other measurement tools. As I have argued in this chapter, making definitions, setting indicators and their criteria, and defining border values inevitably involve normative choices.

From the perspective of the broader media policy debate, however, there are also some very positive aspects about the MPM. For instance, it places high premium on the full transparency of measurement methods and their scoring. In contrast to the Diversity Index in the United States, this means the monitoring tool can be used by others as well, not only regulators, but also nongovernmental organizations, academic scholars, and stakeholders (ICRI et al. 2009, 152). The authors of the study also emphasize that the monitor is a dynamic tool that can be updated and further developed based on stakeholder comments and experiences from its use.

Furthermore, despite the recurring rhetoric of neutrality and objectivity, the authors do not claim that theirs is an ultimate response to the challenges of media pluralism. Instead, the MPM is presented as a practical instrument for collecting empirical data on a set of indicators that is considered the most relevant in the contemporary media environment. These data can then be used to stimulate public debate and underpin policy making.

In the end, the most valuable contribution of the monitor is probably that it illustrates the complexity of media pluralism as a policy goal and hopefully leads to some critical self-reflection in the use of some of the narrower indicators. In all, the MPM is an ambitious and interesting experiment that has already furthered debate by assembling a specific research network, organizing the consultation processes and seminars, and simply by keeping the issue of pluralism on the European media policy agenda. Even though it seems that the study will not lead to any concrete political results, it remains to be seen whether it succeeds in influencing the future terms of debate.

TOWARD SELF-REFLECTIVE ASSESSMENT

There are many principled reasons to criticize the enchantment with empirical measurement in general. The representation of media pluralism as a measurable variable, instead of a contested political value, turns media policy away from values and public deliberation towards instrumental rationality and technocratic decision making. Overall, it can hardly be assumed that the paradoxes of pluralism will be solved by doing away with politics and turning political considerations into matters of either individual choice or expert consideration.

This is not to say that empirical information could not serve a purpose in policy making, in defining policy problems and in evaluating the effects of policies. Even if pluralism is understood more broadly in terms of power relations and communicative inequalities between different social actors, there is an obvious need for policy-relevant empirical information.

Despite the attempts through the Media Pluralism Monitor to broaden the existing scope of measurement, there are a number of still other possible approaches that could conceivably be used in debates on media pluralism. In one interesting attempt to develop alternative conceptions of policy-relevant empirical data, a concept of "social demand" has been proposed as a way of combining the policy studies and audience research in a way that exceeds economic and market considerations (Raboy et al. 2003). As an empirical notion, the term social demand refers to the expectations that can be extrapolated from what people actually say about their media use, as well as the efforts of organized social and cultural groups to influence the direction of media policy. The purpose then is to seek new grounds to analyze the objectives of media policy, their legitimacy, and to produce useful and relevant information for the needs of public policy. There are no doubt other comparable ways in which to use relevant empirical data from both political economy and audience research.

The identification of various forms of exclusion and power relations inherent in the structures of the media is also largely an empirical question. Instead of dismissing the relevance of empirical evidence altogether, the argument here is that we need to distinguish between value questions and factual questions. When discussing the justification of policies and what to value, empirical evidence is not enough. It is also important that the content of investigation is not determined by the availability of evidence. Even if the variety of formats available, for instance, is easy to measure, this does not make it the most relevant indicator of media pluralism.

It can be claimed that this emphasis on public debate and democratic politics is rather uncontroversial, even revealing a fair amount of naïve idealism. There will always be a need to make policy decisions on the distribution of various privileges and resources and to base those decisions on deficient information. It is perhaps too easy to criticize empirical assessment from the vantage point of political and normative ideals, since there are always trends that fall outside the chosen indicators and data, and we need no reminder about these shortcomings.

It should therefore be noted that the biggest problem with these studies is not that they are insufficient, but that they create an illusion—not entirely through their own fault—that questions of media pluralism or media performance are conceptually unambiguous problems that can be solved by technical means. From this perspective, indicators of pluralism, some of which are better than others, should be seen more as an addition to the media policy debate rather than as objective instruments that bring closure to political questions.

What should and can be expected of administrative, and especially scholarly, evaluation discourse is critical self-reflection of the concepts, indicators, and criteria it employs. In addition to developing new criteria of assessment, we need to ask what aspects are emphasized by the different criteria, what are their premises, and what are the possible political consequences they have.

Conclusion

In thinking about the role of the media in modern society, the concepts of pluralism and diversity have become part of the common sense of both theoretical and media policy debates. This in part reflects a broader renaissance of pluralism in political thought. At the same time, the changing nature of the media environment seems to be pushing us toward pluralistic conclusions. The fact that pluralism is invoked by almost all political sides, however, does not mean that media policy no longer involves conflicting values and interests.

The aim of this book has been to analyze the political rationalities that lie behind different uses of media pluralism in recent media policy debates, especially within the European Union. Part I focused on different conceptions of democracy and the public space and their implications for conceptualizing pluralism as a media policy goal, whereas Part II reviewed the actual uses and definitions of media pluralism in contemporary media policy practice. As expected, the arguments used in the contexts of political philosophy and policy debates rarely share the same starting points or even a common vocabulary. Yet the book is premised on the idea that these debates have at least some bearing on each other.

Based on current media policy discourses, it can be argued that policy approaches to media pluralism have been means rather than ends based. From this it follows that the underlying values of different policy options are rarely explicated or debated. Instead, issues such as media ownership or the role of public service media have so far been discussed largely in isolation and mostly with reference to technological or economic arguments. The debate on media pluralism has also been skewed by the narrow focus on the effects of competition or the evidence of whether or not ownership concentration actually constitutes a threat to pluralism. Similarly, the discussion on the role of public service media has largely focused on different funding mechanisms and feuds over distortion of competition. All parties to these debates routinely appeal to pluralism or diversity, usually without clarifying the values and aims that lie behind their use of the concept.

I have argued in this book that a more constructive approach would start by addressing the underlying values and aims of media policy and by clarifying the nature of the media system aimed at. To have any real use in such debates, the concept of media pluralism should be understood more broadly, not in terms of regulatory means, but in terms of basic normative principles. It is only after the political aims have been defined that we can discuss the efficacy of different regulatory means or develop meaningful indicators for measuring them. In order to do that, I have argued that media policy research needs richer intellectual resources, which include recent debates on contemporary political philosophy and democratic theory.

Clarifying the values and principles at stake does not necessarily mean that there has to be consensus on the basic values themselves. Pluralism, as viewed in this book, remains an essentially contested concept whose specific meaning and proper realization will always remain open-ended. Like other normative concepts in political thought, its meanings are essentially open and indeterminate. Therefore, the aim of this book to disarticulate the concept of media pluralism from the discourses of free market competition and consumer choice and rearticulate it with questions of the distribution of communicative power, should also be seen as a normative contribution.

From the perspective adopted in this book, such contestability can in fact be viewed as desirable. Drawing from radical pluralist theories of politics, democratic politics is best conceived as an ongoing contestation of all normative principles, not as their ultimate realization. As John Keane (1992, 129) has emphasized, no ideal model is a "recipe for creating a heaven of communication on earth" that would stifle controversies about the meaning of democracy, pluralism, freedom of speech, or the accompanying criticism of paternalism or elitism. There is no single solution to the problems of the media; normative principles such as media pluralism are therefore not something that can be realized in any definitive or perfect sense. Instead, this is an ongoing project without an ultimate solution and a goal that constantly throws up new contradictions and dilemmas.

In the words of William Connolly (1995, xiv), pluralism never simply is, because existing forms of diversity are always challenged by new movements as they struggle to come into existence. Respectively, there is no particular institutional model that can ensure a perfectly fair distribution of communicative power. Instead, media pluralism as an abstract notion denotes many goals that can be achieved through many different means, some of which have yet to be imagined.

Rather than the contested nature of the concept of media pluralism, the problem I identified in this book is the inability of media policy to deal with such questions in normative terms, as requiring not simply technical but genuinely political decisions. In line with this, I set out to demystify and deconstruct some of the premises upon which the public legitimation of contemporary media policy is based. The primary purpose has therefore been to illustrate the inherently contested nature of media pluralism as a policy value and to reveal the normative commitments, implicit or explicit, in its different uses and definitions both in actual policy rhetoric and in media policy research.

The aim of deconstructing totalizing claims and revealing the contestability of media pluralism as a normative value does not, however, imply judgmental or political relativism. Following a critical realist approach, the acceptance of epistemological relativism or the open-endedness of normative concepts does not mean that it is impossible to make judgments on why some theories or political ideals are better or more useful than others (see Sayer 2000). Rather than demonstrably correct definitions, my argument has been guided by a more dialogic aim of criticizing existing paradigms and providing arguments for alternative conceptions.

EVASION OF VALUES IN POLICY AND RESEARCH

Both of the actual policy cases discussed in this book illustrate that appeals to empirical evidence or objectivity are popular rhetorical tools in media policy. As Maria Michalis (2007, 17) notes in her study of European media policy, although governance is always a political affair, "its portrayal as apolitical, technocratic and objective enhances its chances of being accepted."

Based on recent policy discourses, the notion of media pluralism seems especially susceptible to such apolitical forms of arguments. For instance, the argument that policy issues related to media pluralism or public service media should be considered with empirical rigor rather than on the basis of abstract or emotional criteria is a typical way of presenting some political rationalities as commonsensical and others as ideological. As I demonstrated, the shift towards pragmatic or technocratic argumentation is embedded in certain political rationalities, and thus only highlights the need to criticize all political arguments that claim to be objective or apolitical.

Political rationalities and normative assumptions, however, are not constructed only in policy discourses. Although much of the critique is directed at the way in which pluralism is conceptualized in media policy and in administrative policy research, it is clear that the concepts and discourses of academic research are not free from normative assumptions either. In this sense, my contribution can be conceived as an attempt at scholarly self-reflection, since academic research is one of the main institutions of intellectual machinery that produce the conceptual framings used in political discourse.

This applies to both media policy research and other strands of media and cultural studies. If media policy analysts have typically been long on realism, anxious to appear economically and technologically literate, and rather short on idealism and fundamental criticism, as Denis McQuail (1997) suggests, then most other strands of media and communication studies have largely shunned the formal legal-economic discourse and preferred more qualitative and interpretative approaches.

It can be argued that both approaches are apolitical in a different way. It has often been argued that in their incapacity or reluctance to deal with the broader structures of communication and its political and social contexts, the mainstream of media and cultural studies has not contributed very much to the debate on the norms and values of media regulation (Garnham 2000; Gitlin 1997; McGuigan 1997; Mosco 1996). Many critical political economists, in particular, have argued that the stress on popular consumption, active audiences and individual creation of meaning in cultural studies is actually rather complicit with the neoliberal idea of consumer sovereignty.

The same can be said of many analyses of new technologies and their implications for media pluralism. Notions such as "cultural chaos" (McNair 2006) and "semiotic democracy" (Jacka 2003), and their acknowledgment of the current abundance of media outlets and forms, seem to point to a situation in which all hierarchies and rigid structures of power would have disappeared. Thus, they are largely void of any critical potential or institutional vision. In this sense, repeated appeals to the complexity, plurality and contingency of media cultures may also reflect the inability of researchers to tackle the politically sensitive issues of media performance and the norms of evaluation.

This echoes the criticism that the preoccupation with pluralism has stripped researchers of their ability to provide real political alternatives. As historian Russell Jacoby (1999, 33) has argued, pluralism and diversity have "become blank checks payable to anyone in any amount, lacking meaning or content." Criticizing liberals and leftists who celebrate diversity in the name of progress, Jacoby argues that "with few ideas on how a future should be shaped, they embrace all ideas." So "pluralism becomes the catch-all, the alpha and omega of political thinking . . . opium of disillusioned intellectuals, the ideology of an era without an ideology" (ibid., 33).

In effect, it can be argued that the mainstream of policy discourses and cultural studies both share a reductive perspective on media pluralism. As Vincent Mosco (1996, 258–59) observes, in their own particular way, both conflate pluralism with mere multiplicity and thus refuse to acknowledge it as an issue that may require concerted political action. By equating pluralism with the sheer number of voices in the market, orthodox policy studies tend to deal with pluralism in the framework of competition policy only. Seen from this vantage point, pluralism is relatively easy to achieve simply by means of increasing the number of units, producers, and distributors—and since technological development often does this anyway, pluralism tends not to become a concern. But as I argued, this perspective fails to account for the difference between the sheer number of voices, the number of different voices, and their relationship with existing structures of power in society.

Despite their theoretical and epistemological differences, cultural studies approaches to the media often lead to similar conclusions about the politics of media pluralism. Starting from the vantage point of audiences, media pluralism is not a substantial problem because media contents are polysemic and subject to multiple readings and interpretations anyway. Audiences, in essence, thus create their own diversity, regardless of the formal structures or political economy of media industries.

The arguments of this book are thus directed against interpretations of pluralism in both these forms. In contrast to these—perhaps somewhat caricatured—views of both policy studies and cultural studies, the critical notion of pluralism espoused in this book relies on a more holistic approach that places the media in a broader social context and recognizes the wider economic, political, and cultural relations of power. In short, the main argument of the book is thus that pluralism is about social relations and about the role of the media in the overall distribution of power in society, not about multiplicity itself or about defining or defending differences as such.

THE MEDIA AND RADICAL PLURALISM

Questions of media structure and performance are essentially political and ideological questions that imply a dialogue between different values and different conceptions of democracy. In essence, different conceptions of democracy lead to different conceptions of pluralism and its institutionalization and realization. Accordingly, the choices made in assessing the state of various demands posed to the structure of communication will inevitably depend not only on the choice of the objective method of assessment, but on different visions of society and a democratic public sphere. Even though it is acknowledged that such visions are rarely discussed in media policy, different actors still rely on assumptions about the meaning of notions such as democracy and public interest.

I have distinguished roughly two dominant conceptions of media pluralism in contemporary media policy debates. The discourse of the marketplace, as the dominant logic in contemporary media policy practice, links pluralism to the political rationalities of the free-marketplace-of-ideas metaphor and its corresponding conflation of pluralism and individual consumer choice. In line with this, the main aims of European media policies have been to promote the free flow of media content and to provide maximum choice for consumers in the market.

The second main discourse can broadly be identified as the public sphere approach. As a common name for the critical approaches that defend public interest beyond the markets, it constitutes an influential counter-discourse that has been adopted by most academic researchers, but also by some progressive policy makers and politicians. Relying loosely on theoretical justifications drawn from ideas about deliberative democracy and the public sphere, this discourse has been especially associated with the ethos of public service broadcasting and the public interest values of universal service, equal access and representation of minorities.

The theoretical argument presented in this book is that, for purposes of conceptualizing media pluralism as a critical concept, both the liberal discourse of the free marketplace of ideas and the more critical public sphere approach are wedded to unhelpful idealizations. Liberal notions of consumer choice and the free marketplace of ideas obscure the existing asymmetries of power by unnecessarily treating the market as some kind of neutral mediator of interests. On the other hand the ideals of deliberative democracy and the public sphere can also obscure existing asymmetries of power by postulating impossible and transcendent forms of rational communication. As a consequence, both tend to incorporate current social forms and relations of power into their ideal models as justifiable and permanent features of the social landscape (see also Kuper 2004, 197).

The ideals of the free marketplace of ideas and the rational-critical public sphere both tend to assume a sphere of unlimited participation or free-floating discourse. Yet the public sphere is always also constituted as a representative order linked to particular institutions that confine and filter public discourse in various ways. While the advocates of free market ignore the relations of power inherent in the market and the forms of censorship it produces, the defenders of public interest in media policy tend to defend existing public service institutions as embodiments of balance and representativeness in a way that ignores the necessary exclusions and biases of all existing systems.

I argue then that media reformers and advocates of public interest would be better off drawing on the recent theorizing of radical pluralism in democratic theory. This implies an emerging third discourse of pluralism, which relies not on idealizations of unrestricted communication or perfect representation but on recognizing the inevitable asymmetries of communicative power. In short, this means that all media are essentially institutions that unevenly distribute entitlements to speak and to be heard and seen. This does not imply a nihilistic acceptance of the status quo, but a more radical aim of democratizing or leveling the distribution of communicative power on all levels. As John Keane (1992) has argued, democratic forms of public intervention in the media can be conceived above all as correctives against the wishful belief in the decentralized anonymity of the market, public service institutions, or any other superior or natural self-correcting mechanisms.

In a sense, this implies a negative definition of media pluralism not as a state of affairs, but as a critical counter-discourse to all forms of monisms. While no one expects that all citizens' voices can be reflected in the media and the public sphere exactly equally, radical pluralism emphasizes the capacity of different groups and perspectives to challenge the established hegemonic order and provide new alternatives and new forces of pluralization. The realist standpoint of recognizing that all media are subject to asymmetries of power arguably opens up perspectives on envisioning institutions or practices that help identify power and knowledge differentials and aim to level them out. Accordingly, in the radical pluralist approach, media pluralism is viewed in terms of contestation and the leveling of the unequal distribution of power, instead of the idealization of free choice or the illusion of balanced representation through regulated pluralism.

Of course, this remains an abstract idea and does not imply a readily enforceable institutional model. Yet it is not difficult to identify ways in which the radical pluralist ethos already informs some forms of media activism and practice. The aims of contestation and dislocation can easily be associated with the growth of grassroots projects and nonprofit and community media initiatives. Various movements for alternative, autonomous, or independent media are often portrayed as voices of dissent that challenge the hegemony of mainstream media. Secondly, such ideas can be found in recent initiatives to rethink the role of public service media in decentered forms; not as a single, centralized institution, but as an alternative logic of media production and distribution. Thirdly, the Internet and new forms of media also provide opportunities for new media forms that explicitly seek to challenge the gatekeeper role of traditional journalism. From the perspective of the aim of supporting the different operating logics and principles of different media sectors, many of these new media forms can be viewed as emancipatory developments that challenge the hegemonic role of professional media and their established sources. In this way, although still marginal in media policy discourse, they already provide seeds for genuine pluralization, which goes beyond the standard rites of consumer choice and balanced professional journalism.

One of the most prominent examples of such counter-hegemonic is provided by new modes of "radical journalism" like Wikileaks, which not only provide alternative sources of information but also seek to disrupt the established routines and norms of the mainstream media. It is not difficult to forecast the proliferation of many other movements that seek to emulate these counter-hegemonic aims.

Yet radical pluralism does not just mean more diversity. The ideal of contesting hegemonic structures of power must be distinguished from the mere proliferation of different media outlets and information sources. Even when they do disrupt the established media order, the proliferation of different media outlets in no way eradicates the fact that some groups and individuals will always have more power and influence than others. A critical concept of media pluralism must thus be able to answer questions about the role of the media with regard to the distribution of power and influence in society. Above all, radical pluralism points to a need to identify the new forms of concentration and asymmetries of power that both old and new media continue to exhibit. For example, it is by no means given that new media and their challenge to mainstream journalism will lead automatically to a more egalitarian and inclusive public sphere—they can just as easily lead to further inequalities in communicative power and give further tools for powerful elites and corporations to dominate public communication. The various forms alternative media movements thus continue to require public support and acknowledgment in official media policy, too.

Finally, the argument that the most fundamental rationale for defending media pluralism derives from the egalitarian commitment to the democratic distribution of communicative power in the public sphere is admittedly contestable, too. However, it represents one attempt to provide a holistic normative basis for debates on media pluralism. To summarize the main arguments of the book, the critical notion of media pluralism proposed above involves at least three contentions:

Pluralism is not a linear variable and it cannot be unambiguously measured, let alone conflated with choice or any other quantifiable criteria. Instead, media pluralism needs to be posited as a broader social and political principle that is best seen as a critical orientation, rather than a concrete state of affairs. As a political goal, its justification cannot be drawn from empirical evidence alone. This does not rule out the use of empirical evidence in analyzing various trends in media structures and contents, but it does emphasize that as a broader underlying value, the principle of media pluralism itself should not be reduced to these indicators.

The promotion of pluralism in this sense requires political action to balance out unequal relations of power and to support different forms of media that are independent not only from government influence, but also from market forces. While the forms of regulation will and should always be debated, this book has emphasized that contrary to the discourse of deregulation or liberalization, all media institutions entail forms of regulation or hegemonic "rules of the game" that privilege some voices and exclude others. Therefore, it is argued that the aims of policies designed to promote media pluralism should be articulated critically as means of disrupting or leveling out existing power structures and supporting disadvantaged actors, rather than as means of safeguarding purportedly neutral or representative media structures.

Media pluralism, even in a revised, critical meaning, does not provide a catchall value or a coherent vision of a democratic media system. Pluralism is not an absolute value and it has its limits and contradictions. A broader conception of pluralism will not solve the problem of ambiguous guiding principles in media policy. Not only is pluralism, like freedom, something that can never be achieved in a perfect sense, but there will always remain conflict between pluralism and other values, such as quality, commonality and coherence. Therefore, the principle of equal distribution of communicative power is not meant to provide universal validity that can be applied in any media policy situation.

Promoting pluralism does not mean that the setting of meaningful policy goals will no longer involve substantial values, such as quality or responsibility, which in some cases may even be in conflict with the principle of pluralism. Following the antiessentialist reasoning, there can be no final reconciliation or a single right balance between these conflicting values. Instead, questions about the interpretation and prioritization of guiding principles remain, above all, political matters, not something that can be settled empirically.

REFERENCE LIST

ACT (The Association of Commercial Television in Europe). 2009a. Comments on the second draft Communication on State Aid and Public Broadcasting. http://www.acte.be/EPUB/easnet.dll/GetDoc?APPL=1& DAT_IM=028CBE.

———. 2009b. ACT Response to the Questionnaire on the Independent Study on Indicators for Media Pluralism in the Member States.

Adamic, Lada A., and Natalie Glance. 2005. "The political blogosphere and the 2004 U.S. Election: Divided they blog." In LinkKDD '05: Proceedings of the 3rd International Workshop on Link Discovery, 36–43. New York: ACM Press.

Anderson, Charles W. 1987. "Political Philosophy, Practical Reason and Policy Analysis." In *Confronting Values in Policy Analysis*, edited by Frank Fischer and John Forester, 22–44. Newbury Park: Sage.

Ariño, Mónica. 2004. "Competition Law and Pluralism in European Digital Broadcasting: Addressing the Gaps." *Communications & Strategies* 54 (2): 97–128.

Aslama, Minna. 2009. "Participation as Position and Practice: Rethinking Media Diversity and Policy in the Web 2.0 Era." Donald McGannon Communication Research Center Working Paper.

Aslama, Minna, Heikki Hellman, and Tuomo Sauri. 2004. "Does Market-Entry Regulation Matter?" *Gazette: The International Journal for Communication Studies* 66 (2): 113–32.

Aslama, Minna, Els De Bens, Jan van Cuilenburg, Kaarle Nordenstreng, Winfried Schulz, and Richard van der Wurff, with contributions from Ildiko Kovats, Gianpietro Mazzoleni, and Ralph Negrine. 2007. "Measuring and Assessing Empirical Media Diversity: Some European Cases." In *Media Between Commerce and Culture*, edited by Els de Bens, 55–98. Bristol: Intellect Books.

Audiovisual Media Services Directive. 2007. Directive 2007/65/EC of the European Parliament and of the Council. *Official Journal of the European Union*, L332, 27–45.

Bagdikian, Ben H. 2004. *The New Media Monopoly*. Boston: Beacon Press.

Baker, C. Edwin. 2007. *Media Concentration and Democracy. Why Ownership Matters*. New York: Cambridge University Press.

Bardoel, Jo, Leen d'Haenens, and Allerd Peeters. 2005. "Defining Distinctiveness. In Search of Public Broadcasting Performance and Quality Criteria." In *Cultural Dilemmas in Public Service Broadcasting*, edited by Gregory Ferrell Lowe and Per Jauert, 57–78. Göteborg: Nordicom.

Bardoel, Jo, and Gregory Ferrell Lowe. 2007. "From Public Service Broadcasting to Public Service Media: The Core Challenge." In *From Public Service Broadcasting to Public Service Media*, edited by Gregory F. Lowe and Jo Bardoel, 9–26. Göteborg: Nordicom.

Barnett, Steven. 2009. "Journalism, Democracy and the Public Interest: Rethinking Media Pluralism for the Digital Age." Working Paper. Oxford: Reuters Institute for the Study of Journalism.

Baum, Bruce. 2001. "Freedom, Power and Public Opinion: J.S. Mill on the Public Sphere." *History of Political Thought*. 22 (3): 501–24.

Bauman, Zygmunt. 1997. *Postmodernity and its Discontents*. Cambridge: Polity Press.

———. 1999. *In Search of Politics*. Cambridge: Polity Press.

Baumeister, Andrea. 2003. "Habermas: Discourse and Cultural Diversity." *Political Studies* 51 (4): 740–58.

Beck, Ulrich and Elisabeth Beck-Gernsheim. 2001. *Individualization*. London: Sage.

Benhabib, Seyla. 1996. "Toward a Deliberative Model of Democratic Legitimacy." In *Democracy and Difference*, edited by Seyla Benhabib, 67–94. Princeton: Princeton University Press.

———. 2002. *Claims of Culture: Equality and Diversity in the Global Era*. Princeton: Princeton University Press.

Bennett, W. Lance. 2003. "New Media Power: The Internet and Global Activism." In *Contesting Media Power: Alternative Media in a Networked World*, edited by Nick Couldry and James Curran, 17–37. Oxford: Rowman & Littlefield.

Berlin, Isaiah. 1969. *Four Essays on Liberty*. Oxford: Oxford University Press.

Bessette, Joseph M. 1981. "Deliberative Democracy: The Majority Principle in Republican Government." In *How Democratic is the Constitution?*, edited by Robert Goldwin and William Shambra, 102–16. Washington, DC: American Enterprise Institute.

Blumler, Jay G. 1992. "Public Service Broadcasting before the Commercial Deluge." In *Television and the Public Interest. Vulnerable Values in West European Broadcasting*, edited by Jay G. Blumler, 7–21. London: Sage.

Bobbio, Norberto. 1990. *Liberalism and Democracy*. London: Verso.

Bohman, James. 2000. "The Division of Labor in Democratic Discourse: Media, Experts, and Deliberative Democracy." In *Deliberation, Democracy, and the Media,* edited by Simone Chambers and Anne Costain, 47–64. Lanham: Rowman & Littlefield.

———. 2007. "Political Communication and the Epistemic Value of Diversity: Deliberation and Legitimation in Media Societies." *Communication Theory* 17 (4): 348–55.

Bohman, James, and William Rehg. 1997. "Introduction." In *Deliberative Democracy: Essays on Reason and Politics*, edited by James Bohman and William Rehg, ix–xxx. Cambridge: MIT Press.

Born, Georgina. 2006. "Digitising Democracy." *The Political Quarterly* 76 (s1): 102–23.

Bourdieu, Pierre, and Loic Wanquant. 2001. "NewLiberalSpeak—Notes on the new planetary vulgate." *Radical Philosophy* 105 (Jan.–Feb. 2001): 2–5.

Braman, Sandra. 2004. "Where Has Media Policy Gone? Defining the Field in the Twenty-First Century." *Communication Law and Policy* 9 (2): 153–82.

———. 2007. "The Limits of Diversity." In *Media Diversity and Localism: Meaning and Metrics,* edited by Philip M. Napoli, 139–50. Mahwah, NJ: Lawrence Erlbaum Associates.

———. 2008. "Policy Research in an Evidence-Averse Environment." *International Journal of Communication* 2 (Feature): 433–49.

Brady, John S. 2004. "Assessing the Agonistic Critiques of Jürgen Habermas's Theory of the Public Sphere." *Philosophy & Social Criticism* 30 (3): 331–54.

Carpentier, Nico. 2011. *Media and Participation: A Site of Ideological-Democratic Struggle*. Bristol: Intellect.

Carpentier, Nico, and Bart Cammaerts. 2006. "Hegemony, Democracy, Agonism, and Journalism. An Interview with Chantal Mouffe." *Journalism Studies* 7 (6): 964–75.

Castells, Manuel. 2007. "Communication, Power and Counter-power in the Network Society." *International Journal of Communication* 1 (1): 238–66.

———. 2009. *Communication Power*. Oxford: Oxford University Press.

Cavallin, Jens. 1998. "European Policies and Regulations on Media Concentration." *International Journal of Communication Law and Policy* 1(summer 1998). http://www.ijclp.net/files/ijclp_web-doc_3-1-1998.rtf.

Charter of Fundamental Rights of the European Union. 2007. *Official Journal of the European Union* C 303/01.

Christians, Clifford, Theodore L. Glasser, Denis McQuail, Kaarle Nordenstreng, and Robert A. White. 2009. *Normative Theories of the Media. Journalism in Democratic Societies.* Urbana and Chicago: University of Illinois Press.

Coleman, Stephen. 2004. "From Service to Commons: Re-inventing a Space for Public Communication." In *From Public Service Broadcasting to Public Service Communications*, edited by Damian Tambini and Jamie Cowling, 88–99. London: IPPR.

Collins, Richard. 1998. *From Satellite to Single Market: New Communication Technology and European Public Service Television.* London: Routledge.

Compaine, Benjamin M., and Douglas Gomery. 2000. *Who Owns the Media?* Mahwah, NJ: Lawrence Erlbaum Associates.

Compaine, Benjamin M. 2001. "The myths of encroaching global media ownership." *OpenDemocracy,* November 9, 2001. http://www .opendemocracy.net/media-globalmediaownership/article_87.jsp.

Connolly, William. 1991. *Identity\Difference: Democratic Negotiations of Political Paradox.* Ithaca and London: Cornell University Press.

———. 1995. *The Ethos of Pluralization.* Minneapolis: Minnesota University Press.

———. 2005. *Pluralism.* Durham: Duke University Press.

Convention for the Protection of Human Rights and Fundamental Freedoms. 1950. Rome, November 4, 1950.

Convention on the Protection and Promotion of the Diversity of Cultural Expressions. 2005. Paris: Unesco, October 20, 2005.

Coppens, Tomas. 2005. "Fine-tuned or Out-of-key? Critical Reflections on Frameworks for Assessing PSB Performance." In *Cultural Dilemmas in Public Service Broadcasting*, edited by Gregory Ferrell Lowe and Per Jauert, 79–100. Göteborg: Nordicom.

Couldry, Nick. 2008. "Form and Power in an Age of Continuous Spectacle." In *The Media and Social Theory*, edited by David Hesmondhalgh and Jason Toynbee, 161–76. Abingdon and New York: Routledge.

Couldry, Nick, and James Curran. 2003. "The Paradox of Media Power." In *Contesting Media Power: Alternative Media in a Networked World,* edited by Nick Couldry and James Curran, 3–15. Lanham: Rowman & Littlefield.

Council of Europe. 1994a. The Activity Report of the Committee of Experts on Media Concentration and Pluralism MM-CM. Submitted to the 4th European Ministerial Conference on Mass Media Policy. Prague, December 1994.

———. 1994b. Resolution No 1: The Future of Public Service Broadcasting. Adopted by the Ministers of the states participating in the 4th European Ministerial Conference on Mass Media Policy. Prague, December 1994.

———. 1996. Recommendation No. R(96)10 of the Committee of Ministers on the guarantee of the independence of public service broadcasting. Strasbourg, September 1996.

———. 1997. Report on media concentrations and pluralism in Europe. Committee of Experts on Media Concentrations and Pluralism (MM-CM). Strasbourg, January 1997.

———. 1999. Recommendation No. R(99)1 of the Committee of Ministers to Member States on measures to promote media pluralism. Strasbourg, January 1999.

———. 2000. Report on Media Pluralism in the Digital Environment. CDMM(2000)pde. Adopted by the Steering Committee on the Mass Media in October 2000.

———. 2002. Media Diversity in Europe. Report prepared by the Advisory Panel to the CDMM on Media Concentrations, Pluralism and Diversity Questions. H/APMD(2003)001. Strasbourg, December 2002.

———. 2003. Recommendation (2003)9 of the Committee of Ministers to member states on measures to promote the democratic and social contribution of digital broadcasting. Strasbourg, May 2003.

———. 2004a. Recommendation 1641(2004) of the Parliamentary Assembly of the Council of Europe on public service broadcasting. Strasbourg, January 2004.

———. 2004b. Transnational Media Concentrations in Europe. Report prepared by the Advisory Panel to the CDMM on Media Concentrations, Pluralism and Diversity Questions. APMD(2004)7. Strasbourg, November 2004.

———. 2007a. Recommendation Rec(2007)2 of the Committee of Ministers to Member States on media pluralism and diversity of media content. Strasbourg, January 2007.

————. 2007b. Recommendation CM/Rec(2007)3 of the Committee of Ministers to Member States on the remit of public service media in the information society. Strasbourg, January 2007.

————. 2009. Methodology for measuring media concentration and media content diversity. Report prepared by the Group of Specialists on Media Diversity MC-S-MD. H/Inf(2009)9. Strasbourg, June 2009.

————. 2012. Recommendation CM/Rec(2012)3 of the Committee of Ministers to Member States on the protection of human rights with regard to search engines. Strasbourg, April 2012.

CPBF (Campaign for Press and Broadcasting Freedom). 2005. Response to the European Commission Issues Paper on Media Pluralism. http://ec.europa.eu/avpolicy/docs/reg/modernisation/issue_papers/contributions/ip6-cpbf.pdf.

Craig, Geoffrey. 2000. "Perpetual Crisis: The Politics of Saving the ABC." *Media International Australia* 95: 105–16.

Crowder, George. 2006. "Chantal Mouffe's Agonistic Pluralism." Paper presented at the APSA Annual Conference, University of Newcastle, 26–27 September 2006.

Cunningham, Frank. 2002. *Theories of Democracy: A Critical Introduction.* London: Routledge.

Currah, Andrew. 2009. *What's Happening to Our News? An Investigation into the Likely Impact of the Digital Revolution on the Economics of News Publishing in the UK.* Oxford: Reuters Institute for the Study of Journalism.

Curran, James. 1991. "Rethinking the media as a public sphere." In *Communication and Citizenship: Journalism and the Public Sphere,* edited by Peter Dahlgren and Colin Sparks, 27–57. London: Routledge.

————. 2002. *Media and Power.* London: Routledge.

————. 2011. *Media and Democracy.* London: Routledge.

Curran, James, Shanto Ieyngar, Anker Brink Lund, and Inka Salovaara-Moring. 2009. "Media System, Public Knowledge and Democracy: A Comparative Study." *European Journal of Communication* 24 (1): 5–26.

Czepek, Andrea, Melanie Hellwig, and Eva Novak. 2009. "Introduction: Structural Inhibition of Media Freedom and Plurality across Europe." In *Press Freedom and Pluralism in Europe: Concepts and Conditions,* edited by Andrea Czepek, Melanie Hellwig, and Eva Novak, 9–22. Bristol: Intellect.

Dahl, Robert. 1956. *A Preface to Democratic Theory.* Chicago: University of Chicago Press.

Dahlberg, Lincoln. 2001. "Computer-Mediated Communication and the Public Sphere: A Critical Analysis." *Journal of Computer Mediated Communication* 7 (1). http://jcmc.indiana.edu/vol7/issue1/dahlberg.html.

———. 2005a. "The Corporate Colonization of Online Attention and the Marginalization of Critical Communication." *Journal of Communication Inquiry* 29 (2): 160–80.

———. 2005b. "The Habermasian Public Sphere: Taking Difference Seriously?" *Theory and Society* 34 (2): 111–36.

Dalhberg, Lincoln, and Sean Phelan, eds. 2011. *Discourse Theory and Critical Media Politics.* New York: Palgrave Macmillan.

Dahlgren, Peter. 1995. *Television and the Public Sphere.* London: Sage.

Dean, Mitchell. 1999. *Governmentality. Power and Rule in Modern Society.* London: Sage.

De Bens, Els. 2007. "Media Between Culture and Commerce: An Introduction." In *Media Between Commerce and Culture*, edited by Els de Bens, 9–24. Bristol: Intellect.

Donders, Karen, and Caroline Pauwels. 2008. "Does EU Policy Challenge the Digital Future of Public Service Broadcasting?" *Convergence: The International Journal of Research into New Media Technologies* 14 (3): 295–311.

———. 2010. "The Introduction of an *ex ante* evaluation for new media services: Is 'Europe' asking for it, or does public service broadcasting need it?" *International Journal of Media and Cultural Politics* 6 (2): 133–48.

Dowding, Keith. 1992. "Choice: Its Increase and its Value." *British Journal of Political Science* 22 (3): 301–14.

Doyle, Gillian. 1997. "From 'Pluralism' to 'Ownership': Europe's emergent policy on Media Concentrations navigates the doldrums." *Journal of Information, Law and Technology* 1997 (3). http://www2.warwick.ac.uk/fac/soc/law/elj/jilt/1997_3/doyle/.

———. 2002. *Media Ownership.* London: Sage.

———. 2007. "Undermining Media Diversity: Inaction on Media Concentration and Pluralism in the EU." In *Media and Cultural Policy in the European Union*, edited by Katherine Sarikakis, 135–56. Amsterdam and New York: Rodopi.

Dryzek, John S. 1990. *Discursive Democracy. Politics, Policy, and Political Science.* Cambridge: Cambridge University Press.

———. 2000. *Deliberative Democracy and Beyond. Liberals, Critics, Contestations.* Oxford: Oxford University Press.

Dryzek, John S., and Simon Niemeyer. 2006. "Reconciling Pluralism and Consensus as Political Ideals." *American Journal of Political Science* 50 (3): 634–49.

Dutton, William. 2007. "Through the network (of Networks)—the Fifth Estate." Inaugural Lecture, Examination Schools, Oxford University, October 15, 2007.

EBU (The European Broadcasting Union) 2004. "The Position of Public Broadcasting in Europe: An Essential Territory for Cohesion." Speech by Werner Rumphorst, Legal Director. Madrid, November 3, 2004.

———. 2009. EBU contribution to the Commission's second public consultation. Review of the Communication from the Commission on the application of State aid rules to public service broadcasting. Geneva, January 2009.

Edkins, Jenny. 1999. *Poststructuralism and International Relations: Bringing the Political Back in.* Boulder: Lynn Rienner.

EFJ (European Federation of Journalists). 2005a. Submission to the Issue Paper for the Audiovisual Conference in Liverpool: Media Pluralism. Brussels, August 2005.

———. 2005b. *Media Power in Europe: The Big Picture of Ownership.* Brussels, August 2005.

Ellis, John. 2000. *Seeing Things: Television in the Era of Uncertainty.* London and New York: I. B. Tauris.

Enli, Gunn Sara. 2008. "Redefining Public Service Broadcasting." *Convergence: The International Journal of Research into New Media Technologies* 14 (1): 105–20.

ENPA (European Newspaper Publishers' Association). 2005. ENPA Response to the Commission Issues Paper on Media Pluralism—What Should Be the European Union's Role? Brussels, August 2005.

European Commission. 1984. Television without Frontiers: Green Paper on the Establishment of the Common Market for Broadcasting, Especially by Satellite and Cable. COM (84)300. Brussels, June 14, 1984.

———. 1992. Green Paper on Pluralism and Media Concentration in the Internal Market: An Assessment of the Need for Community Action. COM(92)480. Brussels, December 1992.

———. 1994a. Follow-up to the Consultation Process Relating to the Green Paper on "Pluralism and Media Concentration in the Internal Market—An Assessment for the Need of Community Action." COM (94)354. Brussels, October 1994.

———. 1994b. Europe and the Global Information Society. Bangemann Report Recommendations to the European Council. Brussels, May 1994.

————. 1999. Principles and Guidelines for the Community's Audiovisual Policy in the Digital Age. Communication from the Commission to the Council, the European Parliament, the Economic and Social Committee and the Committee of the Regions. COM(1999)657. Brussels, December 1999.

————. 2001. Communication on the Application of State Aid Rules to Public Service Broadcasting. Official Journal of the European Union C320/04, November 2001.

————. 2003. Green Paper on Services of General Interest. COM(2003) 270 final. Brussels, May 2003

————. 2005. Issues Paper for the Liverpool Audiovisual Conference: Media Pluralism—What should be the European Union's role? Brussels: DG Information Society and Media. July 2005.

————. 2007a. Media pluralism in the Member States of the European Union. Commission Staff Working Document. SEC(2007)32. Brussels, January 2007.

————. 2007b. Indicators for media pluralism in the Member States— towards a risk-based approach. Tender Specifications. SMART 007A 2007/0002. Brussels, March 2007.

————. 2009. Communication from the Commission on the Application of State Aid Rules to Public Service Broadcasting. Official Journal of the European Union C257/01, October 2009.

European Parliament. 1996. Resolution on the Role of Public Service Television in a Multi-Media Society. A4-0243/96. Committee on Culture, Youth, Education and the Media. September 1996.

————. 2004. Resolution on the risks of violation, in the EU and especially in Italy, of freedom of expression and information (Article 11(2) of the Charter of Fundamental Rights). 2003/2237(INI). Official Journal of the European Union C 104 E, 1026–40. April 2004.

————. 2006. Draft Report on the proposal for a directive of the European Parliament and the Council amending Council Directive 89/552/EEC, Committee on Culture and Education, 2005/0260 (COD). August 2006.

————. 2008a. Resolution on concentration and pluralism in the media in the European Union 2007/2253(INI). Brussels, September 2008.

————. 2008b. Resolution on Community Media in Europe. 2008/2011(INI). Brussels, September 2008.

————. 2010. Resolution on public service broadcasting in the digital era: the future of the dual system. 2010/2028(INI). Strasbourg, November 2010.

———. 2011. Resolution on media law in Hungary. 2011/2510 (RSP). Brussels, March 2011.

FACT (Finnish Association of Commercial Television). 2009. Comments on the second draft Communication on State Aid and Public Broadcasting. Helsinki, January 2009.

Fay, Brian. 1975. *Social Theory and Political Practice*. London: Allen & Unwin.

FCC (Federal Communications Commission). 2003. Report and Order and Notice of Proposed Rulemaking. FCC 03–127.

———. 2008. Report and Order and Order on Reconsideration. FCC 07–216.

Fenton, Natalie. 2009. "Drowning or Waving? New Media, Journalism and Democracy." In *New Media, Old News. Journalism and Democracy in the Digital Age*, edited by Natalie Fenton, 3–16. LoFerree, Myra Marx, William A. Gamson, Jürgen Gerhards, and Dieter Rucht. 2002. "Four Models of the Public Sphere in Modern Democracies." *Theory & Society* 31 (3): 289–324.

Finlayson, Alan. 2004. "Political Science, Political Ideas and Rhetoric." *Economy and Society* 33 (4): 528–49.

Fischer, Frank. 1998. "Beyond Empiricism: Policy Inquiry in Postpositivist Perspective." *Policy Studies Journal* 26 (1): 129–46.

———. 2003. *Reframing Public Policy. Discursive Politics and Deliberative Practices*. Oxford: Oxford University Press.

Fiske, John. 1987. *Television Culture*. London: Methuen & Co.

Fraser, Nancy. 1992. "Rethinking the Public Sphere: A Contribution to the Critique of Actually Existing Democracy." In *Habermas and the Public Sphere*, edited by Craig Calhoun, 108–42. Cambridge: MIT Press.

———. 1997. *Justice Interruptus. Critical Reflections on the "Postsocialist" Condition*. New York and London: Routledge.

———. 2007. "Transnationalizing the Public Sphere: On the Legitimacy and Efficacy of Public Opinion in a Postwestphalian World." In *Identities, Affiliations, and Allegiances*, edited by Seyla Benhabib, Ian Shapiro, and Danilo Petrnovich, 45–66. Cambridge: Cambridge University Press.

Freedman, Des. 2003. *Television Policies of the Labour Party 1951–2001*. London: Frank Cass.

———. 2005. "Promoting Diversity and Pluralism in Contemporary Communication Policies in the United States and the United Kingdom." *The International Journal on Media Management* 7 (1–2): 16–23.

———. 2008. *The Politics of Media Policy*. Cambridge: Polity Press.

———. 2012. "The Phone Hacking Scandal: Implications for Regulation. *Television & New Media* 13 (1): 17–20.

Fossen, Thomas. 2008. "Agonistic Critiques of Liberalism: Perfection and Emancipation." *Contemporary Political Theory* 7 (4): 376–94.

Foucault, Michel. 1991. "Governmentality." In *The Foucault Effect: Studies in Governmentality*, edited by Graham Burchell, Colin Gordon, and Peter Miller, 87–104. London: Harvester Wheatsheaf.

Gardiner, Michael. 2004. "Wild Publics and Grotesque Symposiums: Habermas and Bakhtin on Dialogue, Everyday Life, and the Public Sphere." In *After Habermas: New Perspectives on the Public Sphere*, edited by Nick Crossley, and John Michael Roberts, 28–48. Oxford: Blackwell.

Garnham, Nicholas. 1992. "The Media and the Public Sphere." In *Habermas and the Public Sphere*, edited by Craig Calhoun, 359–76. Cambridge: MIT Press.

———. 1999a. "Amartya Sen's Capabilities Approach to the Evaluation of Welfare: Its Application to Communications." In *Communication, Citizenship, and Social Policy*, edited by Andrew Calabrese, and Jean-Claude Burgelman, 113–24. Lanham: Rowman & Littlefield.

———. 1999b. "Information Politics: The Study of Communicative Power." In *Society on the Line: Information Politics in the Digital Age*, edited by William Dutton, 77–78. Oxford: Oxford University Press.

———. 2000. *Emancipation, the Media, and Modernity*. Oxford: Oxford University Press.

———. 2003. "A Response to Elizabet Jacka's 'Democracy as Defeat.'" *Television & New Media* 4 (2): 193–200.

———. 2007. "Habermas and the public sphere." *Global Media and Communication* 3 (2): 201–14.

Gibbons, Thomas. 2000. "Pluralism, guidance and the new media." In *Regulating the Global Information Society*, edited by Christopher C. Marsden, 304–15. London: Routledge.

Gitlin, Todd. 1997. "The Anti-political Populism of Cultural Studies." In *Cultural Studies in Question*, edited by Marjorie Ferguson, and Peter Golding, 25–38. London: Sage.

———. 1998. "Public sphere or public sphericules." In *Media, Ritual and Identity*, edited by Tamar Liebes, and James Curran, 168–75. London: Routledge.

———. 2002. *Media Unlimited. How the Torrent of Images and Sounds Overwhelms Our Lives*. New York: Henry Holt.

Golding, Peter, and Graham Murdock. 2000. "Culture, Communications and Political Economy." In *Mass Media and Society*, edited by James Curran, and Michael Gurevitch, 70–92. 3rd Edition. London: Arnold.

Goodman, Ellen P. 2004. "Media Policy Out of the Box: Content Abundance, Attention Scarcity, and the Failures of Digital Markets." *Berkeley Technology Law Journal* 19 (4): 1389–472.

———. 2007. "Proactive Media Policy in an Age of Content Abundance." In *Media Diversity and Localism. Meaning and Metrics*, edited by Philip M. Napoli, 363–83. Mahwah, NJ: Lawrence Erlbaum.

Gordon, Jill. 1997. "John Stuart Mill and the 'Marketplace of Ideas.'" *Social Theory and Practice* 23 (2): 235–50.

Graham, Todd. 2009. What's Wife Swap got to do with it? Talking politics in the net-based public sphere. Academic dissertation, University of Amsterdam.

Habermas, Jürgen. 1989. *The Structural Transformation of the Public Sphere: An Inquiry into a Category of Bourgeois Society.* Cambridge: Polity Press. First published in German in 1962.

———. 1992. "Further Reflections on the Public Sphere." In *Habermas and the Public Sphere*, edited by Craig Calhoun, 421–61. Cambridge: MIT Press.

———. 1996a. *Between Facts and Norms: Contributions to a Discourse Theory of Law and Democracy.* Cambridge: Polity Press.

———. 1996b. "The Scientization of Politics and Public Opinion." In *Habermas Reader*, edited by William Outhwaite, 44–52. Cambridge: Polity Press.

———. 1998. *The Inclusion of the Other.* Cambridge: Polity Press.

———. 2006. "Political Communication in Media Society: Does Democracy Still Enjoy an Epistemic Dimension? The Impact of Normative Theory on Empirical Research." *Communication Theory* 16 (4): 411–26.

Hall, Stuart. 1997. "The Centrality of Culture: Notes on the Cultural Revolutions of Our Time." In *Media and Cultural Regulation*, edited by Kenneth Thompson, 207–38. London: Sage.

Hallin, Daniel C., and Paolo Mancini. 2004. *Comparing Media Systems. Three Models of Media and Politics.* Cambridge: Cambridge University Press.

Harcourt, Alison. 2005. *The European Union and the Regulation of the Media Markets.* Manchester and New York: Manchester University Press.

———. 2008. "Institutionalizing Soft Governance in the European Information Society." In *The European Union and the Culture Industries*, edited by David Ward, 7–31. Aldershot: Ashgate.

Harcourt, Alison, and Robert Picard. 2009. "Policy, Economic, and Business Challenges of Media Ownership Regulation." *Journal of Media Business Studies* 6 (3): 1–17.

Hargittai, Eszter. 2007. "Content Diversity Online: Myth or Reality?" In *Media Diversity and Localism: Meaning and Metrics,* edited by Philip M. Napoli, 349–62. Mahwah, NJ: Lawrence Erlbaum.

Harrison, Jackie, and Lorna Woods. 2001. "Defining European Public Service Broadcasting." *European Journal of Communication* 16 (4): 477–504.

Harrison, Jackie, and Bridgitte Wessels. 2005. "A New Public Service Communication Environment? Public Service Broadcasting Values in the Reconfiguring Media." *New Media & Society* 7 (6): 834–53.

Hartley, John. 1999. *Uses of Television.* London: Routledge.

———. 2004. " 'Republic of Letters' to 'Television Republic'? Citizen readers in the era of broadcast television." In *Television after TV: Essays on a Medium in Transition,* edited by Lynn Spigel and Jan Olsson, 386–417. Durham and London: Duke University Press.

———. 2009. "The History and Future of Ideas." *Television & New Media* 10 (1): 69–71.

Hay, Colin. 2002. *Political Analysis: A Critical Introduction.* Basingstoke: Palgrave.

———. 2004. "The Normalizing Role of Rationalist Assumption in the Institutional Embedding of Neoliberalism." *Economy and Society* 33 (4): 500–27.

Held, David. 2006. *Models of Democracy.* Cambridge: Polity Press.

Hellman, Heikki. 1999. "Legitimations of Television Programme Policies. Patterns of Argumentation and Discursive Convergencies in a Multichannel Age." In *Rethinking the Media Audience,* edited by Pertti Alasuutari, 105–29. London: Sage.

———. "Diversity—An End in Itself? Developing a Multimeasure Methodology of Television Programme Variety Studies." *European Journal of Communication* 16 (2): 181–208.

Herman, Edward, and Robert McChesney. 1998. *Global Media: The Missionaries of Global Capitalism.* London: Cassell.

Hesmondhalgh, David. 2001. "Ownership is only part of the media picture." *OpenDemocracy,* 29 November 2001. http://www.opendemocracy.net/node/46/.

Hindman, Matthew. 2007. "A Mile Wide and an Inch Deep: Measuring Media Diversity Online and Offline." In *Media Diversity and Localism. Meaning and Metrics,* edited by Philip M. Napoli, 327–48. Mahwah, NJ: Lawrence Erlbaum.

———. 2009. *The Myth of Digital Democracy.* Princeton: Princeton University Press.

Hitchens, Lesley. 2006. *Broadcasting Pluralism and Diversity: A Comparative Study of Policy and Regulation.* Oxford: Hart Publishing.

Honig, Bonnie. 1993. *Political Theory and the Displacement of Politics.* Ithaca and London: Cornell University Press.

Horwitz, Robert. 2007. "On Media Concentration and the Diversity Question." *Media Diversity and Localism: Meaning and Metrics,* edited by Philip M. Napoli, 9–56. Mahwah, NJ: Lawrence Erlbaum.

Howley, Kevin. 2005. "Diversity, localism and the public interest: The politics of assessing media performance." *International Journal of Media and Cultural Politics* 1 (1): 103–6.

Humphreys, Peter. 1996. *Mass Media and Media Policy in Europe.* Manchester and New York: Manchester University Press.

———. 2007. "The EU, Communications Liberalisation and the Future of Public Service Broadcasting." In *Media and Cultural Policy in the European Union,* edited by Katherine Sarikakis, 91–112. Amsterdam and New York: Rodopi.

ICRI—K.U. Leuven (lead contractor), Jönköping International Business School—MMTC, Central European University—CMCS, and Ernst and Young. 2009. Indicators for Media Pluralism in the Member States— Towards a Risk-Based Approach (Final Report and Annexes: User Guide, MPM, Country Reports). Brussels: European Commission, July 2009.

Ingber, Stanley. 1984. "The Marketplace of Ideas. A Legitimizing Myth." *Duke Law Journal* 1984 (1): 1–91.

Jacka, Elizabeth. 2003. "Democracy as Defeat." *Television & New Media* 4 (2): 177–91.

Jacoby, Russell. 1999. *The End of Utopia. The Politics and Culture in the Age of Apathy.* New York: Basic Books.

Jakubowicz, Karol. 2004a. "A Square Peg in a Round Hole. The EU's Policy on Public Service Broadcasting." In *European Culture and the Media,* edited by Ibn Bondebjerg, and Peter Golding, 277–301. Bristol: Intellect.

———. 2004b. "Another threat to public service broadcasting." *Intermedia* 32 (1): 20–23.

———. 2007. "Public Service Broadcasting: A Pawn on an Ideological Chessboard." In *Media Between Commerce and Culture,* edited by Els de Bens, 115–50. Bristol: Intellect.

Jensen, Klaus Bruhn. 2002. "The Qualitative Research Process." In *A Handbook of Media and Communication Research—Qualitative and Quantitative Methodologies,* edited by Klaus Bruhn Jensen, 235–54. London and New York: Routledge.

Jones, Paul. 2000. "Democratic Norms and Means of Communication: Public Sphere, Fourth Estate, Freedom of Communication." *Critical Horizons* 1 (2): 307–39.

Just, Natascha. 2009. "Measuring media concentration and diversity: New approaches and instruments in Europe and the USA." *Media, Culture & Society* 39 (1): 97–117.

Kaitatzi-Whitlock, Sophia. 1996. "Pluralism and Media Concentration in Europe. Media Policy as Industrial Policy." *European Journal of Communication* 11 (4): 453–83.

———. 2005. *Europe's Political Communication Deficit*. Bury St. Edmunds: Arima Publishing.

Karppinen, Kari. 2006. "Media Diversity and the Politics of Criteria. Diversity Assessment and Technocratisation of European Media Policy." *Nordicom Review* 27 (2): 53–68.

———. 2007. "Against naïve pluralism in media politics: On the implications of the radical pluralist approach to the public sphere." *Media, Culture & Society* 29 (3): 495–508.

———. 2008. "Media and the paradoxes of pluralism." In *Media and Social Theory*, edited by David Hesmondhalgh, and Jason Toynbee, 27–42. London: Routledge.

Karppinen, Kari, Hallvard Moe, and Jakob Svensson. 2008. "Habermas, Mouffe and Political Communication: A Case for Theoretical Eclecticism." *Javnost—The Public* 15 (3): 5–22.

Keane, John. 1991. *Media and Democracy*. Cambridge: Polity Press.

———. 1992. "Democracy and the Media—Without Foundations." *Political Studies* 40 (special issue): 116–29.

———. 1999. "On Communicative Abundance." CSD Perspectives working paper. Centre for the Study of Democracy. http://johnkeane.net/wp-content/uploads/2011/01/on_communicative_abundance.pdf.

———. 2009. *The Life and Death of Democracy*. London: Simon & Schuster.

Keen, Andrew. 2007. *The Cult of the Amateur. How Today's Internet is Killing Our Culture*. New York: Doubleday.

Kelly, John, Danyel Fisher, and Marc Smith. 2009. "Friends, Foes, and Fringe: Norms and Structure in Political Discussion Networks." In *Online Deliberation: Design, Research, and Practice*, edited by Todd Davis and Seeta Peña Gangadharan, 83–93. CLSI Publications, http://odbook.stanford.edu/.

Klimkiewicz, Beata. 2008. "Media Pluralism and Enlargement: The Limits and Potential for Media Policy Change." In *The European Union and* the Culture Industries: Regulation and the Public Interest, edited by David Ward, 81–104. London: Ashgate.

Knops, Andrew. 2007. "Debate: Agonism as Deliberation—on Mouffe's Theory of Democracy." Journal of Political Philosophy 15 (1): 115–26.

Komorek, Ewa. 2009. "The European Commission's 'Three-Step Approach' to Media Pluralism—a Conduit for the Protection of Freedom of Expression in the European Union?" Amsterdam Law Forum 2 (1): 49–54.

Kretzschmar, Sonja. 2007. "Diverse Journalists in a Diverse Europe? Impulses for a Discussion on Media and Integration." In Media and Cultural Policy in the European Union, edited by Katherine Sarikakis, 203–26. Amsterdam and New York: Rodopi.

Kuper, Andrew. 2004. Democracy Beyond Borders. Justice and Representation in Global Institutions. Oxford: Oxford University Press.

Laclau, Ernesto, and Chantal Mouffe. 1985. Hegemony and Socialist Strategy. Towards a Radical Democratic Politics. London: Verso.

Larsen, Håkon. 2010. "Legitimation strategies of public service broadcasters: The divergent rhetoric in Norway and Sweden." Media, Culture & Society 32 (2): 267–83.

Lehtinen, Pauliina, and Minna Aslama. 2009. Finnish Television Programming 2008. Helsinki: Ministry of Transport and Communications.

Levy, David. 1999. Europe's Digital Revolution. London: Routledge.

Lewis, Peter. 2008. Promoting social cohesion: The role of community media. Report prepared for the Council of Europe's Group of Specialists on Media Diversity (MC-S-MD). Strasbourg: Council of Europe.

Lowe, Gregory Ferrell. 2008. The role of public service media for widening individual participation in European democracy. Report prepared for the Council of Europe's Group of Specialists on Public Service Media in the Information Society (MC-S-PSM). Strasbourg: Council of Europe.

Lumby, Catharine. 1999. Gotcha! Life in a Tabloid World. Allen and Unwin: St Leonards.

Machill, Marcel, Markus Beiler, and Martin Zenker. 2008. "Search-engine research: a European-American overview and systematization of an interdisciplinary and international research field." Media, Culture & Society 30 (5): 591–608.

Marcil-Lacoste, Louise. 1992. "The Paradoxes of Pluralism." In Dimensions of Radical Democracy, edited by Chantal Mouffe, 128–42. London: Verso.

Mattelaart, Armand. 2003. The Information Society. An Introduction. Sage: London.

McChesney, Robert. 2007. Communication Revolution: Critical Junctures and the Future of Media. New York and London: The New Press.

McClure, Kirstie. 1992. "On the Subject of Rights: Pluralism, Plurality and Political Identity." In *Dimensions of Radical Democracy*, edited by Chantal Mouffe, 108–27. London: Verso.

McDonald, Daniel, and John Dimmick. 2003. "The Conceptualization and Measurement of Diversity." *Communication Research* 30 (1): 60–79.

McGuigan, Jim. 1997. "Cultural Populism Revisited." In *Cultural Studies in Question*, edited by Marjorie Ferguson and Peter Golding, 138–54. London: Sage.

McLennan, Gregor. 1995. *Pluralism*. Buckingham: Open University Press.

McNair, Brian. 2006. *Cultural Chaos: Journalism, News and Power in a Globalised World*. London: Routledge.

McQuail, Denis. 1992. *Media Performance. Mass Communication and the Public Interest*. London: Sage.

———. 1997. "Policy Help Wanted. Willing and Able Media Culturalists Please Apply." In *Cultural Studies in Question*, edited by Marjorie Ferguson, and Peter Golding, 39–55. London: Sage.

———. 2003. *Media Accountability and Freedom of Publication*. Oxford: Oxford University Press.

———. 2007a. "Introduction: Reflections on Media Policy in Europe." In *Power, Performance and Politics: Media Policy in Europe*, edited by Werner A. Meier, and Josef Trappel, 9–20. Baden-Baden: Nomos.

———. 2007b. "Revisiting Diversity as a Media Policy Goal." In *Power, Performance and Politics: Media Policy in Europe*, edited by Werner A. Meier, and Josef Trappel, 41–58. Baden-Baden: Nomos.

Meier, Werner E., and Joseph Trappel. 1998. "Media Concentration and the Public Interest." In *Media Policy: Convergence, Concentration and Commerce*, edited by Denis McQuail, and Karen Siune, 38–59. London: Sage.

Meier, Werner A. 2007. "National and Transnational Media Ownership Concentration in Europe: A Burden for Democracy?" In *Power, Performance and Politics: Media Policy in Europe*, edited by Werner A. Meier and Josef Trappel, 75–104. Baden-Baden: Nomos.

Michalis, Maria. 2007. *Governing European Communication. From Unification to Coordination*. Lanham: Lexington Books.

Mill, John Stuart. 1948. *On Liberty* and *Considerations on Representative Government*. Oxford: Basil Blackwell. First published in 1859.

Moe, Hallvard. 2008. "Dissemination and dialogue in the public sphere: a case for public service media online." *Media, Culture & Society* 30 (3): 319–36.

———. 2009. "Between Supranational Competition and National Culture? Emerging EU Policy and Public Broadcasters' Online Services." In

Media, Democracy and European Culture, edited by Ib Bondebjerg and Peter Madsen, 307–24. Bristol: Intellect.

―――. 2010. "Governing Public Service Broadcasting: 'Public Value Tests' in Different National Contexts." *Communication, Culture & Critique* 3 (2010): 207–23.

Moe, Hallvard, and Trine Syvertsen. 2008. "Researching Public Service Broadcasting." In *Handbook of Journalism Studies*, edited by Karin Wahl-Jorgensen and Thomas Hanitzsch, 398–412. New York and London: Lawrence Erlbaum.

Mosco, Vincent. 1996. *The Political Economy of Communication. Rethinking and Renewal*. London: Sage.

Mouffe, Chantal. 1993. *The Return of the Political*. London: Verso.

―――. 2000. *Democratic Paradox*. London: Verso.

―――. 2005. *On the Political*. London: Routledge.

―――. 2007. "Artistic Activism and Agonistic Spaces." *Art and Research* 1 (2). http://www.artandresearch.org.uk/v1n2/mouffe.html.

Murdock, Graham. 1999. "Rights and Representations. Public Discourse and Cultural Citizenship." In *Television and Common Knowledge*, edited by Jostein Gripsrud, 7–17. London & New York: Routledge.

―――. 2005. "Building the Digital Commons." In *Cultural Dilemmas in Public Service Broadcasting*, edited by Gregory Ferrell Lowe and Per Jauert, 213–31. Göteborg: Nordicom.

Napoli, Philip M. 1999. "Deconstructing the Diversity Principle." *Journal of Communication* 49 (4): 7–34.

―――. 2001. *Foundations of Communications Policy: Principles and Process in the Regulation of Electronic Media*. Creskill, NJ: Hampton Press.

―――. 2005. "The Broadening of the Media Policy Research Agenda." Social Science Research Council Working Paper.

―――. 2007. "Introduction." In *Media Diversity and Localism. Meaning and Metrics*, edited by Philip M. Napoli, xv–xiv. Mahwah, NJ: Lawrence Erlbaum.

―――. 2008. "Paradoxes Of Media Policy Analysis: Implications For Public Interest Media Regulation." *Administrative Law Review* 60 (4): 801–12.

―――. 2011. "Diminished, Enduring, and Emergent Diversity Policy Concerns in an Evolving Media Environment." *International Journal of Communication* 5 (2011): 1182–96.

Napoli, Philip M., and Michelle Seaton. 2007. "Necessary Knowledge for Communications Policy: Information Asymmetries and Commercial Data Access and Usage in the Policymaking Process." *Federal Communications Law Journal* 59 (2): 295Napoli, Philip M., and Nancy

Gillis. 2008. "Media Ownership and the Diversity Index: Outlining a Social Science Research Agenda." Donald McGannon Communication Research Center Working Paper.

Negroponte, Nicholas. 1996. *Being Digital*. New York: Vintage Books.

Nesti, Giorgia. 2007. "Inter-institutional bargaining and emergent policy networks in the European debate on media pluralism." Paper presented at the ECREA Symposium: Equal Opportunities and Communication Rights. Brussels October 11–12.

Nielsen, Henrik Kaare. 2003. "Cultural Policy and Evaluation of Quality." *International Journal of Cultural Policy* 9 (3): 237–45.

Nieminen, Hannu. 2000. *Hegemony and the Public Sphere. Essays on the Democratisation of Communication*. Department of Media Studies, School of Art, Literature and Music Series A no. 44. Turku: University of Turku.

———. 2010. "Towards democratic regulation of European media and communication." In *Media Freedom and Pluralism: Media Policy Challenges in the Enlarged Europe*. edited by Beata Klimkiewicz, 3–26. Budapest: CEU Press.

Nordic Public Service Broadcasters (Nordic PSB). 2009. Public service broadcasting, more important than ever. Contribution to the Commission's second public consultation on the review of the Communication from the Commission on the application of State aid rules to public service broadcasting. January 14, 2009.

O'Loughlin, Ben. 2006. "The operationalisation of the concept 'cultural diversity' in British television policy." Working Paper No. 27, ESRC Centre for Research on Socio-Cultural Change (CRESC). http://www .cresc.ac.uk/sites/default/files/wp27.pdf.

Open Society Institute (OSI). 2009. Comments on the Communication from the Commission on the Application of State Aid Rules to Public Service Broadcasting. January 2009.

Papathanassopoulos, Stylianos. 2002. *European Television in the Digital Age. Issues, Dynamics and Realities*. Cambridge: Polity Press.

Patomäki, Heikki. 2001. *After International Relations: Critical Realism and the (Re)Construction of World Politics*. Routledge: London and New York.

Pauwels, Caroline. 1998. "From Citizenship to Consumer Sovereignty: The Paradigm Shift in the European Audiovisual Policy." In *Communication, Citizenship, and Social Policy*, edited by Andrew Calabrese, and Jean-Claude Burgelman, 65–76. Lanham: Rowman & Littlefield.

Pauwels, Caroline, and Jo Bauwens. 2007. " 'Power to the People'? The myth of television consumer sovereignty revisited." *International Journal of Media and Cultural Politics* 3 (2): 149–65.

Peña Gangadharan, Seeta. 2009. "Understanding Diversity in the Field of Online Deliberation." In *Online Deliberation: Design, Research, and Practice*, edited by Todd Davis, and Seeta Peña Gangadharan. CLSI Publications. http://odbook.stanford.edu/.

Peters, John Durham. 2001. "Realism in Social Representation and the Fate of the Public." In *Public Opinion and Democracy: Vox Populi—Vox Dei*, edited by Slavko Splichal, 85–102. Creskill, NJ: Hampton Press.

———. 2004. "'The Marketplace of Ideas': A History of the Concept." In *Toward a Political Economy of Culture*, edited by Andrew Calabrese and Colin Sparks, 65–82. Lanham: Rowman & Littlefield.

Phillips, Anne. 1996. "Dealing with Difference: A Politics of Ideas, or a Politics of Presence." In *Democracy and Difference: Contesting the Boundaries of the Political*, edited by Seyla Benhabib, 139–52. Princeton: Princeton University Press.

———. 2000. "Equality, Pluralism, Universality: Current Concerns in Normative Theory." *British Journal of Politics and International Relations* 2 (2): 237–55.

Prior, Markus. 2007. *Post-Broadcast Democracy: How Media Choice Increases Inequality in Political Involvement and Polarizes Elections*. New York: Cambridge University Press.

Puppis, Manuel. 2009. "Introduction: Media Regulation is Small States." *The International Communication Gazette* 71 (1–2): 7–17.

Raboy, Marc, Serge Proulx, and Peter Dahlgren. 2003. "The Dilemma of Social Demand: Shaping Media Policy in New Civic Contexts." *Gazette* 65 (4–5): 323–29.

Rasmussen, Terje. 2008. "The Internet and Differentiation in the Political Public Sphere." *Nordicom Review* 29 (2): 73–83

Rawls, John. 1996. *Political Liberalism*. New York: Columbia University Press.

Raycheva, Lilia. 2009. "The Challenges of ICT to Media Pluralism." In *Press Freedom and Pluralism in Europe: Concepts and Conditions,* edited by Andrea Czepek, Melanie Hellwig, and Eva Novak, 75–90. Bristol: Intellect.

Rescher, Nicholas. 1993. *Pluralism. Against the Demand for Consensus*. Oxford: Clarendon Press.

Rogers, Richard. 2004. *Information Politics on the Web*. Cambridge, MA: MIT Press.

Rose, Nikolas, and Peter Miller. 1992. "Political Power Beyond the State: Problematics of Government." *British Journal of Sociology* 43 (2): 173–205.

Rose, Nikolas. 1999. *Powers of Freedom. Reframing Political Thought.* Cambridge University Press.

Sack, Warren, John Kelly, and Michael Dale. 2009. "Searching the Net for Differences of Opinion." In *Online Deliberation: Design, Research, and Practice,* edited by Todd Davis and Seeta Peña Gangadharan, 95–103. CLSI Publications. http://odbook.stanford.edu/.

Sarikakis, Katherine. 2004. *Powers in Media Policy. The Challenge of the European Parliament.* Oxford: Peter Lang.

Sayer, Andrew. 2000. *Realism and Social Science.* London: Sage.

Sen, Amartya. 2010. *The Idea of Justice.* London: Penguin.

Scott, John. 2001. *Power.* Cambridge: Polity Press.

Siebert, Fred, Theodore Peterson, and Wilbur Schramm. 1963. *Four Theories of the Press.* Urbana: University of Illinois Press. First published in 1956

Smith, Martin. 2006. "Pluralism." In *The State: Theories and Issues,* edited by Colin Hay, Michael Lister, and David Marsh, 21–38. New York: Palgrave McMillan.

Splichal, Slavko. 1999. *Public Opinion: Developments and Controversies in the 20th Century.* Lanham: Rowman & Littlefield.

———. 2002. *Principles of Publicity and Press Freedom.* Lanham: Rowman & Littlefield.

Stokes, Susan. 1998. "Pathologies of Deliberation." In *Deliberative Democracy,* edited by Jon Elster, 123–39. Cambridge: Cambridge University Press.

Sunstein, Cass. 2002. "The Future of Free Speech." In *Eternally Vigilant. Free Speech in the Modern Era,* edited by Lee C. Bollinger and Geoffrey R. Stone, 285–310. Chicago: University of Chicago Press.

———. 2003. "The Law of Group Polarization." In *Debating Deliberative Democracy,* edited by James Fishkin and Peter Laslett, 80–101. Oxford: Blackwell.

———. 2007. *Republic.com 2.0.* Princeton: Princeton University Press.

Suoranta, Juha, and Tere Vadén. 2008. *Wikiworld. Political Economy of Digital Literacy and the Promise of Participatory Media.* Paolo Freire Research Center and Open Source Research Center, Hypermedialab, University of Tampere. http://wikiworld.wordpress.com.

Syvertsen, Trine. 1999. "The Many Uses of the 'Public Service' Concept." *Nordicom Review* 20 (1): 5–12.

———. 2003. "Challenges to Public Television in the Era of Convergence and Commercialisation." *Television and New Media* 4 (2): 155–75.

———. 2004. Citizens, Audiences, Customers and Players. A Conceptual Discussion of the Relationship Between Broadcasters and their Publics. *European Journal of Cultural Studies* 7 (3): 363–80.

Tambini, Damian. 2001. *Communications: Revolution and Reform.* London: The Institute for Public Policy Research.

Thompson, John B. 1995. *Media and Modernity: A Social Theory of the Media.* Stanford: Stanford University Press.

Treaty of Amsterdam. 1997. Protocol on the system of public broadcasting in the Member States. Official Journal of the European Communities C 340/109. November 10, 1997.

Trenz, Hans-Jörg. 2009. "Digital Media and the Return of the Representative Public Sphere." ARENA Working Paper Series 06/2009. University of Oslo.

Valcke, Peggy. 2009. "From Ownership Regulations to Legal Indicators of Media Pluralism: Background, Typologies and Methods." *Journal of Media Business Studies* 6 (3): 19–42.

———. 2011. "A European Risk Barometer for Media Pluralism: Why Assess Damage When You Can Map Risk?" *Journal of Information Policy* 1 (2011): 185–216.

Valcke, Peggy, Robert Picard, Miklos Sükösd, Beata Klimkiewicz, Brankica Petkovic, Cinzia dal Zotto, and Robin Kerremans. 2010. "The European Media Pluralism Monitor: Bridging Law, Economics and Media Studies as a First Step towards Risk-Based Regulation of Media Markets." *Journal of Media Law* 2 (1): 85–113.

Van Cuilenburg, Jan. 1998. "Diversity Revisited: Towards a Critical Rational Model of Media Diversity." In *Media in Question*, edited by Kees Brants, Joke Hermes, and Liesbet Van Zoonen, 38–49. London: Sage.

———. 2007. "Media Diversity, Competition and Concentration: Concepts and Theories." In *Media Between Commerce and Culture*, edited by Els de Bens, 25–54. Bristol: Intellect Books.

Van Cuilenburg, Jan, and Denis McQuail. 2003. "Media Policy Paradigm Shifts. Towards a New Communications Policy Paradigm." *European Journal of Communication* 18 (2): 181–207.

Van Cuilenburg, Jan, and Richard van der Wurff. 2007. "Toward Easy-to-Measure Media Diversity Indicators." In *Media Between Commerce and Culture,* edited by Els de Bens, 99–114. Bristol: Intellect Books.

Van der Wurff, Richard. 2004. "Supplying and Viewing Diversity. The Role of Competition and Viewer Choice in Dutch Broadcasting." *European Journal of Communication* 19 (2): 215–37.

———. 2005. "Competition, Concentration and Diversity in European Television Markets." *Journal of Cultural Economics* 29 (4): 249–75.

Villa, Dana R. 1992. "Postmodernism and the Public Sphere." *American Political Science Review* 86 (3): 712–21.

Venturelli, Shalini. 1998. *Liberalizing the European Media: Politics, Regulation, and the Public Sphere.* Oxford: Oxford University Press.

Verhulst, Stefaan G. 2007. "Mediation, Mediators and New Intermediaries. Implications for the Design of New Communications Policies." In *Media Diversity and Localism: Meaning and Metrics,* edited by Philip M. Napoli, 113–38. Mahwah, NJ: Lawrence Erlbaum.

Ward, David. 2001. "The Democratic Deficit and European Union Communication Policy. An Evaluation of the Commission's Approach to Broadcasting." *Javnost—The Public* 8 (1): 75–94.

———. 2006. The Assessment of content diversity in newspapers and television in the context of increasing trends towards concentration of media markets. Final Report on the study commissioned by the Group of Specialists on Media Diversity (MC-S-MD). Strasbourg: Council of Europe.

———. 2008. "The European Commission's State Aid Regime and Public Service Broadcasting." In *The European Union and the Culture Industries,* edited by David Ward, 59–80. Aldershot: Ashgate.

Webster, James G. 2007. "Diversity of Exposure." In *Media Diversity and Localism: Meaning and Metrics,* edited by Philip M. Napoli, 309–26. Mahwah, NJ: Lawrence Erlbaum.

Wenman, Mark. 2003. "What is Politics: The Approach of Radical Pluralism." *Politics* 23 (1): 57–65.

———. 2008. "William E. Connolly: Pluralism without Transcendence." *The British Journal of Politics and International Relations* 10 (2): 156–70.

Wheeler, Mark. 2007. "Whither Cultural Diversity: The European Union's Market Vision for the Review of Television without Frontiers Directive." In *Media and Cultural Policy in the European Union,* edited by Katherine Sarikakis, 227–49. Amsterdam and New York: Rodopi.

Wildman, Steven S. 2007. "Indexing Diversity." In *Media Diversity and Localism: Meaning and Metrics,* edited by Philip M. Napoli, 151–76. Mahwah, NJ: Lawrence Erlbaum.

Williams, Raymond. 1975. *Television: Technology and Cultural Form.* London: Routledge.

Williams, Bruce A., and Michael X. Delli Carpini. 2004. "Monica and Bill all the time and everywhere: The collapse of gatekeeping and agenda setting in the new media environment." *American Behavioral Scientist* 47 (9): 1208–30.

WSIS (World Summit on Information Society). 2003. Declaration of Principles. Document WSIS-03/GENEVA/DOC/4-E. Geneva, December 2003.

Young, Iris Marion. 1997. "Difference as a Resource for Democratic Communication." In *Deliberative Democracy: Essays on Reason and Politics*, edited by James Bohman, and William Rehg, 383–406. Cambridge: MIT Press.

———. 2000. *Inclusion and Democracy*. Oxford: Oxford University Press.

Zittrain, Jonathan. 2008. *The Future of the Internet—and How to Stop it*. New Haven: Yale University Press.

INDEX

active audience theory, 54, 64, 204
agonistic democracy, 9, 29, 41–46, 56–57, 72–76, 117. *See also* radical pluralism
alternative media, 5, 11, 67, 74–78, 99, 105–6, 207–8. *See also* community media
Association of Commercial Television in Europe (ACT), 142, 170

Baker, C. Edwin, 14, 111–12, 152, 185, 191
Barnett, Steven, 97
Baum, Bruce, 34
Bauman, Zygmunt, 40, 66
Beck, Ulrich, 48–49
Benhabib, Seyla, 48, 69
Bennett, Lance, 120
Berlin, Isaiah, 30–31
Berlusconi, Silvio, 11, 93
blogs, 105, 112, 114, 116, 118
Bohman, James, 38, 62, 71, 77
Born, Georgina, 16, 76, 176
Braman, Sandra, 50

Campaign for Press and Broadcasting Freedom (CPBF), 141
capabilities approach, 121
capitalism, 33, 35, 107
Cavallin, Jens, 95, 98, 192
Castells, Manuel, 105, 110, 114, 121

censorship 8, 32, 65–66, 207
citizen journalism, 77, 109
citizenship, 36; do-it-yourself, 53, 56; and public service media 120, 156–57, 160, 163, 170, 190
civil society, 36, 41, 49, 66, 74, 77, 79, 105, 176; participation in media policy, 23, 131, 137, 140–41, 143–44, 147, 160, 166
Collins, Richard, 156, 175
commodification: of culture, 107; and intellectual property, 113; in media policy, 152–53, 158, 165, 177, 186–87
communication rights, 35, 90, 96
communicative abundance, 5, 14, 51, 80, 103–23, 184, 204
communicative power: asymmetries of, 60–63; definition, 61n2; democratization of, 76–81; distribution of, 1, 4, 14–15, 49, 68, 70, 83, 88, 97, 105, 152, 190, 202–3, 207–9; and Internet, 5, 103–4, 110–14, 120–23; and media regulation, 101–2
community media, 5, 78, 99, 144, 147, 207. *See also* alternative media
competition: in democratic theory, 30, 41; among information sources, 111, 122; and media ownership, 93–97; and media pluralism, 2, 4, 11–12, 14, 32–33, 35, 77, 88, 91, 128–30, 135, 151–53, 156, 184, 186,

expert power, 13, 17, 19, 153, 169, 171, 179–80, 188, 191

exposure diversity, 5, 91–93, 192–93; and Internet 110, 112, 114, 116, 121–23

Federal Communications Commission (FCC), 183–86

filtering, 92, 113–14

Finland, 194

Fischer, Frank, 17, 24

Four Theories of the Press, 31–32

fragmentation, 55, 73; in the Internet, 115–20; of media audience and public sphere 3, 5, 49–50, 92, 105, 111, 175–76

Fraser, Nancy, 49, 63, 74–75

Freedman, Des, 2, 11, 64, 67, 86, 128, 132, 151, 171, 182

freedom: articulation with markets, 33–34, 66; of choice, 8, 11, 34, 63–68, 96, 134–35, 156, 175; of information, 123, 137, 142, 168; journalistic 146, 151; of media, 11, 32–36, 90, 126, 130–31, 144, 152; negative/positive conception of, 35–36, 152; political and philosophical value, 12, 24, 28, 30, 40, 48, 89, 209; of speech, 8, 10, 31, 34–35, 47, 130, 132, 139, 152, 168, 182n1, 192, 197, 202

free markets, 8, 32, 65–66, 94, 98, 102, 133–35, 172, 174, 202, 206

Garnham, Nicholas, 32, 39, 50, 54–55, 60, 80, 108, 111, 121, 176

gatekeepers: and Internet, 101, 104, 107n1, 110–14, 119–20, 123, 208; media as, 61, 127, 184

Gibbons, Thomas, 118, 128

Gitlin, Todd, 49, 108

globalization, 127, 132

global markets, 87, 138, 140–41, 144, 150, 172, 174

global networks, 105–6, 120

Gordon, Jill, 34

governmentality, 19, 180

governmental technologies, 18–19, 179–81, 195

Habermas, Jürgen: criticisms of, 38–41, 43–45, 52, 61–62, 176; on democracy and public sphere, 8–9, 29, 36–38, 191; on Internet and mass media, 61, 75, 117; later work, 47, 71–77

Hall, Stuart, 66

Hartley, John, 52–54

Hay, Colin, 18–19, 182

Hesmondhalgh, David, 96

Hindman, Matthew, 111–13

Hitchens, Lesley, 86, 186

Honig, Bonnie, 9, 45, 73

Humphreys, Peter, 138

Hutchins Commission, 126

identity politics, 27, 55, 64, 69, 72

intellectual property. *See* copyright

Internet: concentration and hierarchies, 108–14; fragmentation, 115–18; governance, 109; implications for media pluralism, 4–5, 75, 95, 103–7, 127, 142, 148, 184, 208; and public service media, 165–69

Italy, 97, 127, 137

Jacka, Elizabeth, 52–54

Jacoby, Russell, 204–5

Jakubowicz, Karol, 164, 173

Jones, Paul, 35

journalism: and democracy, 51, 77; effect of media ownership on, 95–96, 142; and Internet, 106, 108, 208; workforce, 91, 100

Kaitatzi-Whitlock, Sophia, 123, 133, 136, 141

Keane, John, 2, 33, 35, 47, 51, 62, 70, 79, 110, 176, 202, 207

Klimkiewicz, Beata, 87, 153

liberalism, 8; liberal democracy, 2, 6; liberal pluralism, 8, 28–35, 37, 41–44, 56–57, 72

liberty of the press. *See* freedom: of media

mainstream media, 68, 76, 106–8, 111, 114, 116, 128, 207–8

Marcil-Lacoste, Louis, 7

market censorship, 8, 65–66, 207

market failure, 33, 128, 151, 154, 178

marketization, 11, 120, 129

marketplace of ideas, 3, 8; criticism of, 37, 43, 45, 56, 62–65, 66, 81; meaning and origin, 25, 28–35; uses in media policy, 86–87, 89, 94, 106, 110, 206

Marxism, 36

7–10, 21, 25–26, 28–29; unitary *versus* multiple, 72–76
public sphericules, 49, 92

radical journalism, 208
radical pluralism: criticisms of, 42, 45, 55; in media politics, 52, 54–57, 62–63, 78, 80, 121, 197, 205–8; in political theory, 9–10, 29, 41–46, 48, 72, 75, 202; and public service media, 77, 177
Rawls, John, 30–31
relativism, 7, 21, 54–55, 73, 203
representation, 68–72, 88–89
Rogers, Richard, 106
Rose, Nikolas, 18–20
Russia, 97, 127

Sayer, Andrew, 21
search engines, 101, 112–14, 119, 123
semiotic democracy, 53, 56–57, 177, 204
Sen, Amartya, 30, 121
social cohesion, 79, 156, 163, 168, 175
social media, 54, 77, 116
social movements, 78–79, 105–6, 120
social responsibility, 32, 172, 174, 180
soft governance, 144–45, 171
source diversity, 91–92, 192–93
Splichal, Slavko, 65
subsidies: for broadband access, 123;

for media and culture, 11, 70, 79–80, 98–100, 108, 119n4
Sunstein, Cass, 67, 71, 115–19, 177

tabloidization, 39, 52

UNESCO, 188; Convention on the Protection and Promotion of the Diversity of Cultural Expressions, 131
United Kingdom (UK), 2, 93, 97
United States (US), 3n1, 12, 23, 33, 91; debate on media ownership and diversity, 98, 182–87, 189–90, 196, 198; media policy, 126, 173; media use, 112n2, 118
user competence, 93, 121. *See also* media literacy
user-generated content, 77, 109

value pluralism, 30–31, 44
van Cuilenburg, Jan, 88–89, 122
Verhulst, Stefaan, 104, 113–14

Ward, David, 134, 161–62
Williams, Bruce, 104, 120
World Summit on the Information Society (WSIS), 131

Young, Iris Marion, 20, 40, 44, 69, 72